ROMAN
BRITAIN

LEO

ROMAN
BRITAIN

T.W. Potter *and*
Catherine Johns

THE BRITISH MUSEUM PRESS

FOR BELINDA

© 1992 T.W. Potter and Catherine Johns
Published by The British Museum Press
A division of The British Museum Company Ltd
46 Bloomsbury Street, London WC1B 3QQ

First published 1992
First published in paperback 2002

British Library Cataloguing in Publication Data
A catalogue record for this book is available from
the British Library
ISBN 0 7141 2774 4

Designed by Harry Green

Printed in Great Britain by
Butler & Tanner Ltd, Frome

References to illustrations appear in the margins.
Roman numerals indicate colour plates, which can
be found between pages 48 and 49 (Plates I to VI)
and pages 144 and 145 (Plates VII to XII).

Half-title page Dragonesque brooch from Norton,
North Yorkshire (see Fig. 60).
Title page Mosaic floor from the villa at Rudston,
North Yorkshire. The main figure in the central
roundel is Venus, represented in a highly
provincial style. Fourth century AD.
Hull Museum.

Roman Britain is part of the 'Exploring the
Roman World' series. Other titles include:
Roman Gaul and Germany by Anthony King
Roman Italy by T.W. Potter
Roman Spain by S.J. Keay

CONTENTS

ACKNOWLEDGEMENTS

One of the pleasures of working in the British Museum is that we are constantly visited by people – scholars, students and lay persons alike – with interests in Roman Britain and its material culture. It is always fun and profitable to discuss our subject with them, and our debts of gratitude could therefore be extremely long. Practicalities compel us, however, to keep them within reason; but we would like to offer our particular thanks to the following, who have aided the publication of this book in especial ways, namely Lindsay Allason-Jones, Guy de la Bédoyère, Kevin Greene, Martin Henig, Ralph Jackson, Anthony King, Ian Longworth, Jack Ogden, Jenny Price, Val Rigby, Ian Stead and Steve Trow. We would also like to thank Stephen Crummy, both for his splendid drawings and for his major contribution to the study of the Meonstoke façade and the Stonea building complex; Simon James, for reading the entire text, to its great advantage; and our recently retired Director, Sir David Wilson, for his great encouragement and leadership over the past fifteen years. We are also enormously grateful to Judith Cash, who has typed most of this volume with fortitude and remarkable enthusiasm; the many people, acknowledged elsewhere, who have provided illustrative material; and our kind and sympathetic editors, Teresa Francis and Celia Clear. Finally, we would like to offer particular gratitude to Don Bailey and Sandra Potter, who have in so many senses shared the burden of producing what has never seemed an easy book to write.

INTRODUCTION

T here was a time, sixty years or so ago, when to some eyes many of the problems of Roman Britain had been largely sorted out. Thus in 1932, Kendrick and Hawkes, then both Assistant Keepers at the British Museum, could write that 'prehistoric studies require an interim report [on the present state of research], but our knowledge of Roman Britain has advanced some way beyond this and ... it is actually the stage of historical revision that is setting in.'[1] Likewise, a reviewer in 1932 could write that a discussion of Hadrian's Wall was 'a clear and spirited statement of difficult problems that are nearing solution'.[2]

There are more than a few echoes here of a confident intellectual environment, so much so that when the brilliant philosopher, historian and archaeologist R.G. Collingwood published (with J.N.L. Myres) *Roman Britain and the English Settlements*, in 1936, it was criticised by I.A. Richmond for 'driving the evidence hard' and 'building upon it a series of conclusions whose very artistry disguised the weakness of foundation'.[3] Richmond – himself a scholar of the greatest stature – alas never produced more than a short *Roman Britain* (1955, revised in 1963) in which the treatment was 'dictated by the subjects upon which evidence rather than conjecture holds the field'.[4] Collingwood's powerfully written volume remained, however, the main textbook down into the 1960s, along with F. Haverfield's *Romanisation of Roman Britain* (1912). This still influential work was particularly concerned to gauge the impact of Roman traditions upon indigenous peoples, and was most unusual for its time in recognising and defining the *British* component of the culture of Roman Britain.

Sir Mortimer Wheeler, whose outstanding contribution, *inter alia*, to the development of excavation methodology is universally recognised, was also, one feels, much influenced by Haverfield. Despite his many seasons

of digging on Roman military sites in Wales and, in the early 1930s, at the town of Verulamium, by modern St Albans, he later admitted that he abjured things Roman. Like Haverfield, what really interested him was the interaction between foreign and indigenous cultures; indeed, his work at Verulamium, which originated as an important British capital, was partly directed at elucidating this very theme.[5]

In the post-war years, the pace of discovery accelerated, with such outstanding finds as the Mildenhall, Water Newton and Thetford treasures, the London mithraeum and the Fishbourne 'palace', the Vindolanda writing tablets and the Hinton St Mary mosaic, to name but a few. Many of these came to light through chance, but there has also been an enormous increase in the number of excavations, many on a very considerable scale. Some, like Richmond's inspired investigation of the legionary fortress at Inchtuthil in Scotland, were carried out solely for reasons of research,[6] but most have been rescue projects, reflecting the much greater level of public and, more recently, developer funding that has been available since the

early 1970s. Virtually every class of site, urban and rural, military and religious, has benefited, accompanied these days with commensurate and fitting attention to environmental, floral and faunal evidence. Some of the conclusions from the examination of plant remains and animal bones have been particularly fascinating: by way of instance, the conquest of AD 43 is now beginning to appear as much less of a watershed in the life of the province of Britannia than was once thought, although there were highly significant agricultural innovations in the later third and early fourth centuries – just when the villa was to enter its real heyday in Britain.

Two other advances of recent decades require particular emphasis. One is the enormous progress that has been made in artefact studies, especially pottery. Well over 1,000 pottery production centres, major and minor, are now known in Britain, and most imports from elsewhere in the Roman world are easily recognisable to the specialist eye.[7] Markets, marketing trends and broader aspects of the ancient economy are therefore much defined and debated these days, aided by a zest for all manner of quantification. It may be that the resulting figures convey an impression of precision which is not always justified by the quality of the evidence; but the broad thrust of the approach is probably right. The other major advance is the stress that is now placed upon setting a site within the context of its broader landscape. Aerial photography has long played an essential role, and remains a crucial tool in the discovery of buried features: but it is now increasingly supplemented by field-walking and allied methods of landscape investigation, especially geomorphological studies of soils and sediments. Moreover, it is now appreciated that sites of the Roman period are the heirs of a long tradition of landscape organisation and exploitation, the understanding of which is often essential for a grasp of a site's context and purpose. The landscape maps currently being produced for areas such as the Yorkshire Wolds reflect millennia of human activity, with Roman-period sites as just one component in a matrix of immense complexity.

1 Rescue work in progress in 1988 on the oak floor-joists and sills of a timber warehouse at Southwark, on the south bank of the Thames in London. The planks of the floor have already been lifted, and the structure owes its preservation to its low-lying position.

It must here be said that in recent years some of the methodological approaches employed in Romano-British studies have come under fiery criticism, especially from those brought up on the theoretical 'models' so widely used by prehistorians. Roman Britannia has been portrayed as 'an aged, cosseted old lady ... fawned on by a bevy of tireless, dedicated servants',[8] while many contributors to a survey of work on Roman Britain undertaken between 1960 and 1989 (one of the present authors included) have been described as 'trapped in a culture-historical pre-processual paradigm'.[9] Put elsewhere more clearly, we are vigorously enjoined 'to cross period- and subject-boundaries and ... focus on processes and trajectories rather than personalities and campaigns'.[10]

We are far from being against new approaches (as long as they are couched in language that does not instantly mystify), and there are in this book more than a few echoes of some current thinking of this sort. However, nearly forty years' experience between us in the British Museum, curating

the Romano-British collections, have undoubtedly coloured our views. We live with exotic finds, like the Mildenhall silver or the extraordinary collection of late Iron-Age gold and silver currently coming to light at Snettisham in Norfolk;[11] and we also work on a day-to-day basis with the no less fascinating bric-à-brac of Romano-British times. Material culture is central to our lives, and we make no apology for giving it due prominence in the pages that follow.

2 Hoard of silver drinking-cups from Hockwold, Norfolk. The cups were buried in a damaged and fragmentary state, and are shown here after restoration. First century AD. British Museum.

People also feature much more conspicuously than will no doubt be thought proper by some prehistorians. Individuals *were* important in the Roman world, as Classicianus' tombstone, a highlight of the British Museum collections, constantly reminds us; it is a precious link between an important figure in the Roman histories and his tangible appearance in the archaeological record. Similarly, the Vindolanda tablets open a remarkable window into ordinary life on the province's frontier, and we shall talk later of what sounds like shady wheeling and dealing, and of the delightful invitation to a birthday party extended by one commandant's wife to another. People like Claudia Severa and Sulpicia Lepidina are to us very real, and they must not be forgotten in our attempts to identify 'processes and trajectories'.

We are also very aware that, however remote Britannia may have been, it was a province of a great empire. It cannot therefore be properly understood in isolation, as the currently fashionable 'core and periphery' model quite rightly reminds us. Even though Rome (or for that matter warfare) hardly figures in the Vindolanda tablets, decisions taken at the heart of the empire were important for Britain and its populace, and it would be imprudent to ignore this. Every province had its peculiarities and regional characteristics, as the series 'Exploring the Roman World' as a whole clearly shows. But the broader context is also important, and not infrequently intervenes in our narrative. As chance would have it, there has been a stream of recent works on Roman Britain, and both the general and the specialist reader can be considered well served, as the bibliographies make clear; but this has allowed us to stray more often into specialist interests than has been possible with other volumes in the series.

There must be one final cautionary observation. Although we have more or less parallel jobs at the British Museum, our joint authorship of this book has not always brought about academic consensus. The debates have been more or less daily, always lively, and often far from resolution. Rather than conceal this with artificial disguise, we have chosen to let some of our differing viewpoints stand, despite the pitfalls of inconsistency. For working in this museum has at least taught us one thing: that, however well explored the province of Britannia may be, major new discoveries seem never to abate, bringing forth fresh ideas and novel perspectives. Of one thing we are certain: the last word on Roman Britain can surely never be written.

T.W. POTTER
British Museum, 1992

NOTE ON THE NEW EDITION

Since this book was first published ten years ago, there has been much new research on Roman Britain and on the immediately pre- and post-Roman periods in Britain. Numerous important publications have appeared, and new finds, both planned and fortuitous, have come to light. To take account of these, a number of changes have been made to this edition, including several new or updated photographs, references to important new discoveries, and the addition of a short supplementary bibliography (p. 232) listing significant and relevant publications since 1992.

Tim Potter died in January 2000. Though he and I had discussed a new edition of this volume, it has therefore fallen to me alone to make the revisions. I have benefited greatly from the advice of my colleagues, especially Ralph Jackson, J.D. Hill, Jonathan Williams and Sam Moorhead, and I hope they will forgive me for being unable to fit in all their suggestions. I have made some amendments to my own sections of the book, but I have not wished to make radical changes to the chapters (1, 2, 3 and 7) written by my late friend and colleague. They summarise the views of one of the leading scholars of Roman Britain at the end of the twentieth century, and remain valid in their present form.

CATHERINE JOHNS
British Museum, December 2001

BRITAIN BEFORE AD 43

W ho the first inhabitants of Britannia were, whether natives or immigrants, remains obscure, as is usual with barbarians. (Tacitus, *Agricola* 11.)

Few Romans knew much about Britain. Published sources were scant, and the gossip trivial, inaccurate and sometimes bizarre. Moreover, most had only a hazy idea of the island's location and geography. Gaius Iulius Solinus, for example, was an educated Roman who wrote a highly plagiarised geography soon after AD 200. By that time Britain had been a Roman province for more than 150 years; even so, Solinus could write of Britain as being 'another world', adjacent to islands which were notable for the 'inhuman and savage practices of the inhabitants'.[1] Similarly Cassius Dio, also writing in the early third century AD, could speak of the Caledonii of Scotland as a people who 'live in tents, naked and unshod, holding their women in common and rearing all their offspring together. They can bear … all kinds of hardship, for having plunged into the marshes they endure many days with only their head out of water.'[2] Dio, we can be sure, knew nothing of the realities of life in Scotland, despite the fact that the emperor Septimius Severus, whom he knew well, campaigned there in AD 208–10.

That there should have been deep-rooted ignorance about Britain amongst the educated Romans of Italy (and other parts of the empire) is hardly surprising. Duty reasons apart (especially military service), few Romans will have been tempted to visit Britain, a province which, at times, will have seemed much more bother than it was worth. Even so, contacts between Britain and the Mediterranean world were of long standing. According to Pliny, a Greek trader called Midacritus is said to have imported tin from the island of Cassiterus – the Cassiterides, or 'Tin Islands', are to be identified as the Scillies and Cornwall – perhaps as early as about 600 BC.[3] Herodotus (c. 485–420 BC) doubted the existence of the Cassiterides,[4] but the voyage of Pytheas to Britain in the fourth century BC is mentioned by several ancient writers. Pytheas, a navigator from Massalia (modern Marseilles), is reported to have visited Ictis (perhaps St Michael's Mount, by Penzance in Cornwall), where tin ore was collected, circumnavigated the island, and even sighted distant Thule (perhaps Iceland or Norway).[5]

Fabulous stories such as these did not command much credence in antiquity. However, they accord well with other stories of early maritime exploration, especially by Greek and Phoenician merchants. Around 600 BC, for example, one Kolaios, a sea captain from Samos in the Aegean, made himself a huge fortune with one cargo from Tartessos, the metal-rich region of south-western Spain.[6] Even in northern Europe, scrap metal was being traded across the Channel by the middle Bronze Age (c. 1200–1100 BC). This much is clear from wreck cargoes recently discovered lying on the seabed. One was from a ship that foundered off Salcombe in Devon, while another was swept off course into Langdon Bay (Kent) as it attempted to make the safe anchorage that is today the harbour at Dover. Short-haul voyages of this sort may well have become increasingly common during the first millennium BC, notwithstanding the undoubted perils of the Channel crossing.[7]

Despite intrepid adventurers like Kolaios and Pytheas, Britain seems largely to have been ignored by the Mediterranean world, while Rome was building up its young Republic. The Greek writer Eratosthenes of Cyrene, in modern Libya, who lived from about 275 to 194 BC, alluded to Britain in his *Geography*; but it was a shadowy and distant land to which he referred. Only when Rome began to lay the foundations for an empire, by acquiring large parts of Spain during the second century BC and Gallia Narbonensis in the south of France between 125 and 121 BC, did matters begin to change. Cornish tin was apparently transported to Massalia via a depot called Corbilo on the Loire estuary, and thence overland, even though 'no-one of all the Massiliotes ... was able when questioned by Scipio [Africanus, the great Roman general] to tell anything worth recording about Britain'.[8] But land transport was expensive, and no doubt the Gallic tribes whose territory the convoys traversed were not always friendly.[9] The problem, as Strabo explains, was that the Phoenicians, who knew a convenient sea route to the British Tin Islands, kept it a closely guarded secret. They even lured a Roman, who was following them in an early act of commercial espionage, into shoal waters; adding insult to injury, the Phoenician sea captain 'escaped by a piece of wreckage, and received from the State the value of the cargo he had lost'.[10]

Eventually, however, one Publius Crassus, a governor of part of Spain (Hispania Ulterior) between 96 and 93 BC, journeyed the route successfully. 'He crossed over to these people [presumably the Cornish] and saw that the metals were being dug from only a slight depth, and that the men there

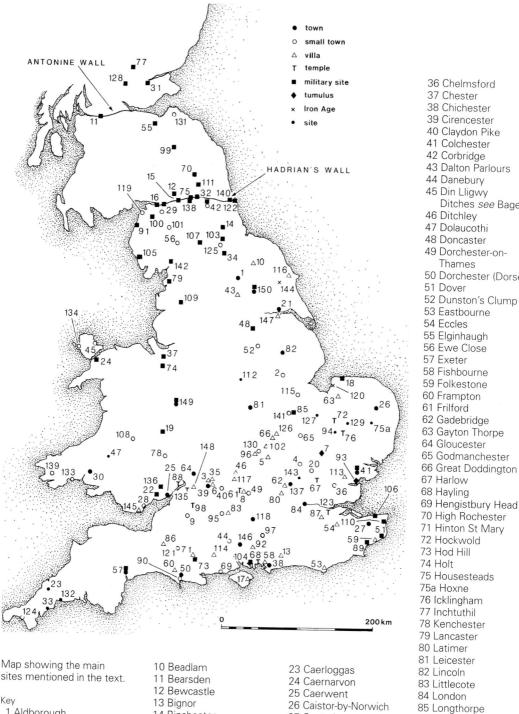

ANTONINE WALL

HADRIAN'S WALL

- town
○ small town
△ villa
T temple
■ military site
◆ tumulus
× Iron Age
• site

36 Chelmsford
37 Chester
38 Chichester
39 Cirencester
40 Claydon Pike
41 Colchester
42 Corbridge
43 Dalton Parlours
44 Danebury
45 Din Lligwy
   Ditches *see* Bagendon
46 Ditchley
47 Dolaucothi
48 Doncaster
49 Dorchester-on-
   Thames
50 Dorchester (Dorset)
51 Dover
52 Dunston's Clump
53 Eastbourne
54 Eccles
55 Elginhaugh
56 Ewe Close
57 Exeter
58 Fishbourne
59 Folkestone
60 Frampton
61 Frilford
62 Gadebridge
63 Gayton Thorpe
64 Gloucester
65 Godmanchester
66 Great Doddington
67 Harlow
68 Hayling
69 Hengistbury Head
70 High Rochester
71 Hinton St Mary
72 Hockwold
73 Hod Hill
74 Holt
75 Housesteads
75a Hoxne
76 Icklingham
77 Inchtuthil
78 Kenchester
79 Lancaster
80 Latimer
81 Leicester
82 Lincoln
83 Littlecote
84 London
85 Longthorpe
86 Low Ham
87 Lullingstone
88 Lydney
89 Lympne
90 Maiden Castle
91 Maryport
92 Meonstoke
93 Mersea
94 Mildenhall (Suffolk)

Map showing the main
sites mentioned in the text.

Key
1 Aldborough
2 Ancaster
3 Bagendon
4 Baldock
5 Bancroft
6 Barnsley Park
7 Bartlow Hills
8 Barton Court Farm
9 Bath

10 Beadlam
11 Bearsden
12 Bewcastle
13 Bignor
14 Binchester
15 Birdoswald
16 Bowness-on-Solway
17 Brading
18 Brancaster
19 Brandon Camp
20 Braughing
21 Brough-on-Humber
22 Caerleon

23 Caerloggas
24 Caernarvon
25 Caerwent
26 Caistor-by-Norwich
27 Canterbury
28 Cardiff
29 Carlisle
30 Carmarthen
31 Carpow
32 Carrawburgh
33 Carvossa
34 Catterick
35 Chedworth

were peaceable. He forthwith laid abundant information before all who wished to traffic over this sea.'[11] From then on, trade in tin certainly flourished. Diodorus Siculus, writing about the time of Caesar and Augustus (but possibly using an older source such as Pytheas), provides us with a quite detailed account of the process of tin extraction, its conversion into ingots shaped like astralagi, and its stockpiling by the wagon-load at Ictis. 'From there', Diodorus goes on, 'the [Roman] merchants buy the tin from the natives and carry it across to Gaul. Travelling on foot across Gaul for about thirty days, they bring their load on horseback to the mouth of the Rhone' – where the great port of Massalia was located.[12]

Tin was of course an essential component of the alloy bronze, and the Cornish deposits remained an important source throughout the Roman period. However, it was only one element in the economic and political relationship which gradually emerged between Britain and Rome during the latter part of the first millennium BC. We shall come to examine the consequences of Caesar's two expeditions of 55 and 54 BC, but it will be useful first to say something of the archaeological contribution to our understanding of Iron-Age Britain.

Iron-Age studies have been revolutionised in the course of the last twenty years or so. In part this is due to a series of dramatic new excavations and chance discoveries, but it also reflects some sharp changes in intellectual perspectives, mirroring those that we sketched out for Roman Britain in the Introduction. Until recently, the British Iron Age was seen in terms of three main 'cultural groups', known as A, B and C.[13] Each was thought to have been introduced into Britain by invading peoples from the Continent: A, from about 600 BC by folk of the Hallstatt culture; B, about 250 BC by Celtic warriors of the La Tène culture; and C, about 150–100 BC by the Belgae, mentioned by Caesar, who lived within the region bounded by the Seine, Marne and Rhine rivers. However, only the invasion of the Belgae could be documented in historical terms, in a famous passage in Caesar's *Gallic War*: 'The coastal area [of Britain] was inhabited by invaders who crossed from Belgium for the sake of plunder and war; and then, when the fighting was over, settled there and began to work the land.'[14]

This classificatory scheme, first mapped out in 1931, was with increasing elaboration to hold the field for close on forty years. That it was a brilliant means of organising the archaeological data then available is not in doubt; but from the early 1960s the underlying assumptions began to come under attack. Boiled down to essentials, the evidence for successive invasions, once rescrutinised, seemed ever more tenuous; not even the Belgic incursions referred to by Caesar could be satisfactorily correlated with the archaeological material, since the cemeteries of late Iron-Age cremations in south-east England (which had hitherto been correlated with the Belgae) all now seemed to belong to the period after Caesar's expeditions. In archaeological terms, the Belgae had, to all intents and purposes, lost their identity.[15]

The furore of debate that ensued during the 1960s and 1970s can be

easily imagined, for not everyone accepted the rejection of the old views. Gradually, however, new ideas have emerged, whereby many of the developments in the Iron-Age cultures of Britain are explained much more in terms of social and economic changes (often influenced by events on the Continent) than by militaristic interventions from abroad.[16] If the result is a much less clear-cut picture of Iron-Age Britain, it nevertheless reflects the huge intellectual advances that have taken place in archaeological discovery and thinking over recent decades. This is of major consequence. Given that the great bulk of the population of Roman Britain was made up of indigenous, Celtic-speaking peoples, the nature of their society and traditions prior to the conquest is of prime importance. Only by knowing this can we fully appreciate the impact that the imposition of Roman ways had upon the country.

It is as well to start with hillforts. Not only are these the most conspicuous monuments of Iron-Age Britain, but they have always played a central role in the interpretation of the period. Around 1,400 are known, ranging from modest enclosures of a hectare or less to huge fortified centres like Maiden Castle (18.5 ha) and Hod Hill (22 ha), both in Dorset. They are by no means evenly distributed, however. There are comparatively few, for example, in

3 The decorated bronze 'crown' of an Iron-Age warrior buried at Deal, Kent. The grave also contained an iron sword in a highly decorated scabbard, and a brooch and belt fitting, also much embellished. Third century BC. British Museum.

4 Maiden Castle, Dorset: a view of the massive ramparts of one of the largest Iron-Age hillforts in Britain. It was eventually superseded by the Roman town of Durnovaria, modern Dorchester.

East Anglia and the Midlands, in complete contrast with regions such as Wessex, the Cotswolds and the Welsh Marches, where they are exceptionally prolific. Moreover, they are highly variable not only in terms of their size but also in their form, complexity of defences and internal arrangements. Indeed, a significant proportion are found not on hilltops but in lower and much less impregnable locations. Clearly, therefore, the surviving evidence points to a highly complex state of affairs, in which hillforts may have assumed a variety of roles.

The first hillforts were constructed well before the beginning of the Iron Age. It is not easy for us to comprehend why people should have chosen to occupy bleak summits such as that of Mam Tor in Derbyshire – and, eventually, to have girdled it with ramparts – but radiocarbon dates from that site show that they did so from the later Bronze Age, about the twelfth century BC. We may suppose that in some areas of Britain pressures became such that people found it prudent to create settlements in locations with strong natural defences.[17]

The main thrust of hillfort building came, however, rather later. A number, surrounded by simple palisades or ramparts contained within a timber box-frame, can be dated to the first half of the first millennium BC, but it was after about 600 BC that they really proliferated. Thenceforth the architecture of the defences underwent steady modification, with imposing stone-faced ramparts appearing in some regions from about 400 BC. However, most of the so-called 'multivallate' hillforts – such as Maiden Castle – with line after line of massive ramparts and elaborately protected gates, seem to date to after 100 BC, an archaeological reflection, perhaps, of Strabo's verdict that the Continental Celts were 'war-mad, high-spirited and quick to battle'.[18]

The investigation of hillfort interiors has proceeded apace in recent years, even though it is a task made daunting by their often huge size. Whilst some have yielded only sparse evidence for occupation – they may have been temporary refuges or foci for tribal fairs and festivals – most are proving to have been densely inhabited. It was Wheeler's brilliant campaigns at Maiden Castle in 1934–7 that first demonstrated the almost urban character of settlement there, with a medley of wooden houses, pits for the storage of grain (and, doubtless, other commodities), and a comparatively orderly system of streets. One building was probably a shrine, pointing to an early emergence of 'public' buildings within the settlement – a very faint echo, perhaps, of the planning and order that was by then the norm in so many towns around the Mediterranean.[19]

Wheeler's demonstration of these 'proto-urban' characteristics of Iron-Age Maiden Castle has been considerably amplified by the more recent large-scale investigation of other sites such as South Cadbury (Somerset) and Danebury (Hampshire).[20] Both proved to have a rectangular building, placed more or less in the centre, which probably served a religious function – that at South Cadbury was approached by an avenue flanked with animal burials – and a dense arrangement of other structures and pits. Nearly half of the five-hectare area enclosed by the ramparts at Danebury has been explored, permitting an intriguing reconstruction of the hillfort's history, layout and social and economic make-up. This is being considerably facilitated by detailed study of the farms and field systems within the fort's environs, which must have formed its main territory.[21]

Danebury had a long history. The first defences were built about 550 BC, enclosing a settlement with circular wooden houses and square post-built constructions which were probably used as granaries. Around 400 BC the defences were drastically remodelled and the internal arrangements replanned. There were at least four streets, some lined with granaries, and another leading to the shrines, while round houses clustered in the lee of the rampart. Calculations suggest a population in the order of 250 to 350, and the archaeological evidence indicates a wide range of activities: the growing of winter-sown spelt wheat and six-row barley, as well as the spinning and weaving of wool, the production of some objects in bronze and iron, and the acquisition, probably by exchange, of commodities such as salt and items in coveted materials such as shale from Kimmeridge in Dorset.

Who, then, were the people who lived at Danebury, and what was their social status? They may well have belonged to the great Celtic-speaking group of northern Europe, and from what the classical writers tell us – and their remarks are supported by the stories of later Irish legends – this was a highly stratified society. At the top was an aristocracy of, in Caesar's word, *equites* ('knights'), normally led by a supreme king. These nobles practised a system of clientage, whereby individuals of lesser social rank swore allegiance to particular aristocrats in return for loans and favours. This social and political mechanism was also a feature of the Roman world, and our classical authorities may therefore have overstressed its importance in Celtic society, but there does seem to have been a substantial body of lower-ranking freemen, with whom the nobles could well have maintained a client-patron relationship. Many will have been farmers; however, there is evidence that craftsmen such as blacksmiths also shared this status, a conclusion borne out by the manifest importance of items of metalwork intended for display, which, as we shall see, are so conspicuous a feature of the archaeological record.[22]

The ancient writers also stress the importance of other social groups in the Celtic world. Strabo notes that, in Gaul of the first century BC, 'among all the tribes ... there are three classes of men held in special esteem: the Bards, the Vates and the Druids. The Bards are singers and poets; the Vates interpreters of sacrifice and natural philosophy; while the Druids, in addition to the science of nature, also study moral philosophy.' Caesar rated the Druids with the knights in the social hierarchy, emphasising the priests' role as judges and their exemption from taxation, military service and other obligations.[23]

The great mass of the population, however, was at a near servile level: 'they possess no initiative', remarks Caesar, 'and their views are never invited on any question. Most ... hand themselves over into slavery to the upper classes, who have all the same legal rights against these men that a master has towards his slave.' Here Caesar may perhaps have been couching his narrative in exaggerated fashion so that it would be more familiar to his Roman readers, whose world was one where slaves were commonplace – two to three million in Italy alone.[24] Moreover, the Celtic world was vast, and its society had evolved over a period of many centuries; it may not, therefore, be legitimate to apply the observations of the classical writers to an interpretation of the sites of Iron-Age Britain.

That there were Iron-Age aristocrats in Britain is not in doubt. Lindow Man, who met a gruesome end in a Cheshire peat bog towards the end of the Iron Age – the dating evidence is somewhat ambiguous – may well have been one of them. Ritually executed by axe-blows to the head, followed by garotting and then the slitting of his throat, 'Pete Marsh's' remains are those of a well-to-do gentleman of about 25 years of age, unaccustomed to hard manual labour. This much is clear from his well-nourished appearance, neatly trimmed moustache and beard and his unbroken nails. His was not the life of a peasant farmer, nor of a working craftsman,

and the mistletoe in his stomach may link him to arcane Druidic rites of sacrifice.[25]

Similarly, the chalk wolds and limestone uplands of eastern Yorkshire have yielded striking evidence for the burial of rich men and women, who must have occupied a very privileged rank within their society. It is a curious fact that, before the latest phases of the Iron Age, very few burials of the period are known in Britain. Yorkshire is a marked exception, for reasons that have never been satisfactorily explained. Most were placed in graves under barrow mounds, surrounded by square ditches, but yield comparatively little in the way of grave goods, other than the occasional pot or brooch. However, a few are outstanding in that the deceased was interred in, or with, a two-wheeled cart or hearse (often described as a chariot).[26]

Most are old discoveries, like the so-called King's Barrow excavated between 1815 and 1817 at Arras, a farm near Market Weighton (Humberside). A large mound, 8 metres across, covered a grave with an inhumed body, the dismantled remains of a two-wheeled vehicle, various items of harness, the skulls of two pigs and the bones of the two horses that pulled the cart. It was one of about a hundred barrows, two of which also contained dismantled carts (the 'Charioteer's' and the 'Lady's'), while three

5 The corpse of a late Iron-Age aristocrat, from Lindow Moss, Cheshire. He appears to have been ritually slain, and mistletoe in the stomach hints at Druidic connections. British Museum.

6 Cart burial with the skeleton of a young adult woman, from Wetwang Slack, Yorkshire. The iron tyres of the dismantled wheels and the line of the pole are clearly visible. The grave goods included an iron mirror, a decorated bronze box and chain, and an iron and gold dress pin. Probably third century BC.

others possessed no vehicle but did include rich items of jewellery. In the 'Queen's Barrow', for example, there was a brooch, rings of gold, amber and bronze, a necklace of glass beads, two bracelets, a pendant and even a toilet set.

Until 1971, fewer than a dozen cart burials were known. Since then, however, a further six have been discovered, some partly by accident but others through systematic programmes of research. They come from a shallow valley which runs through Wetwang and Garton, to the west of Driffield (Humberside). Three clustered together at Wetwang and contained the bodies of two men and one young adult woman. All the burials contained dismantled carts and and horse fittings, and the men were fully armed with swords and scabbards and the remains of shields. The woman, by contrast, was buried with an iron mirror – seemingly an important and comparatively rare status symbol in Iron-Age Britain – and a mysterious, highly decorated, sealed bronze canister with an attached chain: it may well have held organic matter, such as sacred water, but the problem is unresolved, since the object cannot be opened without causing unacceptable damage.[27]

The cart burial found at Garton Station in 1985 contained the body of a man, but no weapons. However, within the same cemetery were other interments which lacked vehicles but did yield a sword and a shield, in separate graves. The sword had been placed on the back of the corpse, a tradition attested elsewhere in Yorkshire, not least on small chalk figurines; and there were traces of what may have been a wooden shield. The body had then been impaled with seven spears, while a further seven spearheads were found in the fill of the grave. This macabre burial rite, conjuring up – as it irresistibly does – images of ghost-slaying, is found in three other graves at Garton Station, one at Wetwang, and in other Iron-Age cemeteries in Yorkshire. Thus, in 1987, at nearby Kirkburn three spears were found to have been thrust into the chest of a body that was accompanied by a magnificently decorated sword and scabbard. Still more remarkably, a cart burial in the same cemetery yielded a skeleton covered by a coat of iron mail; it is the most complete example to survive from the Celtic world.[28]

Together with the weaponry in the richer graves, and the abundant signs on the skeletons of all manner of gruesome wounds, the funerary evidence from these sites points to a society in which military combat was a significant factor in everyday life. Caesar tells us that 'the Gallic states used to fight offensive or defensive wars almost every year', and the ancient sources are consistent in their portrayal of a society in which individual contests between the nobles of different tribes was a normal feature of battle. Despite the immense difficulties in interpreting the picture afforded by the comparatively few graves that have been excavated (only a thousand or so), it is tempting to interpret them as a broad reflection of Celtic customs as described for us by the classical writers.[29]

The very few datable objects from the Yorkshire cemeteries suggest that they were being used from at least as early as 350 BC, while the latest graves belong to the first century BC. This would place them in the same broad chronological bracket as a widespread and numerous series of cemeteries in the Champagne region of northern France which have certain similarities with the Yorkshire burials, in particular the ubiquitous use of square ditches around barrows, the occasional interment of carts and the presence of weapons in the male graves. There are significant differences between the two regions, not least that the French burials are much richer, the carts were placed in the ground intact and the bodies extended; by contrast, only one (or possibly two) of the Yorkshire vehicles was not dismantled, the grave furnishings are poorer, the corpses placed in a crouched position, and the artefacts have many distinctive British traits. Even so, there seems to be a case for suggesting a family link – cousins, rather than siblings, perhaps – between the two areas.

It has long been considered possible that some Celts may have migrated from France to Yorkshire, a hypothesis which has always seemed plausible given that we know that the Celts did expand widely from their homeland during and after the fifth century BC. They settled *en masse* in northern Italy, sacked Rome itself in 390 BC and even invaded Greece and Asia Minor. When, much later, St Paul preached to the Galatians, in what is now central

Turkey, he was addressing Galli, or Gauls, who had settled there in the third century BC. St Jerome tell us that, as well as Greek, they still spoke their Celtic tongue 700 years later.[30]

With such evidence for Celtic migrations before us, it seems inconceivable – despite the current unpopularity of 'invasion hypotheses' – not to infer the presence of some Gauls from Champagne amongst the Iron-Age peoples of eastern Yorkshire. It is easy to imagine how a marauding Gallic band may eventually have found its way into the north of England, there to introduce new ideas and customs, albeit in adapted form. Indeed, when Ptolemy drew up his *Geography* in the second century AD, he was to place the tribe known as the Parisi in eastern Yorkshire, a name that is to this day enshrined in the French capital, Paris, ancient Lutetia Parisiorum: a link of some sort between France and Yorkshire seems to be assured.[31]

But we must readdress the question concerning the identity and social position of the people who resided in hillforts such as Danebury. Was it a township where all classes of society lived and worked, with an open market for the exchange of goods and produce; or was it the citadel of a Celtic noble, surrounded by his knights, bards, priests and craftsmen, and with a territory farmed by the freemen? The truth is that we really do not know. There is no obvious architectural distinction in surviving traces of the buildings, and it may well be that we are quite wrong in attempting to apply what little is known of Celtic Gaul to an anonymous hillfort in Hampshire. Most archaeologists would agree that the evidence of the square 'granaries', together with the grain seeds (which seem to derive from the cultivation of many different environments), points to Danebury's role as a central storage and distribution centre: but beyond that there is little consensus.[32]

What is certain is that the environs of the hillfort were tightly packed with fields, trackways and, at roughly one-kilometre intervals, small farms. This much is clear from aerial photographs, which provide an extraordinarily clear impression of the ancient landscape even though, without excavation, we cannot say which farms were in occupation at the same time.[33] However, a good many such smaller rural sites, situated elsewhere on the chalklands of southern England, have been investigated. Pride of place is always given, rightly, to Little Woodbury, near Salisbury. The examination in 1938–9 of about one-third of this defended enclosure of 1.6 hectares disclosed a settlement which shared many of the features encountered within larger hillforts: circular houses, square 'granaries' and deep storage pits. Despite a paucity of objects suggestive of high social status, the great circular wooden house, 14 metres in width, at the centre of the settlement, has always seemed an appropriate residence for a well-to-do farmer and his family – even, some scholars believe, people who ranked with the Celtic nobles described by Caesar.[34]

Conjectures of this sort have derived some support from the results of work at more recently excavated sites such as Gussage All Saints (Dorset), which lies some 24 kilometres to the south-west of Salisbury.[35] Gussage was also a defended farm on the chalkland, and at 1.2 hectares was much the same size as Little Woodbury. However, whilst it proved possible to excavate Gussage in its entirety, the site had suffered much more heavily from ploughing. Although traces of some buildings remained – including a group of four-post 'granaries' constructed early in the site's history at the centre of the enclosure – it was clear that much of the structural evidence had been totally erased in recent years. Even so, three successive phases of defences were identified, as well as 477 pits, designed originally, we may assume, for the storage of grain.

The finds from the pits and other features, in combination with radio-carbon dates, point to more or less continuous occupation from perhaps 400 BC or before, down into the early Roman period. That crop cultivation and stock raising were prime activities is not in doubt, for both have left their characteristic detritus, botanical and faunal, on the site; however, more surprisingly, the manufacture of prestigious items of metalwork also seems to have been a significant element in the economy. Not only is there metallurgical debris in deposits spanning the entire history of the site, but one pit yielded a vast, and unprecedented, concentration of broken clay moulds. This material, which is thought to represent no more than the work of a year or two, sometime in the first century BC, turned out to consist solely of elaborately decorated bronze chariot fittings and harness items for the horses that pulled them. No fewer than fifty chariots, it is calculated, could have been equipped using the objects represented by the moulds.[36]

Whilst the Gauls had by this time abandoned chariots in favour of cavalry, the Britons still used them extensively. Caesar tells us that his British opponent, Cassivellaunus, could muster 4,000, a figure that gains credence in view of the evidence from Gussage. What is more puzzling is the mass-production of chariot and horse fittings by an accomplished craftsman within the confines of a comparatively small farm. The exca-vators initially assumed him to have been an itinerant metalworker, pro-ducing objects as gifts or exchange for various wealthy patrons; but they later reverted to the view that such metallurgical activity was an integral part of the economy of the Gussage All Saints settlement. As so often in archaeological debate, the matter remains unresolved, pending further evidence from comparable sites.[37]

We have so far considered Iron-Age settlements solely in terms of hillforts and the comparatively small farms of the Wessex chalklands. Whilst this might have been broadly acceptable a few decades ago, we now know that the range of settlement types was much more diverse and, moreover, that there were profound changes in many regions during the Iron Age. The evidence now available points to a complex array of social groupings, which cannot always be matched with ideas about the nature of Celtic society as depicted in our ancient sources. Village communities seem, in particular, to have been widespread, especially in areas such as East Anglia and the east Midlands, where hillforts are largely absent. This much is clear from sites like Cats Water, on the western edge of the Cambridgeshire Fens, and Little Waltham in Essex, both of which proved to be packed with houses, indicating substantial populations.[38] They may be compared with the long-known Somerset villages at Meare and Glastonbury, with their remarkable harvest of artefacts in wood, leather and other organic materials. Glastonbury yielded traces of no fewer than ninety houses, concentrated into an area measuring only 122 x 90 metres. However, not all were occupied at the same time: a sensitive reappraisal of the excavations has suggested that the settlement originated as just twelve buildings which housed four family units, amounting to about sixty people in all. During three subsequent episodes of rebuilding, it was enlarged, reaching a population of over a hundred. Figures of this sort are no more than educated guesswork, but they are probably reliable as a rough order of magnitude.[39]

This suggestion of an increasing population during the lifetime of Iron-Age Glastonbury (about third to first century BC) is of particular interest, for it can be matched with similar evidence from other regions. Intensive study through aerial photography and excavation of the gravel reaches of the middle and upper Thames valley – to take one instance of conspicuously excellent recent research – has disclosed an intricate but consistent pattern. The gravel terraces that border the Thames were being steadily developed from as early as the eighth and seventh centuries BC; indeed, at places like Runnymede, where there was a small island in the river channel, impressively large settlements surrounded by a wooden palisade came into being. During the middle period of the Iron Age, from the third century, the scale of settlement did, however, alter: sites became more numerous, and the landscape was increasingly divided up with ditched field systems and trackways. At Claydon Pike near Lechlade, for example, there were three separate groups of round houses, each complex on a gravel hummock which was surrounded by a highly organised arrangement of field divisions. Indeed, by the first century BC, many of the small settlement units had been reformed into larger communities, and what little unexploited terrain remained was brought into cultivation: the impression is of a sharply rising population responding to an ever increasing pressure on land.[40]

Some of these riverside settlements can only have been occupied during the summer months, taking advantage of the rich pastures left by the receding winter flood waters. Flooding of the low-lying meadows seems, however, to have become steadily more frequent during the Iron Age. This was in all probability the result of intensive cultivation of the uplands bordering the Thames valley, which gradually led to a clogging-up of the drainage systems by silt washed into the river.[41] Subtle environmental changes of this sort must have been widespread in Britain at this time. However, they seem to have been presaged by a broad climatic trend towards rather colder and wetter conditions which affected much of Britain during the first few centuries of the first millennium BC. The consequences seem in the long term to have been catastrophic. Recent work on Dartmoor, for example, has shown that the settlements and field systems – many of which are still magnificently preserved – had been largely abandoned by about 500 BC; the same may well be true of many other upland regions, such as parts of Northumberland. The reason for this is to this day fossilised in the botanical record built up in the peat bogs, which indicates an average drop in temperature of about 2°C; this, it is calculated, would have reduced the growing season by nearly six weeks, sufficient to have upset drastically the precarious farming regime of a relatively primitive Bronze-Age society.[42]

There were also environmental changes along the coasts. The most conspicuous example is the East Anglian Fenland, where a rise in sea-level around 600 BC resulted in the inundation of several hundred square kilometres of once fertile flatlands. Only in the first century AD were they gradually to dry out again. In combination with an enforced desertion of the settlements in the uplands, and the hints in the archaeological record of an increasing population, it is not surprising that regions like the Thames valley should manifest signs of more intensive occupation – a telling demonstration of the pervasive power that unchecked environmental changes can have upon the pattern of human settlement.

The cumulative picture, therefore, is of a diverse series of Iron-Age landscapes, into which archaeology has opened some windows, although the focus often remains blurred. Even so, some fascinating chronological perspectives can be inferred from the data. Whilst the pace of change in northern England (and probably Scotland, too) is likely to have been comparatively slow, in parts of the south matters were rather different. In regions such as Wessex, where hillforts are the most durable monuments of the period, it can now be shown that some continued as major centres of wealth for much of the Iron Age, while others dwindled in importance. It is hard not to interpret this in terms of political and economic domination, especially when we recall the militaristic society that existed in Celtic Gaul by this time. Hillforts in southern Britain could well have become centres for tribal affiliation, a regulation of society that would correspond with the much more tightly controlled landscape that the archaeological evidence independently attests. Thus Danebury, for example, was to become preeminent within its region, while its immediate neighbours either went into a sharp decline or were completely abandoned.

It is against this background of a complex mosaic of emergent, competing societies that we must now turn to review the later phases of the Iron Age. We have already said something of the way in which a trade in tin grew up between south-western Britain and the classical world. This, however, was merely one facet of a cross-Channel commercial interchange which steadily escalated from about 100 BC or before. As we hinted earlier, there is little doubt that the Roman conquest of southern Gaul in the 120s BC was the critical catalyst. The Romans required both metal ore and slaves,

7 Reconstruction of an Iron-Age cremation burial of the late first century BC found in 1965 at Welwyn Garden City, Hertfordshire. Among the grave-goods were a superb set of glass gaming-counters (not visible in this photograph), a Roman silver wine-cup (centre front, behind the lidded pottery box) and five Roman amphorae in which wine had been imported from the Continent. British Museum.

commodities which could yield vast profits. According to Diodorus, a slave could be purchased for a single amphora – about 25 litres – of wine, a beverage for which the Gallic nobility had a singular fondness: 'Many Italian merchants', he goes on, 'regard the Gaul's taste for wine as a godsend. They take the wine to them by ship up the navigable rivers, or by chariot travelling overland, and it fetches incredible prices.'[43]

There was no shortage of Italian wine to sell. Many Roman landowners invested in its production, and achieved vast surpluses. The so-called Dressel 1 amphorae – the distinctive vessels used to carry Italian wine from about 150 BC until the late first century BC – are found in enormous quantities in southern Gaul, and in comparatively large numbers in most other parts of what is now France. Their distribution also extends to southern Britain, although here they are nothing like as numerous. Archaeologists distinguish two types of Dressel 1 amphorae, 1A and 1B, based on slight changes in shape. It is thought that production of the Dressel 1A gave way to 1B about 50 BC – roughly the time when Caesar was bringing Gaul under the Roman yoke. In Britain, most of the 1A amphorae have been found south of the Thames, and especially in the Wessex region; by contrast, the 1B form appears to be more prevalent in Hertfordshire and Essex, north of the Thames. This has been taken to suggest a shift in the foci of wealth in the period after Caesar's two expeditions to Britain in 55 and 54 BC, although it has been argued that the distinction is more apparent than real.[44]

This nevertheless fascinating conclusion, first clearly spelt out in the early 1970s, has led to some important new excavations, especially at Hengistbury Head in Dorset.[45] The site, a defended promontory overlooking the natural harbour of Christchurch, is ideally placed to act as a commercial entrepôt between south-western Britain and the Continent. Recent investigations have demonstrated an intensive level of occupation during the late Iron Age and, more importantly, unmistakable indications of widespread trading activity. Metal production seems to have been a particularly important industry, and there is clear evidence to show that iron, copper, silver and tin were brought to Hengistbury from as far afield as Cornwall, the Mendips and Wales. Shale, for manufacture into attractive vessels and other objects, came from Kimmeridge in Dorset, and there must have been commerce in goods that leave little archaeological trace, such as hides. Slavery no doubt figured large. We have it on the authority of Strabo that slaves were exported from Britain (along with corn, cattle, gold, silver, iron, hides and hunting dogs), and his remark implies that the scale of trade in slaves was probably substantial – even though Britain could hardly have rivalled the Aegean island of Delos where, as the same author reports, 10,000 slaves could change hands in a single day.[46]

Hengistbury shows ample signs of the fruits of this commerce: amphorae that contained Italian wine, glass vessels, coins minted in Gaul and other pottery vessels made on the Continent, especially from Brittany. Both the coins and the pottery suggest that the Continental links were predominantly via the ports of Armorica – the Breton peninsula of northwestern France – and especially the site now covered by the modern town of Alet.[47] This much had already been inferred by Sir Mortimer Wheeler in the light of his excavations at Maiden Castle; in 1938–9 he led two expeditions to explore Breton sites, with the aim of establishing the connection between the major local tribes of Brittany – the Veneti and the Coriosolites – and the Iron-Age people of south-western Britain.[48] The outbreak of war interrupted the enquiry, but by then the nature of the contacts had been brilliantly illuminated. The archaeological evidence seemed fully to support the observation of Julius Caesar, who had noted that 'the Veneti have a great many ships ... and regularly sail to and from Britain'. To this Strabo added that the Veneti were prepared 'to hinder his [Caesar's] voyage to Britain, as they were using the emporium there'. We might well wonder if that 'emporium' lay at Hengistbury Head.[49]

As centres such as Hengistbury came into increased prominence, others such as Danebury seem to have gone into decline, hinting at some readjustment to the tribal hierarchy. However, as we pointed out earlier, the concentration of rich imported goods in the Wessex region appears largely to be a phenomenon of the period between about 100 and 50 BC, and we may reasonably suppose that Caesar's intervention in the affairs of Gaul and Britain had a good deal to do with this. The Veneti were conquered in 56 BC, and the two famous expeditions across the Channel followed shortly afterwards, in 55 and 54 BC. Caesar justified these risky ventures because 'in almost all the Gallic campaigns, the Gauls had received reinforcements from the Britons'; this, then, is the likeliest explanation for the large quantities of Gallic gold coinage of this period found in Britain.[50]

We need not dwell on the campaigns in detail. The Britons eventually elected a war leader, Cassivellaunus, 'to whom the chief command and direction of the campaign had been entrusted by common consent'. Caesar goes on to say that Cassivellaunus' territory lay to the north of the Thames and that 'previously he had been continually at war with the other tribes': he had an *oppidum* or stronghold that 'was protected by forests and marshes ... and of great natural strength and excellently fortified'. Even so, the legions successfully stormed the place, so that Caesar could then impose terms: the delivery of hostages, the payment of annual tribute and the undertaking that the Trinovantes – a strong, pro-Roman tribe in Essex, whose king had been killed by Cassivellaunus – should remain unmolested.

The location of Cassivellaunus' *oppidum* is a much-debated matter, for none of the obvious candidates, such as Wheathampstead near St Albans, have produced finds of the right date. There is, however, material of this period at Baldock (Hertfordshire), which has yielded some evidence for settlement around 50 BC and a rich cremation burial; this contained a Dressel 1A Italian wine amphora, a great bronze cauldron, pairs of bronze bowls and wooden buckets and two iron firedogs. Whoever it was that was interred in this splendid tomb must have been an individual of considerable importance, with Mediterranean (or Gallic) tastes and contacts.[51]

The Baldock burial is an archaeological harbinger of a series of late Iron-Age cremations, many with conspicuously fine grave goods. Baldock apart, all date to the period that followed Caesar's expeditions, and the majority cluster within the borders of Hertfordshire, Essex and northern Kent. Sometimes known as the Aylesford culture (after the early excavations of one of the cemeteries), the burials typically contain distinctive wheel-made pottery – a major technological innovation in Britain at this time – placed in flat graves. Some tombs are, however, much richer, with bronze vessels and other metalwork, some imported from as far afield as central and southern Italy. Still more outstanding are tombs in the Baldock tradition, which contain the full paraphernalia of a Roman-style feast. In the well-known example found at Welwyn Garden City (Hertfordshire) in 1965 were five wine amphorae, a silver drinking cup made in Italy, a strainer 7 to remove the sediment, mixing bowls and thirty pottery vessels. Other personal items included a nail-cleaner and a handsome set of decorated glass gaming pieces. We have no idea of the identity of the person whose cremated bones lay on one side of the grave, but his high social status is not in doubt.[52]

As we observed earlier, there was a time when archaeologists believed that they could associate these cremation cemeteries with the Belgic tribe of north-eastern France and Belgium. Caesar tells us that 'the coastal areas [of Britain] are inhabited by invaders who crossed from Belgium for the sake of plunder and war and, once the fighting was over, settled there and began to work the land; these people have almost all kept the names of the tribes from which they originated.' However, it is now clear that the equation works neither geographically nor chronologically, and the British Belgae remain archaeologically invisible. We should probably look for them in the Hampshire region, since the Roman town that lies beneath modern Winchester was named Venta Belgarum, 'the market of the Belgae': but as yet the matter remains completely unresolved.[53]

More is known of the Hampshire town of Silchester, Roman Calleva Atrebatum. The Atrebates were in origin a Gallic tribe, over whom Caesar had placed as king a Gaul named Commius. We are told that Commius was 'greatly respected in Britain', and Caesar therefore used him as an envoy in an attempt to persuade the British tribes to pledge their allegiance to the Romans. However, Commius was eventually to take up arms against Caesar and, in the aftermath of a resounding victory by the Roman forces, took refuge in Britain soon after 51 BC.[54]

Whether Commius established himself at Silchester from the outset is unclear but recent excavations beneath the basilica of the Roman town have shown that occupation began there well back into the first century BC and that by about 25 BC a remarkably regular system of streets was being laid out. It is possible that some Atrebates had already settled on or near the site before Commius' arrival, but it was during the period of Commius' rule (or possibly that of his son, Tincomarus) that the first steps were made to introduce some Mediterranean ideas of urbanisation.[55]

Coins bearing the name *Commios* – the earliest inscribed British issues – are known from the Hampshire, Sussex and Berkshire region, and it makes good sense to link them with the Commius of history. Moreover, other British coins permit us to reconstruct the Atrebatic dynasty, for no fewer than three subsequent rulers, Tincomarus, Eppillus and Verica, claim on their issues to be sons of Commius. Tincomarus was apparently the eldest, ruling until about AD 7, when he was forced to flee to the protection of Rome, as Augustus himself records.[56] Tincomarus seems actively to have promoted contact with the Roman world. This much is clear from the archaeological evidence for imports (including wine amphorae and, doubtless, other goods) and from a famous coin issue, bearing a finely lettered TINC on one side and a horse and rider on the other: expert numismatic

8 Coin of Tincomarus, ruler of the Atrebates of Hampshire, *c.* 30–10 BC. His name, usually abbreviated to TINC on his coinage (as seen here), was long presumed to have been Tincommius, but a full clear reading has now been obtained from a coin in a hoard from Alton, Hampshire, found in 1995. British Museum.

opinion regards this as the work of a highly skilled die-cutter, trained in Roman techniques of moneying.[57]

This coin of Tincomarus was minted about 15 BC, coinciding with a marked escalation in trade between Britain and the Continent. In part, this is a reflection of the remarkable changes taking place at that time in Italy itself. Octavian's great victory at Actium in 31 BC over the forces of Antony and Cleopatra finally put an end to the factional in-fighting that had characterised the last decades of the Roman Republic. With Octavian securely established as the first Roman emperor, Augustus, the stage was set for peace and commercial expansion. Campaigning continued, especially in Germany, where the Romans were determined to extend control over the lands on the east side of the Rhine – albeit, in the end, unsuccessfully – but even so, the Augustan age brought an unprecedented degree of prosperity. Augustus himself records that he settled over 300,000 soldiers, either in colonies (many founded by him) or in their home towns, and that he gave them land or cash payments.[58] This stimulated the growth of new markets, a challenge which was readily met by profit-seeking merchants: Roman wine amphorae and fine tableware, such as the red-slipped pottery made in Arezzo in central Italy and known as Arretine *terra sigillata*, even turns up on sites as remote as southern India, testifying to a dramatic increase in the scale of trade.

Both our literary sources and the archaeological evidence confirm that some of the British tribes developed ever stronger ties with Rome at this time. The Augustan geographer Strabo tells us that some British chieftains 'procured the friendship of Caesar Augustus by sending embassies and by paying court to him', and goes on to add that virtually the whole of the island became, in effect, Roman property and that the Britons paid heavy duties on the goods they imported: 'ivory chains and necklaces and amber gems, and glass vessels and other petty wares of that sort'.[59] There was thus no point in annexing Britain, Strabo suggests, even though Augustus, according to another ancient source, Cassius Dio, did at one time have this in mind.[60] Indeed, he may have been encouraged by the arrival in Rome of Tincomarus and another chieftain, Dumnobellaunus, both of whom sought the protection of the emperor.[61]

The archaeological material, too, points to close links between Britain and the Continent in the Augustan period. If once major ports like Hengistbury were now in decline, then other regions increasingly benefited. Canterbury, for instance, was fast developing into the pre-eminent centre of eastern Kent, where the Cantiaci had long enjoyed close contact with the Roman world. However, it is Hertfordshire and Essex that have yielded the greatest bulk of imported Augustan goods, continuing a trend that, as we pointed out above, began rather earlier in the first century BC. Until recently, the precursor to Roman Verulamium (close to modern St Albans) and pre-Roman Camulodunum, near Colchester, might have been regarded as the leading centres in the region during Augustan times. However, new discoveries contradict this view. It is now apparent that a key site lay between the two modern villages of Puckeridge and Braughing (Hertfordshire), just 40 kilometres from central London along the Roman Ermine Street.[62] Here, a number of rescue excavations have poured forth an astonishing quantity of imports from the Roman world: fine Italian glass; amphorae that contained Italian wine and oil, and others used to ship Spanish *garum* or fish sauce; numerous Arretine vessels from Etruria; and pottery cups of north Italian manufacture. There were also imported *mortaria* (vessels used in the classical world in the preparation of food) and Roman toilet instruments known as *ligulae*. Particularly interesting are various *styli* or pens for writing upon wooden tablets inlaid with a wax surface; and graffiti on potsherds, one recording the name Graecus.[63] That people who were both literate in Latin and familiar with Roman tastes and customs were present at the site in Augustan times seems certain.

There is some evidence from the Puckeridge–Braughing complex to suggest that British coins were produced there, and we can hardly doubt that it was an important *oppidum*. Although the present indications are that it consisted of modest wooden buildings, far removed architecturally from the pretensions of the Mediterranean world, we are bound to wonder about the population mix in such a settlement. Clearly, it was a centre for a high-ranking Briton and his retinue; but could there have been immigrants from the Roman world too? Caesar makes many references to Roman merchants who were in Gaul before his wars of conquest, while Tacitus tells of 'business men and camp-followers from the Roman provinces' who established themselves in the palace of Maroboduus, leader of the Celtic tribe of the Marcomanni, who lived in Bohemia: 'they had been induced first by a trade agreement, and then by hopes of making more money, to migrate ... to enemy territory. Finally', observes Tacitus, 'they had forgotten their own country.'[64]

Archaeological attestation of communities of Italian merchants in Celtic strongholds is most graphically revealed at the Magdalensburg, near Klagenfurt in southern Austria. Here, an enclave of Roman traders was established about 100 BC, a commercial enterprise directed particularly at exploiting the fine iron deposits for which the region, ancient Noricum, was famous. They lived initially in wooden houses, grouped around a square recalling the so-called Piazza of the Italians on the island of Delos. When the buildings were later reconstructed in stone, some were provided with cellars, the walls of which came to be covered with graffiti: these demonstrate that, while a large proportion of the merchants came from the great Adriatic city of Aquileia, many other towns on the Italian peninsula were represented, and one trader had his home in Volubilis, an African city in what is now Morocco.[65]

With such parallels to hand, it is not difficult to envisage foreign merchants establishing themselves in regions such as Hertfordshire and Essex, especially in the major centres such as Puckeridge–Braughing. Unfortunately, we cannot be certain about the leader who may have held court there, although one plausible candidate is Tasciovanus. Despite being unknown in the pages of the ancient historians, a good deal can be said about him from his inscribed coins. He ruled the Catuvellaunian tribe in the period of Augustus, probably between about 20 BC and AD 10, and his coins have close similarities with Roman issues of the period, so much so that foreign die-cutters may again be considered a possibility. Whether he was related to Cassivellaunus, the Catuvellaunian leader who opposed Caesar, is unclear, but the celebrated British ruler Cunobelin – Suetonius' *rex Britanniorum* and Shakespeare's Cymbeline – claimed on his coins that he was Tasciovanus' son.[66] Tasciovanus also describes himself as king, using a form of the Celtic word *rigonus*, and is sometimes associated with other names (Dias is an example) which might be those of dependent or related leaders.

Some of Tasciovanus' coins have mint marks, most notably a number which bear the legend VER for Verulamium (or, more probably, 'Verlamion'). This must therefore have been a major royal centre, and excavation has indeed brought to light extensive traces of pre-Roman settlement both at Prae Wood, close to Roman Verulamium, and beneath the town itself.[67] The remains include debris from the minting of coins, as well as a ditched enclosure, some 2.2 hectares in extent, beneath the Roman forum; it has been suggested that this might represent the site of a palace compound.[68] One cemetery, that at King Harry Lane, has also been excavated in its entirety; there were some 472 burials, almost all of them containing cremations, mostly accompanied by vessels and some metalwork such as brooches.[69] Although some graves may be as early as 15 BC, none of these sites has yet yielded much material that could be contemporary with Tasciovanus – even the coin-minting debris is later – and it is impossible to draw any meaningful conclusions about the nature, status or even the location of the settlement in Tasciovanus' day.

Tasciovanus also produced a few coins bearing the mint-mark of Camulodunum. Camulodunum was to emerge as the centre for the Trinovantes, the tribe of the Essex region that came under the protective mantle of Caesar. The promontory on which Colchester stands was in the late Iron Age cut off by a system of dykes, enclosing a vast area of more than 30 square kilometres. Within this area were several separate centres of Iron-Age settlement, the oldest of which may have been at Gosbecks Farm, where subsequently there was to be an important Roman religious sanctuary. However, even at Gosbecks, there is little archaeological material even as early as Augustan times, although the coin evidence has been used to associate two British rulers of the period, Addedomarus (*c.* 15–1 BC) and the Kentish king Dubnovellaunus (*c.* AD 1–10), with Camulodunum. This must remain highly conjectural, as is the idea that Tasciovanus led the Catuvellauni in a war of conquest over the Trinovantes, thus explaining the Camulodunum mint-mark on some of his coins.[70]

Attempts to marry our fragmentary archaeological record with the data upon the coins are therefore fraught with difficulties. Tasciovanus comes down to us as a shadowy figure who probably led a peripatetic life, travelling from one royal centre to another. With Cunobelin we are on rather safer ground. His coins bear only a Camulodunum mint-mark, showing that this must have been his major royal centre and suggesting to some scholars that the Catuvellauni had established firm political control over the Trinovantes. Imported goods flooded into Camulodunum from about AD 5–10, especially from, and via, the Rhineland; here the Roman army was gradually becoming locked into a military cordon along the river, especially after the dreadful disaster of AD 9, when Varus' three legions were ambushed and annihilated by German tribesmen. A more or less permanent army provided an enormous incentive for new markets, which soon embraced Camulodunum; indeed, under Cunobelin, this well-placed site may well have come to exercise a near monopoly upon cross-Channel trade.

9 Coin of Cunobelin, ruler of the Catuvellauni of Hertfordshire and the Trinovantes of Essex c. AD 10–40. His mint at Camulodunum (Colchester) has been excavated. British Museum.

Camulodunum's enhanced status at this time is best epitomised by the great Lexden burial, a huge tumulus which today lies within the suburbs of Colchester. Investigated in 1923, it proved to cover the richest of seventeen burials known from the area. The tomb had been disturbed in antiquity, but sufficient survived to show that it contained an elaborate funeral palanquin, interred with an iron-bound chest, chain-mail, a garment or floor-covering woven with gold wire, a dozen or so wine amphorae and numerous metal objects, some of them the decorative fittings from furniture. Perhaps most notable is a medallion made up with a silver coin of the emperor Augustus, minted about 17 BC.[71]

Whilst the contents of this magnificent burial are unambiguously Roman, rather than British, both its date and the identity of its occupant have been much debated. Recent opinion favours a period of interment between about 15 and 1 BC, and Addedomarus has been canvassed as a likely personage for so splendid a tomb; yet our present evidence – which could easily be misleading – indicates that Camulodunum only became a place of importance after about AD 5, hinting at a later date for the burial. In short, we do not know, and it is probable that the name of the occupant (who might well have been a high-placed but to us anonymous individual) will never be established with certainty.

The coins of Cunobelin are widely distributed over Essex and Hertfordshire, and are also found in north-western Kent and even on small late Iron-Age farms in Oxfordshire.[72] Much controversy surrounds the interpretation of these coin-finds: to what extent do they represent an area in which Cunobelin's coins were a recognised medium of exchange, and at what level of society were they used?[73] The debate rumbles on, but it is pertinent to note that recent calculations suggest that around a million gold staters (the highest-value coins) were probably struck during Cunobelin's long reign, down to AD 40, and that issues in bronze were still more prolific.[74]

A partly monetarised economy must have been in existence within Cunobelin's main territory. Verulamium was certainly issuing coins at this time, for contemporary mint debris has been identified in deposits of this date at several points beneath the Roman city (although no mint-marks of the settlement are known on the coins of Cunobelin). The *oppidum* seems to have expanded massively during his reign while, by contrast, the Puckeridge–Braughing complex entered into a period of decline and contraction; we may infer major changes in the balance of power in a complex society which was beginning to develop more stable tendencies. When Suetonius describes Cunobelin as 'king of the Britons', it is clear recognition of his pre-eminence amongst the tribal hierarchy, and it lends credence to Dio's observation that the Dobunni of the Cotswolds and Severn Valley area were subject to the Catuvellaunians at the time of the Roman conquest.[75]

We shall not dwell in detail, however, upon the other emergent tribal units of Britain at this time, such as the Durotriges of Dorset or the Corieltauvi (or Coritani)[76] of the eastern Midlands. The use of inscribed coins, which helps to locate the different tribal groups, spread to all areas of south-eastern Britain during this period of the late Iron Age, and it was only in Wales, beyond the territory of the Dobunni and in the region to the north and west of the Coritani, that locally produced coinage did not become established. Even so, the minting of coins did not necessarily imply tribal unity, a point well brought out by recent studies of the Iceni.[77] This people, heralded in history as the tribe of Queen Boudicca, inhabited Norfolk, north-eastern Cambridgeshire and the northerly parts of Suffolk. Whilst the Iceni are not referred to as such until they staged an uprising in AD 47, there is good reason to believe that they are Caesar's Cenimagni, best interpreted as Iceni Magni, the great Iceni; they were one of five tribes (the others being otherwise unknown) to submit to him after he had placed the Trinovantes under his protection.[78] The earliest coins are gold staters, dating to about the end of the first century BC; however, silver issues of three main types soon became common, known from their motifs as the boar-horse, face-horse and pattern-horse types. These suggest the existence of three separate *pagi* or sub-groups, and present indications are that one may have focused upon the Norwich area, another in the Breckland around Thetford, and the third in the central Fens; there must also have been a fourth group in north-west Norfolk, where Snettisham, with its great tradition of rich metalworking in gold and silver alloys (electrum), was evidently the pre-eminent centre. Indeed, tribal federation, symbolised by coins bearing the legend ECEN or ECE, for Iceni, seems to have come late, probably around the time of the Roman conquest under Prasutagus, the father of Boudicca.

The finds at Snettisham have been greatly enhanced by recent discoveries. In all at least nine hoards are now known, containing some 75 complete torcs (of gold, electrum, silver and bronze); about 100 fragmentary torcs; about 100 ingot rings/bracelets; and 170 coins. This astonishing

collection, weighing over 30 kg, dates to around 70 BC and includes much metalworking debris. Higher-value objects appear to have been buried in pits with false bottoms, above which were placed less valuable items. Everything points to deliberate concealment of the wealth of an individual leader, who may have met his demise in inter-*pagus* warfare, as different sub-groups of the Iceni fought to establish domination. The location of what might be regarded as a treasury (somewhat resembling those of, for example, Delos or Delphi in the Mediterranean world, and probably protected by a deity, as at those sites), may thus have come to be forgotten.[79]

10 Stonea Camp, an *oppidum* in the heart of the Cambridgeshire Fens, occupied at the time of the Roman conquest. The discovery of skeletons in the ditches is one indicator that this may have been the site of the battle between the Iceni and the Romans in AD 47.

This concentration of wealth aptly illustrates the power and importance of the, alas, anonymous owner or owners. Indeed, the display of status by means of high-quality metalwork became an increasingly pronounced feature of the later Iron Age, matching the contemporary growth of 'conspicuous consumption' in the world of Republican Rome. The pyramid mausoleum of C. Cestius (who died in 43 BC), or the bizarre oven tomb built by the affluent baker M. Virgilius Eurysaces, are in many ways the architectural counterparts of the ostentatious 'great torc' from Snettisham or the other fine metalwork that so dominates Iron-Age displays.[80]

This brief and inevitably incomplete sketch of Iron-Age Britain has shown that we can probably infer a steady rise in the size of the population during the period, especially in the south, which was accompanied by an overall increase in the scale of arable cultivation (particularly in the use of bread wheat). At the same time, social and political systems became more complex and diverse, matching the evolution of what was likely to have been a tiered economy, operating at a variety of different levels. Thus, in the south-east there were many more denominations of coins, especially those minted in bronze, than in the adjacent peripheral regions; there coins tended to be produced largely in precious metals and were probably used principally as high-level gifts. Current thinking tends to play down the importance of invasions, but the pendulum may well have swung too far. Changes of long-term significance *were* introduced from the Continent, and Rome clearly wrought a decisive influence upon British affairs from Caesar's day onwards, if not before. Balancing arguments for internal innovation, as opposed to change brought about externally, is never easy; but the evidence for Roman manipulation of British affairs during the late Iron Age seems ever more compelling. Contemporary analogies are not hard to find. The North African kingdom of Mauretania was in Augustus' day ruled by Juba II (25 BC – AD 23). Educated in Rome, and a friend of Augustus, Juba sought to make his capital, Iol Caesarea (modern Cherchel, in Algeria), as 'Roman' as possible: he introduced, in fact, a blend of Greek and Italian traditions, combined with a touch of Egyptian (for his first wife was the daughter of Antony and Cleopatra). Italian craftsmen certainly resided in Juba's city, amongst them stonemasons and potters; and there is now at least some evidence to suggest that, in Britain too, foreigners from the Roman world may have become resident long before Claudius' invasion of AD 43. Could it be, indeed, that some of the richly furnished late Iron-Age graves, such as that found at Welwyn (Hertfordshire), contained not a British dignitary, but an affluent foreigner from the Roman world?[81]

FURTHER READING

Barry Cunliffe's *Iron Age Communities in Britain*, now in its third massive edition (1990), is the basic work of reference, and should be read in conjunction with his *Greeks, Romans and Barbarians: Spheres of Interaction* (1988), John Collis, *The European Iron Age* (1984), and the exhibition catalogue *The Celts* (1991). Some very important monographs have been published in recent years. Pride of place must go to Cunliffe's fine volumes on the hillfort at Danebury (with now *Danebury. An Iron Age Hillfort in Hampshire*, vols 4 and 5 (1991); two more are scheduled); and to Wheeler's classic report on Maiden Castle can be added N.M. Sharples, *Maiden Castle, Excavations and Field Survey 1985–6* (1991). Other important excavation monographs include I.M. Stead and V. Rigby, *Verulamium: the King Harry Lane Site* (1989); I.M. Stead, *Iron Age Cemeteries in East Yorkshire* (1991); C. Partridge, *Skeleton Green: a Late Iron Age and Romano-British Site* (1981); and B. Cunliffe, *Hengistbury Head, Dorset* (1987). Other useful volumes include S. Macready and F.H. Thompson (eds), *Cross-Channel Trade between Gaul and Britain in the Pre-Roman Iron Age* (1984); for Celtic art in Britain, I.M. Stead, *Celtic Art* (1985) and P. Jacobstahl and E.M. Jope, *Early Celtic Art of the British Isles* (1993); and for coinage C. Haselgrove, *Iron Age Coinage* (1987) and R.D. Van Arsdell, *Celtic Coinage of Britain* (1989). Finally, there is I.M. Stead *et al.*, *Lindow Man. The Body in the Bog* (1986).

— 2 —

CONQUEST AND OCCUPATION

Textbooks on Roman Britain to date [1982] make the subject appear like a nice sand-pit in which toddlers can safely be left to play.[1]

Several major syntheses of Roman Britain have appeared in new or revised form in recent years, as well as a host of more chronologically limited studies.[2] They themselves stand in a long list of histories: first Camden's *Britannia* of 1582, which culled much from the snippets in the classical authors; then Horsley's *Britannia Romana* of 1732, which exploited the evidence of inscriptions and coins to brilliant effect – 'till quite recently the best and most scholarly account of any Roman province that had been written anywhere in Europe', as Haverfield was to write in 1907;[3] and then the histories of this century, not least those of Haverfield himself, which increasingly drew on the results of methodical archaeological excavations.[4]

In some senses, therefore, the history of Roman Britain – so far as it can be reconstructed – can be said to be well understood and available in many modern discussions. However, as we commented earlier, perspectives have changed considerably over recent years. One result has been that some archaeologists have taken an increasingly 'minimalist' view of the value of historical data, emphasising not only the dearth of first-hand accounts of the province, but also the partisan and fragmentary nature of the written record.[5] When combined with the difficulty of defining historical events in terms of the archaeological data – and here, again, current interpretation favours a much more circumspect approach than before – then the difficulties of writing a narrative history of Roman Britain today become ever more apparent.

In this chapter, therefore, we shall do no more than present an outline historical framework for the province. It must necessarily highlight areas of modern controversy, almost as much as the sequence of often turbulent and colourful events which so impressed the minds of those in antiquity who chose to chronicle them. Above all, we must draw attention to the remarkable discoveries currently being made up and down the country which help to provide a material context for Rome's acquisition and control of most of a far-flung land.

It has become customary to preface any account of Roman Britain with speculations about the reasons for the conquest. Balance sheets of profit and loss are drawn up, and particular stress is laid on the fact that Claudius, having passed 'an obscure and idle life' before he became emperor, badly needed to make his mark; he thus decided 'that Britain was the country where a real triumph could be most readily earned'.[6] Moreover, as Caligula's acquisition in AD 40 of the vast kingdom of Mauretania (once ruled by Juba) showed, Rome saw no need to call a halt to territorial expansion, and the large and potentially dangerous concentrations of troops on the Rhine frontier had always to be borne in mind; Claudius' own elevation to power, at the hands of the Praetorian Guard, will have been a compelling reminder of this.

11 The emperor Claudius: head of a life-size bronze statue from Saxmundham, Suffolk. British Museum.

Despite the Ocean which to the ordinary man delimited the known world, Britain must have seemed a desirable addition, whether for political, economic or imperialist reasons; thus in AD 43 Aulus Plautius' army of some 40,000 men – four legions (the IInd Augusta, IXth Hispana, XIVth Gemina and XXth Valeria, each of about 5,000 men), together with auxiliaries (units of about 500 or 1,000 men who, their commanders apart, were not Roman citizens) – set sail from Boulogne.[7]

That some or all of the troops disembarked at Richborough, in east Kent, has long been assumed, for excavations have located beach-head defences of the period, which were soon replaced by a massive supply-base with numerous granaries.[8] Richborough (Rutupiae) was indeed to become a main gateway to Britain; a great triumphal arch was put up there in the AD 80s or 90s and must have closely resembled the arch of Trajan which still stands at Ancona, itself the upper Adriatic gateway to Italy. However, the beach-head defences at Richborough cover little more than 4 hectares, quite insufficient for a huge army, and the literary sources nowhere specify that the army landed in Kent. A recent suggestion that it may have headed for the harbours of the Chichester–Portsmouth–Southampton area, where there was pro-Roman support, has much to commend it. Archaeological evidence of the right period exists, and the distance to the main objective, Camulodunum (modern Colchester), is reasonably short. Moreover, the topography of the River Avon best fits the description in Cassius Dio of a hard-fought two-day battle at a river, usually taken to be the Medway. The evidence on the ground may well be there to find.[9]

By the late summer of 43, Camulodunum had fallen. The emperor Claudius was himself present, and the triumph was commemorated in many ways, not least by the construction of a great arch in Rome, dedicated in AD 51, on which it is proclaimed that eleven British kings surrendered to him.[10] Even in the distant town of Aphrodisias in south-western Turkey, a relief (found as recently as 1980) was set up depicting Claudius overwhelming Britannia, a pleading lady shown in the guise of an Amazon.[11]

One of the striking discoveries of the 1970s was the location of the fortress built for the XXth legion at Camulodunum. The fortress covered some 20 hectares, surrounded by a turf rampart and ditch. Some of the barracks for the 5,300 or so troops have recently been excavated, as well as the house of one of the tribunes, the six officers who assisted the legion's commander, himself a high-ranking Roman senator. The bones of six mutilated corpses were found in the ditch outside one of the gates, and hint at executions (whether of legionaries, auxiliaries or Britons we know not) in tense and difficult times.[12]

While the XXth legion was establishing a permanent base at Camulodunum, the other three legions and the auxiliaries pressed on to the north (IXth legion), north-west (XIVth) and west (IInd legion, commanded by the future emperor Vespasian). Reconstructing the course of these campaigns has long exercised scholars. Of critical importance has been the

12 A marble relief showing the emperor Claudius striking down the figure of Britannia, depicted as an Amazon. Erected in the AD 50s at Aphrodisias in south-west Turkey, the relief is a remarkable symbolic representation of Claudius' conquest. W. 1.35 m.

contribution of aerial photography which, year by year, adds ever more sites of marching camps, forts and larger military installations. To the north-east in Norfolk (the territory of the Iceni, ruled by Prasutagus), and in the southern counties of Hampshire, Sussex and part of Berkshire (the territory of Cogidumnus), Rome found allies in the form of client kings:[13] but elsewhere there was mostly opposition, some of it doubtless marshalled by Cunobelin's surviving son, Caratacus. These areas, then, are where the early military sites are to be sought.

Even with excavation, however, the picture remains far from clear-cut. It used to be thought that legionaries and auxiliaries – Roman citizens and non-citizens, crack troops and supplementary support – could be readily distinguished whether by armour, weapons or military installations. Then came the discovery of 'vexillation fortresses', camps of medium size (8–12 ha) which may have been designed to hold relatively mobile mixed legionary and auxiliary units, perhaps as winter quarters. A dozen or so are now known, but only at Longthorpe, a site just to the south-west of Peterborough, have extensive excavations taken place.[14] This work, although partial, disclosed the foundation trenches for the headquarters building, granaries and barracks, all of which were constructed of wood. Some of the structures appear, on the evidence of limited trenching, to have been very eccentrically laid out; but the permanence of the base is not in doubt, and a works depot, making pottery, ironwork and doubtless other goods such as items of leather, was set up a few hundred metres to the east of the fortress.[15]

The fortress at Longthorpe seems to have been built between about AD 44 and 48 (the latter date is more probable) and was held until about AD 61, being much reduced in size later in its history. The garrison is difficult to reconstruct, but it has been suggested that both legionaries and auxiliary cavalry and infantry troops were brigaded there, perhaps amounting to a force of about 2,500 men in all. There are difficulties with this idea, for it is now clear that some military equipment, such as the short *gladius* sword or *lorica segmentata* armour, was not used exclusively by legionaries, as was once thought:[16] but on balance a mixed garrison is the most probable interpretation.

If our archaeological data are by no means easy to interpret, then our historical sources are riddled with almost as many problems. Even so, we can plot in general terms the way in which successive governors after Aulus Plautius gradually brought the province under control, a story that can increasingly be linked with material discoveries on the ground.[17] Plautius himself returned in triumph to Rome in AD 47, having subjugated much of the lowlands. A road, the Fosse Way, which ran from Exeter to Lincoln, effectively marks the limit of his campaigning, and its permanent character is sometimes considered to imply a form of frontier (even though the concept of finite boundaries to the empire would have been incomprehensible to Romans of this time).[18] Be that as it may, Plautius' successor,

P. Ostorius Scapula, soon found himself at war. Caratacus, 'pre-eminent amongst British chieftains',[19] had been stirring up some of the tribes in Wales, especially the Silures in the south but also the Ordovices in the north. Following a brief but successful attack, Ostorius secured his rear by disarming the tribes within the province (as was his right under Roman law), and easily crushed the Icenian revolt that this provoked, a harbinger of things to come. He then marched north-westwards into the lowlands of Cheshire and on into the territory of the Deceangli, who inhabited the north-eastern corner of Wales. It was a shrewd move, since it divided Caratacus and the Deceangli from the powerful confederation that made up the Brigantes of northern England. This tribal grouping was led by their queen, Cartimandua, and it is generally held that she was amongst the eleven British rulers who had submitted to Claudius after the fall of Camulodunum.

Cartimandua was in fact to prove her loyalty. In AD 51 Caratacus, finally defeated in Wales, had sought refuge with her, to which she responded by handing him to the Romans. He was taken to Rome, where Claudius spared his life. 'Why', Caratacus is said to have asked, 'with all these great possessions, do you still covet our poor huts?'[20] Where, then, did Cartimandua live? This has been much debated, but it now seems clear that one royal centre – there may well have been several – must have been at Stanwick, near Scotch Corner (North Yorkshire), a major road-junction even then. Here there is an enormous complex of defences which encloses nearly 300 hectares and was occupied from soon after AD 43. Superficially, the site resembles one of the late Iron-Age *oppida* of southern England, but recent excavations have underlined the *romanitas* of the material remains. Although the houses so far discovered are circular, there is much roofing tile in the Roman tradition, as well as a range of imports, amongst them amphorae, glass, pottery such as the so-called Pompeian Red, and even an obsidian vessel. Coupled with the famous Stanwick metalwork hoard, which consists of 146 items, mainly elaborate equipment for chariots and their ponies, the finds are precisely what one would expect from the residence of a client queen.[21]

If the material evidence from one of Cartimandua's centres symbolises the political pacification of much of the north, then in Wales the struggle was to continue relentlessly, especially with the Silures. Ostorius died in 52, and even before his successor, Aulus Didius Gallus, could arrive, a legion was defeated.[22] But Didius gradually brought matters under control and, even though problems erupted in Brigantia, stirred up by Cartimandua's former husband, Venutius, Britannia was inexorably turning into a Roman province.

This may be measured in various ways. One extremely important facet was the integration of the local indigenous nobility into the Roman way of life. This is a matter that we shall consider in more detail elsewhere, but both in incipient townships and in the countryside, the 50s and especially the 60s saw a gradual acceptance of Roman values amongst the upper classes in many parts of lowland Britain. As we have already seen, many were already predisposed to indulge in such Roman habits as wine-drinking, and the patron-client system of Celtic Gaul may well also have operated in Britain: amongst the more politically aware within the conquered area social pressure to adapt to the new world will have been strong. In addition, from AD 49, a new *colonia* for retired legionary soldiers was rising in Camulodunum. The XXth legion had been brought forward to the front line, perhaps to Kingsholm, near Gloucester, leaving a vacuum in a region very familiar with the Roman world. Tacitus tells us that the *colonia* – the highest status that a town could achieve – 'was founded on conquered territory as a defence against rebels and to imbue the allies with a respect for law', and, when recounting its terrible sack by Boudicca in AD 61, refers to a *curia* (senate house), a theatre, the temple of Claudius and a statue of Victory.[23] Archaeological investigation beneath modern Colchester has confirmed the existence of the temple and theatre, which lie within an annexe to the east of the legionary fortress, probably with other public buildings; and has also shown that the colonists for the most part moved into the vacated barracks, which had been well and durably built.[24] In addition, they levelled the defences, probably with a view to enclosing a larger space, and developed the pre-Roman industrial centre at nearby Sheepen.[25] Here were produced metalwork, pottery, tiles, leather, and perhaps salt, although an earlier view, namely that the workers comprised '*corvées* of conscripted Britons ... packed together in ... hovels', must be resisted. More recent finds have demonstrated a high level of material wealth, not least containers for wine, olive oil and *garum* fish sauce; here, palpably, Romanisation was at work.[26]

It is probable that the temple of Claudius (which is unlikely to have been so designated until after his death) was preceded by an altar to Rome and Augustus, as at Lyon and Cologne.[27] The British aristocracy could here demonstrate their loyalty to the new order, perhaps coupled with some form of provincial assembly. At the same time the old pre-Roman centre at nearby Gosbecks (where Cunobelin himself may have held court) was respected. Although a fort was planted there for a short time, by the late first century a large temple of Romano-Celtic type had been built, placed within one corner of a *temenos* enclosure; a well-known bronze statue of Mercury, now in Colchester Museum, was ploughed up there in 1945 and must represent one of the patron deities. He was of course a god of commerce, a suitable role since nearby were a wooden theatre and many other features covering an enormous area: Gosbecks must have developed into a rural fairground and market, of a sort well known from Gaul, where religious and trading activities harmoniously mingled. Here, too, then, Roman and indigenous traditions were brought together in a manner calculated to promote Romanisation.

Not all members of the local tribe in Essex, the Trinovantes, were, however, susceptible to such manipulation, as the events of the Boudiccan revolt of AD 60–61 were later to show. Indeed, large parts of the province required tight policing from the outset, nowhere better typified than by the fort at Hod Hill in Dorset.[28] Economically tucked into one corner of a huge Iron-Age hillfort, the Roman base covers an area of 4 hectares within the defences, compared with the 22 hectares of its predecessor. Excavation showed that the hillfort, which contained some 200 houses, had been bombarded by *ballistae* – arrow-shooting catapults – probably by the IInd legion in AD 44. The fort must have been built immediately afterwards and had two structures identified as commanders' houses: this is just one of a number of factors which imply the presence of a double garrison which, it has been argued, comprised legionary infantry and auxiliary cavalry.[29] Whether this conclusion is really justified is to be doubted, since it is based mainly on assumed distinctions between legionary and auxiliary equipment which, as we suggested earlier, may be illusory. But Hod Hill, while maintained for only a few years, nevertheless offers a vivid illustration of the measures that the army was prepared to take to intimidate potential opposition, an inference which is further supported by signs of military occupation in other hillforts, such as Hembury (Devon).[30]

Similarly evocative is the so-called 'war-cemetery' at Maiden Castle, where Wheeler discovered thirty-eight skeletons of men and women, ten with cuts on the skull, one with a ballista bolt (or, more probably, a spearhead) in the back, and another with a bolt-shaped hole in the head.[31] His picture of survivors creeping out by night to bury the dead after the assault by the legionaries of Vespasian is brilliantly compelling; but modern opinion tends to date the grave goods later than AD 44,[32] just as the slaughtered bodies in the entrance of the hillfort at South Cadbury (Somerset) – seemingly the result of a Roman attack – may also belong to a post-conquest period.[33] Although Suetonius tells us that Vespasian, 'under the leadership partly of the consular legate Aulus Plautius, partly of Claudius himself, reduced to subjection two most powerful tribes and more than twenty *oppida*',[34] it is quite possible that brute force was not always necessary; a show of arms may well have done the job, leaving conflict to flare up locally later.

Even so, military bases for legionaries and auxiliaries were rapidly constructed over large parts of the province during the late 40s and 50s. Military considerations must have been predominant, but the forts and fortresses also helped to disperse the army – heavy concentrations of troops always posed a danger – and may additionally have served as centres from which to develop new forms of administration. Lead mining was even under way by AD 49 in the Mendips,[35] initially supervised by the soldiers of the IInd Augustan legion, and analysis suggests that the metal was exported as far afield as Pompeii, where it was used for building work.[36]

Working out the disposition of the troops is, however, far from easy: not only is the epigraphic record thin and the archaeological evidence incapable of really fine definition, but new sites turn up not infrequently, and their sheer size renders adequate investigation a monumental task. Moreover, as we hinted earlier, there is no real consensus about the interpretation of the so-called 'vexillation fortresses'. Were detachments from one, or more than one, legion brigaded in them, and could they also house auxiliaries? We can as yet only guess.

As far as the legions were concerned, the current conventional wisdom runs as follows. The IInd Augusta made its way westwards, establishing a full fortress at Exeter in the mid 50s, but perhaps with earlier vexillation bases at Chichester/Fishbourne, Lake Farm near Wimborne (Dorset), and perhaps at Dorchester, where there is a very early amphitheatre.[37] The revelation of the fortress at Exeter has been a particular triumph of recent years, especially its great legionary baths.[38] The IXth Hispana, on the other hand, headed northwards, as we have seen. Longthorpe apart, vexillation fortresses have been identified from the air at Newton on Trent (Lincolnshire) and Rossington Bridge (South Yorkshire), which could be of this period, while there was certainly military occupation in the Lincoln area by AD 47; the known fortress at Lincoln itself does not, however, date before about AD 60, and may have been planted over a substantial settlement of the local Corieltauvi (for the army proceeded by conquest of tribes, rather than territory).

The XIVth Gemina took a north-westerly route, and various vexillation bases in the Midlands have been proposed for it without much real evidence; but the great fortress at Wroxeter (Shropshire) is thought to have become its main base in the late 50s, probably under Veranius. This, too, is another recent discovery, the military remains being deeply embedded beneath the later Roman town.[39] Finally, there was the XXth Valeria, which had vacated Camulodunum in AD 49; one possible destination was the site at Kingsholm, 1.5 km from the city centre of Gloucester, where a large military base is gradually coming to light.[40] Even so, about AD 55, a further major base was being built at Usk, in South Wales, a matter that has also only become clear as a result of new work. The fortress was of full legionary size (19.475 ha); however, although less than ten per cent of this area was excavated in the major campaign of 1965–76, its buildings do not seem to conform to any predicted plan. There was a group of two large and five small granaries by the east gate, and elsewhere what may be workshops and stores.[41] More recently, work in the north-west corner has brought to light both conventional barracks and what could be a combined barrack and stable. Thus, while we should not expect the more rigid planning of later first-century fortresses, the layout of Usk does seem unusual, and it has been suggested that it was intended as a *hiberna* or winter quarters for the army campaigning against the Silures.[42] If so, some of the XXth legion may well have been brigaded here, perhaps in combination with other units. Alternatively, it may be that the whole of the XXth legion was based here, a matter upon which only further discoveries can shed light.

13 Tile antefix from Holt, Clwyd, made in the workshops of the XXth legion. The boar was the legion's symbol. H. 21 cm. British Museum.

However we interpret the legionary dispositions in the late 40s and 50s in detail, the evidence is clearly consistent with the western advance described for us in our literary sources. Less is known about the auxiliary units, but at Brandon Camp, a hillfort in the central Welsh Marches, the remains of what may be a Roman supply base have been investigated.[43] Occupied between about AD 55 and 60, it included a large granary and an irregular medley of other buildings, some possibly belonging to the mass of traders known to have followed the army on campaign. It lies in an area where aerial photography has disclosed many camps and forts, including a substantial enclosure at Brampton Bryan covering 25.4 hectares, large enough to have accommodated three legions. It seems most probable that it relates to the campaigns of the period.

In AD 58, Suetonius Paullinus became governor, and within two years had effectively quelled Welsh opposition. By the year 60, he was in Anglesey, destroying the sanctuary of the Druids, whose practice of human sacrifice, 'to find out the will of the gods by consulting the entrails',[44] the Romans found evil and repugnant. It was then that the first news was brought of the outbreak of a rebellion that threatened to destroy the entire province, the revolt of Boudicca.

The alleged causes and events of the rebellion are well known, and need not detain us overmuch. Tacitus lays stress upon the insufferable behaviour of the veterans at Camulodunum (a view in some conflict with the archaeological evidence discussed earlier), but debt brought about by heavy borrowing – exacerbated, no doubt, by sharp practice from the moneylenders – must have been a still more insidious incitement to revolt. Local Celtic aristocrats were expected to play a large part in 'Romanising' the province, a heavy expense, especially with buildings such as that of the imperial cult at Camulodunum to pay for. Moreover, there was the additional burden of a rapacious procurator, Catus Decianus, who in the late 50s was making moves to call in loans. Feelings ran high and the savagery of the assaults upon Camulodunum, Londinium and Verulamium has been dramatically highlighted in recent years by massive evidence for burning and destruction at these sites. For once, archaeology and history III closely cohere. The site of the final battle remains, however, unknown; but the outcome was decisive. Eighty thousand Britons are said to have fallen, as opposed to a mere 400 Romans, while Boudicca died by her own hand. A revolt that had threatened to topple Roman government was finally extinguished.

The immediately ensuing years were quiet, partly due to a wise new procurator, a provincial rather than an Italian, called Gaius Julius Classicianus; part of his tombstone has been found in London, suggesting that this had now become the seat of administration. It is possible that the town may have been rather less severely damaged than Camulodunum (where nearly every site in the main built-up area has yielded signs of destruction),[45] and London was, geographically, an obvious choice as a centre of government. But there were also moves to consolidate the Roman hold. A number of forts in East Anglia may date to this period – Tacitus tells us that strong reinforcements were sent from the Rhine – and a more general reorganisation is implied archaeologically. By AD 66, the province was sufficiently quiescent to allow the XIVth legion to be withdrawn, probably from Wroxeter, which broadly coincides with a major reorganisation of other legionary dispositions. The known fortress at Lincoln, beneath the modern town, is likely to date to either AD 61–2 or 66–7;[46] Gloucester was founded about AD 66, probably for the IInd Augusta from Exeter (although that fortress was not abandoned for at least a decade); and the XXth may have gone to Wroxeter. Tacitus saw the legions as running 'riot in times of peace' and 'despoiled and impoverished'; in reality, they must have been busy building, an uncongenial task after nearly two decades of relentless but profitable warfare.[47]

Meanwhile, in Rome Nero committed suicide on 9 June 68, and there rapidly developed a struggle for power. The year 69 saw no fewer than four successive emperors, but Vespasian, the first Flavian ruler, finally came out on top. Eight thousand legionaries from Britain were involved, and to Venutius it seemed the ideal moment to attack his former wife, Cartimandua. The governor Bolanus attempted to intervene but apparently without much success, and it was left to his successor, Q. Petillius Cerialis (an appointment of Vespasian), to initiate a decisive thrust northwards. He arrived in Britain with the newly raised IInd Adiutrix legion, and once this had been installed at Lincoln, marched on with the IXth, together with some or all of the XXth. It seems likely that a new base was now created at York, and auxiliary forts of this general period have been identified at Hayton, Malton and Brough.

It is nowhere directly reported that Cerialis defeated Venutius, but this may be presumed: that the battle took place at Stanwick is, however, unlikely for, with an enceinte more than 5.5 kilometres in circumference, it would have been a hopeless place to defend. Our ancient sources and modern scholarship combine to suggest a widespread campaign, which may conceivably have extended into southern Scotland. A series of marching camps, 8–10 hectares in size (sufficient for about 7,000 men), across the Stainmore pass must surely mark his line of march, especially as one, Rey Cross, clearly precedes the Roman road, itself probably a creation of Agricola in the late 70s or early 80s.[48] Indeed, recent examination of timbers used in the rampart of the earliest fort at Carlisle shows that they were felled in the winter of AD 72–3, while internal buildings used wood cut down in AD 73–4 and 74–5. A Cerialian date seems assured.[49]

If Cerialis concentrated his efforts on the north, then his successor, Frontinus, who took over in AD 74, was primarily occupied in Wales, where the legionary fortresses at Caerleon (for the IInd Augusta) and Chester (for the IInd Adiutrix) are to be attributed to him. However, the surviving historical sources have granted us just one sentence about Frontinus' activi-

PLATE I Sword and scabbard from a grave at Kirkburn, Yorkshire. Magnificently decorated with red enamel and engraving, it is as fine an example as any from the Celtic world. Third century BC. British Museum.

PLATE II Snettisham, Norfolk: the lower part of hoard L, excavated in 1990 and comprising twelve torcs, mainly with more than 50 per cent gold. About 70 BC.

PLATE III Excavation in Culver Street, Colchester, showing the remains of a burnt barrack, destroyed in Boudicca's sack of AD 60–61.

PLATE IV *Top* Part of a painted plaster wall from Verulamium, with a conventional classical design of a leafy scroll incorporating panther-heads and birds. British Museum.

PLATE V *Above* Reconstruction of the building at Meonstoke, Hampshire, showing the colourful and elaborate appearance of the façade, even though the building was used mainly for agricultural storage. Early fourth century.

ties in Britain, whereas the governor who followed him in AD 77 or 78 (modern opinion tends to favour the former), Gnaeus Julius Agricola, has by contrast a whole book devoted to him. Written by his son-in-law, Cornelius Tacitus, the *Agricola* was published in AD 98. Evaluating Tacitus as a historian has long exercised modern scholars, a task which is rendered still more difficult by the family ties between the two men and by Tacitus' overt desire to create a heroic character. The result is a eulogy, although justly described by one modern commentator as more 'the portrait of a career than of a man'.[50]

Tacitus relates how, in a mere seven years, Agricola campaigned from north Wales far up into Scotland, perhaps indeed to the area of Inverness, one of many possible locations for the celebrated battle of Mons Graupius, fought in AD 83 or 84.[51] At the same time, he is credited with developing the civilian side of the province, and with much fort- and road-building. Modern opinion has tended to endorse Tacitus' praises, summing Agricola up as 'a great and energetic governor', a verdict that is strongly supported by an abundance of archaeological evidence bearing witness to his activities. Those within the civilian sphere we shall allude to in chapter 3; here we shall consider his military role, albeit briefly as several detailed publications are available on the subject. Amongst the most recent is an assessment that attempts 'to cut this very paragon of a Roman Major-General down to the size of a very penny-plain civil servant and provincial hack', a view that is currently somewhat in vogue.[52] At its heart is the assumption that Agricola's predecessors, especially Cerialis and Frontinus, laid the foundations for the Roman hold over northern England and Wales, while it was his unknown successor who built the great legionary fortress at Inchtuthil and the flanking 'glen-blocking' forts in south-eastern Scotland, such as Strageath and Fendoch.

The debate is healthy, if perhaps over-iconoclastic. There is considerable evidence for Agricolan military building in the north of England, not least a large base at Red House, near Corbridge (Northumberland),[53] and signs of a carefully planned two-pronged line of attack into southern Scotland. Within two years Agricola's forces had reached the Tay, and were ordered to consolidate their position. Identifying these forts has not proved easy, but a recent spectacular excavation at Elginhaugh, on the Dere Street to the south-east of Edinburgh, has shown what may be expected.[54] This fort, which covered 1.26 hectares within its ramparts, was completely stripped, revealing a broadly familiar plan, but with sufficient oddities to underline the value of this type of approach to excavation. Within the central range, as expected, were the timber-built headquarters (*principia*); an extensive commander's house (*praetorium*), with its own kitchens and lavatory; and two granaries. To the north, in the *retentura*, were four barracks, two probably for cavalry, and to the south, in the *praetentura*, a further eight blocks, seven for infantry and one probably for stores. This would give a garrison of about 800 men, a size and composition which is difficult to

parallel; but it does indicate that army units were much less rigidly organised than is sometimes suggested.

There was also a stone-built workshop – an obvious precaution against fire – and a bath-house placed outside the fort, beside the river. A large annexe, nearly a hectare in size, was also provided. It was defended with a turf rampart and ditch, and contained several wooden buildings, kilns and ovens. These annexes are often thought to have been for civilian 'camp-followers', but it is argued that this particular one served to house animals (including the horses of the cavalry), wagons and workshops; some of the rubbish was also buried there.

The men of the fort at Elginhaugh lived comparatively well. Wine, olive oil and figs were brought from the Mediterranean, and wheat and barley (the latter probably for fodder) are abundantly attested. The supply routes

14 Excavations in progress on the fort of Elginhaugh, Lothian, dating from about AD 80. The foundation trenches of a pair of timber barracks are coming to light, with their series of small rooms.

seem to have been well organised, although, as we shall see, the Vindolanda tablets of a slightly later date point to a shadowy world of wheeling and dealing in frontier country. Even so, there is conveyed an impression of relative comfort and permanence and, above all, the intention of staying: Agricola's conquest was not to be ephemeral.

To the south of the Forth–Clyde isthmus, about fifteen forts have yielded evidence for Flavian occupation, and some at least will have been founded by Agricola. A key site was Newstead, a large fort (4.28 ha) also on Dere Street. Situated below a major hillfort at Eildon Hill North, it was destined to remain of great strategic importance throughout the Roman occupation of Scotland. On the other side of the Cheviots, there is another very large fort (3.2 ha) at Dalswinton, another strategic location on the northern corridor through Annandale. Flavian sites are, however, apparently scarce in Dumfries and Galloway, even though it is probably this region that Agricola invaded in the fifth year of his campaign, when 'the whole side of Britain that faces Ireland was lined with his forces'.[55]

In September 81 Domitian became emperor, and it was presumably he who ordered a resumption of the northern campaigns beyond the Forth–Clyde isthmus which were to lead ultimately to the battle of Mons Graupius. Attributed to Agricola (or, less plausibly, to his successor) are the great legionary fortress at Inchtuthil and a string of forts distributed at the mouths of the Highland glens in south-east Scotland, where they could serve to block incursions or act as bases for a forward advance. Two recently published classic excavations illuminate the nature of these military bases, the auxiliary fort at Strageath and the Inchtuthil fortress.[56]

Inchtuthil lies close to the River Tay, near the mouth of the Dunkeld Gorge, a position which might be seen as a springboard for further campaigns in the Highlands. Its plan is now amongst the most complete for a legionary fortress anywhere in the Roman empire, a remarkable tribute to its excavators, Richmond and St Joseph. The fortress, which covers 21.74 hectares, had a full complement of barracks, $65\frac{1}{2}$ in all; a headquarters, six granaries, four houses for officers, *tabernae* (shop-like rooms for storage or, possibly, accommodation), a large hospital and workshops. Interestingly, some buildings, namely the legate's residence, three houses for officers, two granaries and the legionary baths, had not been constructed when the order came to demolish and evacuate the fortress, probably early in AD 87 – an important comment on the order of priorities. However, there were adjacent compounds, notably a large labour camp of 19.9 hectares, where rows of rubbish pits betray a regular layout of tents; a small enclosure of 1.5 hectares, with officers' houses, a bath-house and two barracks; and a further compound (the so-called 'Redoubt') of 1.65 hectares, where stores and wagons may have been kept. Although there is no proof, it seems likely that it was the XXth legion that was based here, and, if the provision in a second phase of a massive stone wall, fronting the original turf rampart, is any guide, permanence was envisaged.

The fort at Strageath lies some 32 kilometres to the south-west of Inch-tuthil, on the south side of the River Earn. It is conjectured that a legionary force may have constructed the defences and a small granary, which was demolished when the auxiliary unit arrived. The permanent garrison then built twelve barracks, a workshop, a stable or store-building, two exceptionally large granaries and the headquarters and commander's house. There was also what was probably a hospital, immediately to the south of the *principia*. Reconstructing the garrison is extremely problematic, but it is suggested that it included parts of two *cohortes equitatae* (mixed units of infantry and cavalry, nominally of 500 men), and possibly one under-strength century (theoretically 80 men) of legionaries.

The large size of the granaries at Strageath may well imply that they served not only the needs of the garrison, but also those of the army on campaign. Moreover, there are some hints of pottery and tile production, while lead and iron ingots (the lead, at least, of northern provenance) point at the rapid development of mineral exploitation within newly conquered territory. At Inchtuthil, too, local pottery production was immediately initiated. Interestingly, Strageath (but less so Inchtuthil) yielded many pots made in the Verulamium region and, it would seem, in Gaul (both *mortaria* and samian), raising fascinating questions about the mechanisms of supply. There are perhaps signs here of enterprising civilian merchants, working side by side with officialdom; the army may well have been concerned to develop local production, whether of food or manufactured goods, but recognised that private enterprise also played its part. Coinage, after all, reached the province primarily through military pay-packets, and, in Agricola's time, a large part of the army was active in the north: the commercial opportunities will not have been lost on those prepared to take the risks.

The complexity of interpreting individual fort sites, even when extensively excavated, is matched by the difficulties of understanding the broader picture: it is a significant comment on the state of our knowledge that between 1977 and 1984 no fewer than eight permanent Flavian military sites were discovered in Scotland. These include a number of small forts or fortlets, and indeed it is now suggested that there may have been a form of frontier stretching north-eastwards from Doune, near Stirling, up to Bertha, near Perth, in effect from the Forth to the Tay. Strageath will have been a pivotal point, especially as a series of watch-towers (the so-called Gask Frontier), which stretches away eastwards, may belong to this period. Close military control of the local population is clearly implied.[57]

The culmination of Agricola's campaigns came in 83 or 84, with the battle of Mons Graupius. Its site is unknown, but the result was a decisive Roman victory. Yet the archaeological evidence is no less unequivocal that there was a massive programme of demolition in or soon after AD 86, followed by a total withdrawal into southern Scotland, to a line well below the Forth–Clyde isthmus. Most modern scholars link this with incursions of Dacians in the Danube area of modern Romania, which began in AD 85,

15 The western defences of the fort at Strageath, Tayside. The turf ramparts of the Flavian (right) and Antonine periods are seen as a variegated pattern in section.

initiating a period of serious warfare. The IInd Adiutrix legion was summoned from Britain (probably from Chester, although exactly when is uncertain), and other troops may have gone too. For Tacitus, who detested the reigning emperor, Domitian, 'the conquest of Britain was completed, and then let slip'; but in reality the withdrawal was prudent, especially as memories of the events of AD 60–61 will scarcely have faded.[58]

Tacitus lived until about AD 120, but Britain was never again to be central to his thoughts; indeed, as far as the ancient written sources are concerned, the province becomes a shadowy world for nearly forty years after the battle of Mons Graupius. The archaeological evidence, on the other hand, suggests that a frontier line eventually settled on Agricola's road, now known as the Stanegate, just south of and parallel with Hadrian's Wall. Although traces of a palisade and ditch, as well as watch-towers, have been identified in parts of the western sector, south of the Solway Firth, we have little clear idea of how it functioned.[59] As understood at present, it consisted mainly of a road, connecting forts and fortlets at places such as Carlisle, Vindolanda (Chesterholm) and Corbridge. The site of Corbridge, which lies at the lowest crossing of the River Tyne and on the line of the great northern route of Dere Street, was destined always to be of importance, as Agricola realised when he built a supply base nearby at Red House (now partially covered by the Corbridge by-pass). The earliest fort dates to about AD 86, and may have been as large as 5.2 hectares within the ramparts.[60] It was dismantled and burnt down about AD 103 (enemy action, often claimed, now seems unlikely) and replaced by a fort half the size, perhaps as part of a reallocation of forces; interestingly, this broadly coincides with Trajan's wars in Dacia (in AD 101–2 and 105–6), which may well have necessitated the requisitioning of troops from Britain.

The most informative source for this period comes, however, from the remarkable cache of documents, written mainly in ink upon wood, from the pre-Hadrianic forts at Vindolanda, just to the south of Hadrian's Wall.[61] More than a thousand are now known, most very fragmentary but some astonishingly complete, and it is intriguing to discover that the handwriting (the so-called Old Roman Cursive) and the language can be very closely paralleled by contemporary *ostraca* (potsherds with writing in ink on them) from the fort at Mons Claudianus in Egypt's eastern desert, not far from the Red Sea port of Safaga. A remarkable diffusion of literary standards amongst the military is indicated.

The Vindolanda tablets date from about AD 90 to 120, and include drafts and file copies of letters; military reports, rosters, recommendations, lists of supplies and requests for leave, and even private correspondence. It would seem that from about AD 90 to about AD 105, the ninth, and probably the eighth, cohorts of Batavians were stationed there, with Flavius Cerialis as commander, at least for part of the time. His wife, Sulpicia Lepidina, corresponded with Claudia Severa, wife of Aelius Brocchus, who must have been in command of another cohort in the area, as is implied by the following letter:[62]

> Claudia Severa to her Lepidina, greetings.
> On the third day before the Ides of September [i.e. 10 September], sister, for the day of the celebration of my birthday, I give you a warm invitation to make sure that you come to us, to make the day more enjoyable for me by your arrival, if you come.
> Give my greetings to your Cerialis. My Aelius and my little son send you their greetings.
> [in a second hand]
> I shall expect you, sister. Farewell, sister, my dearest soul, as I hope to prosper, and hail.
> [on outside]
> To Sulpicia Lepidina (wife) of Flavius Cerialis; from Severa.

The salutation is almost certainly in Claudia Severa's own hand, and this evocative picture of wives on the northern frontier contentedly entertaining each other is as compelling as it is unexpected. Even children are mentioned several times (their shoes have also survived), perhaps providing a context for a tablet with a line from Virgil's *Aeneid*, which may be a handwriting exercise. Indeed, warfare hardly features in the documents, although there is a dismissive note about the military capabilities of the Britons (*Brittones*) who 'are unprotected by armour. There are very many cavalry, but they do not use swords nor do the *Brittunculi* ["Little Brits"] take up fixed positions in order to throw javelins.'

Many of the tablets are taken up with records of building work and

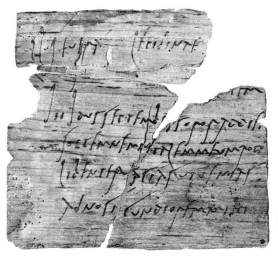

16 The famous birthday invitation from Claudia Severa to Sulpicia Lepidina, wife of the commandant at the Vindolanda fort. British Museum.

supplies. Barley, Celtic beer (*cervesa*, hence the modern Spanish *cerveza*), vintage wine, sour wine, *garum* fish sauce, lard, salt, spices, wheat and various meats – ham, pork, roe-deer and venison – all commonly feature; there is even mention of a gift of fifty oysters and, of course, the now famous 'parcel from home', with pairs of socks, sandals and underpants. The transport of hides, stone and timber also figures, while a remarkable letter records the delivery of 34 hubs, 48 axles for carts, 300+ spokes, 25 planks for beds, [...]8 seats and 6 goatskins. Another official document further describes how 343 soldiers are assigned to duties in the workshops, the tasks including the building of a bath-house and a hospital, plastering, and assignments at the kilns (probably making bricks and tiles).

This picture of a busy programme of building and maintenance is not at all inconsistent with what we know from archaeological sources. On the other hand, there are some surprises in the tablets. A recently discovered letter, written by one Octavius to a man called Candidus, at Vindolanda, complains bitterly about a sum of money – 500 denarii – that is owed to him, and it is evident that he was involved in the supply of grain and cattle-hides and in other purchases.[63] He is also concerned about the state of the roads, which he says are impassable to vehicles, his problem being that he needs to transport cattle-hides from Catterick.[64] Although we know neither who Octavius was, nor where he was writing from, it seems likely that he was a trader who was closely involved in numerous and perhaps shady deals, a practice that may well have been commonplace in military areas (although the Vindolanda tablets do show a considerable emphasis upon book-keeping). Another most interesting feature is a 'strength report', apparently relating to a cohort of Tungrians (from Gallia Belgica), with 761 men. Of these, only 284 were stationed at Vindolanda, and thirty were either ill, wounded (just six) or suffering from an eye complaint (nine). Of the remaining 477, a large number (perhaps 336) were at Corio, probably

17 A bronze plaque found at the legionary fortress at Caerleon, Gwent. It bears a finely modelled figure of a winged Victory, with a trophy that includes a helmet, cuirass, shields and trumpets. It may derive from a piece of parade armour. Probably second century. H. 26.2 cm. Caerleon Museum.

Corbridge, while the others were variously distributed; the one clearly identifiable place is London, where sixteen men were carrying out duties for the governor (*legatus*).

This document provides remarkable confirmation that, whatever the nominal size of a unit, in practice it could be well under strength, at any rate at Vindolanda itself. Moreover, it would seem that mixed forces under a single commander may not have been uncommon, as indeed the evidence of excavation implies. The tablets therefore furnish us with an insight into the Roman world which is as unprejudiced as it is informative. Known figures, like the governor in AD 103, L. Neratius Marcellus, do appear, and even Rome is once mentioned; but, in the main, the concerns are local and mundane, and in many senses all the more valuable for it.

One place that is mentioned in the Vindolanda tablets is Luguvalium (modern Carlisle), where, as we have seen, there was a military base from the early AD 70s. Karus writes a letter to Cerialis, the commander at Vindolanda, soliciting his support for one Brigonius: 'I ask that you think fit to recommend him to Annius Equester, centurion in charge of the region, at Luguvalium.'[65] Equester's title is an interesting one, and it may well imply that he was in charge of organising the western sector of the Stanegate frontier. Certainly Luguvalium must have been a busy place in the late 80s and 90s, and it, too, has recently yielded writing tablets. One is addressed to M. Iulius Martialis, 'Trimontio aut Luguvalio' (at Newstead or Carlisle); perhaps Martialis was involved in both places, and his correspondent did not know where he was at that moment. Sadly, the contents of the letter defy interpretation.[66]

We shall see in a later chapter how the Flavian period (AD 69–96) also witnessed remarkable developments in the civilian area of the province; but the north of England and large parts of Wales were to remain resolutely under military control. There is evidence of building in the permanence of stone at the legionary fortresses of Caerleon, Chester and York early in the second century, and at a number of auxiliary forts. A strong army presence was clearly necessary. When Hadrian became emperor in AD 117, as we learn from his biographer, 'the Britons could no longer be held under Roman control', a hint perhaps of a new generation of warlike tribesmen in northern Britain.[67] Campaigns there surely were, and the result is commemorated in a great war-memorial found at Jarrow but presumably from elsewhere, which, if correctly reconstructed, proclaims how 'after the barbarians had been dispersed and the province of Britain had been recovered, [Hadrian] added a frontier-line between either shore of the Ocean for 80 miles. The army of the province built this defence-work under the charge of Aulus Platorius Nepos, emperor's pro-praetorian legate.'[68] Hadrian's biographer adds that the wall was intended 'to divide the Romans from the barbarians'.

One of the legions involved in this work was the VIth Victrix, which Nepos undoubtedly brought with him in AD 122 from his previous posting as governor of Lower Germany. Whether the IXth Hispana was still in Britain at this time is uncertain. It is not attested in the province after AD 107/8, and may ultimately have been annihilated in the East in 161.[69] It is intriguing to reflect that the last known commander of the legion, L. Aninius Sextius Florentinus, came to be buried in a truly monumental tomb at the great Nabataean city of Petra in Arabia, a province of which he became governor in about AD 126; nothing could illustrate more vividly the mobility of more influential individuals within the vast Roman empire.[70]

18 Building inscription, reused in a later wall, from the fort at Bewcastle, to the north of Hadrian's Wall in Cumbria. It records work done by a vexillation (detachment) of the Legio VI V(ictrix) P(iae) F(idelis).

Hadrian's Wall itself has become so specialised an area of study, backed up by many admirable publications, that we need not dwell unduly upon it. What must be emphasised are the discoveries resulting from new work. Three stretches of the curtain have been investigated in recent years, with an exceptionally clear sequence at Peel Gap in the western part of the central sector.[71] The earliest construction was the Broad Wall (about 3 m wide), which was begun but not completed; silt then accumulated over the footings before the Narrow Wall (about 2.40 m wide) was constructed, a change probably associated with the decision in the mid-Hadrianic period to add sixteen forts to the Wall. Finally, a still narrower wall (about 2 m wide) was built in the early third century, when various renovations were put in hand during the reign of Septimius Severus. Interestingly, the excavations revealed a wholly unsuspected tower between the two known, normally spaced, turrets. It is a reminder that the 'blueprint' was not always rigorously adhered to.

It is also now clear that elaborate provision was made for the protection of the vulnerable coastline of north-west Cumbria, beyond the western end of the Wall itself. There was a regular system of fortlets and towers, spaced, as on most of the Wall, at intervals of one Roman mile (1480 m) and one-third of a Roman mile respectively. In some sectors these were set within a cordon of two parallel wooden palisades (although of slight construction). The system carried on for at least 40 kilometres beyond the end of the Wall, and there may have been further fortlets in the Ravenglass area, 94 kilometres beyond. The massiveness of these measures to regulate life and to contain opposition in northern Britain could not be more sharply manifested, a remarkable contrast with the expansionist policy of the previous century.[72]

If the Vindolanda Tablets disclose to us some of the personalities and preoccupations of the Roman community in the north, then recent excavations at Wallsend, Housesteads and, currently, at Birdoswald, tell us much about the layout and history of the forts. Wallsend, in particular, has yielded a remarkably complete plan, especially given the fact that the site was totally covered until recently by modern buildings. At least eight barracks of the Hadrianic period were found, as well as stables, a workshop, a hospital, two conjoined granaries, the headquarters building and the commander's residence, by far the largest structure in the fort. The plan is therefore relatively standard, and was probably designed for a part-mounted unit of about 480 men.[73]

The underlying strategy behind the Wall and its constituent parts has been much debated. The rigidity of its layout would seem to stem from a high-level edict – most probably of Hadrian himself – issued without detailed local knowledge and possibly with little forethought. It remained for the men on the spot to work out the details and, by adapting the original design, to make the frontier work. Tight control of those who wished to cross it, which attracted levies, was clearly important, while the paper strength of the auxiliaries on the Wall – about 15,000 troops – was sufficient to quell the local opposition that so gigantic a barrier must have from time to time provoked. But little more than this can safely be said.[74]

Still more difficult to understand are the reasons behind the creation of the Antonine Wall, a completely new frontier between the Forth and the Clyde, only two decades or so after Hadrian's Wall was initiated. The evidence needed to understand this seemingly strange decision simply does not exist, although modern scholarship tends to stress the fact that

19 Excavations on Hadrians' Wall at Highshield Crag near Castle Nick (milecastle 39).

the order to advance came very soon after the accession of Antoninus Pius on 10 July 138, and that he may therefore have been seeking military prestige.[75] This does not, however, seem particularly consistent with his temperament, which, according to the contemporary orator Aelius Aristides, was that of an enlightened monarch who created a Golden Age,[76] and it seems more probable that the decision was largely a consequence of a new phase of tribal opposition. At any rate, we know that the new governor, Lollius Urbicus, was making preparations in AD 139, building granaries at Corbridge[77] and refurbishing the fort at High Rochester,[78] both on Dere Street. By 142–3 victory had been achieved.

As with Hadrian's Wall, we shall here highlight only a few features of its Antonine successor. It, too, had a complex history, but only in 1975 was it realised that the original plan appears to have been for only six forts, spaced at intervals of about 12.8 kilometres, with fortlets at every Roman mile between.[79] This brilliant inference from the data then available is rapidly being confirmed by fieldwork directed at locating the mile fortlets; five more have now been found, bringing the total known to nine. Turrets seem, however, to have been excluded from the blueprint, and ten forts were added later, at intervals of about 2 miles. The Wall itself was made of turf, with a stone base, while the forts generally contain a far from regular series of buildings. Bearsden, for example, a small fort of 1.1 hectares which has been as completely excavated as possible, has yielded barracks, stables, store buildings, a workshop and two granaries, but lacks both a headquarters and a commandant's residence. Interestingly, meat seems to have played only a small part in the men's diet, although they did eat wild strawberries, raspberries and figs, and flavoured their food with opium poppies and coriander seeds: such, at any rate, are the results of a study of the sewage.[80]

20 Sestertius of Antoninus Pius, showing on the reverse Britannia seated on rocks and holding a standard and shield. Struck in AD 142–3 to commemorate Lollius Urbicus' victories in Scotland. British Museum.

The force stationed on the Antonine Wall was almost as large as that deployed on Hadrian's Wall, even though the new frontier was less than half the length, only 60 kilometres. Southern Scotland was also heavily garrisoned, and there were several outpost forts, stretching up to the northeast. Strageath was amongst them; the old Agricolan ramparts were refaced with turf, and buildings appropriate to a part-mounted cohort constructed. They were much more conventionally laid out than on the Antonine Wall itself, and were evidently intended to be permanent.[81]

In the event, the Antonine frontier in southern Scotland was held only briefly. An inscription records building work on Hadrian's Wall between milecastles 11 and 13 in AD 158,[82] and archaeological evidence suggests that the Antonine Wall was abandoned at this time. It is conventionally held today that this was the outcome of a rebellion within the province, a conclusion supported by an inscription from the Tyne at Newcastle, which is best interpreted as indicating the arrival of reinforcements for all three British legions from Germany (perhaps a force that had been sent there some years earlier).[83] Certainly trouble in the north of England is implied, and it would have been logical to withdraw from the Antonine frontier. The archaeological evidence is also explicit in showing that the Antonine Wall was subsequently recommissioned, albeit with a reduced force. The question, however, is when, and for how long, a matter which has inspired much debate and controversy. The issues are too complex to be considered in detail here; but the view, currently widely accepted, that the Antonine Wall was recommissioned in about AD 159 and soon again abandoned, about AD 163, is not without its difficulties. Although it has been argued that the pottery supports this date, there are later coins and, it would seem, inscriptions. Moreover, Dio tells us that the Maeatae, a tribe based in the Falkirk–Stirling area, 'live close to the wall that divides the island in two'.[84] This should therefore refer to the Antonine Wall and, since Dio began collecting information about AD 197, may relate to the situation in the later second century. A possible context for the remanning of the Antonine Wall might therefore be in the aftermath of the war of about AD 181, when northern tribes crossed 'the wall' (which one is not stated) and killed a general. The emperor Commodus sent Ulpius Marcellus to deal with the situation, and coins of AD 184 commemorate both a victory and Commodus' adoption of the title Britannicus; this, then, might have been the moment when the Antonine Wall was recommissioned, although the matter is far from decided.[85]

The accession in AD 193 of the African dynasty of the Severi was a turning point in the long saga of the Roman empire; Italy finally lost its supremacy and, from then onwards, power came to be concentrated in the hands of provincials. One of the two other claimants for the purple was the governor of Britain, Clodius Albinus; but he was decisively defeated by Septimius Severus outside Lyon early in 197, and the new governor, Virius Lupus, was obliged to buy off the Maeatae. Whether they invaded the province is still hotly argued (the ancient sources are silent), since identifying destruction deposits caused by enemy hands in the archaeological record is extremely difficult; but what is not in doubt is that Hadrian's Wall was extensively reconstructed – so much so, that Severus was later credited as its builder.[86] Inscriptions show that much of this work was carried out between 205 and 207, when Alfenus Senecio was governor, and it could be that this followed the ultimate withdrawal from the Antonine Wall. Whatever the truth of that, both literary and archaeological sources help to document campaigns led first by Severus and then by his son, Caracalla, in south-east Scotland between about 208 and 211. Severus was to die in February 211, in York (where part of what may have been his palace has recently been discovered), and Caracalla may have fought one more campaign later that year, before imposing terms on the Maeatae and Caledonians. Marching camps probably of this period have been identified stretching up into south-east Scotland, and a large base of nearly 10 hectares has been partially investigated at Carpow, on the south side of the Tay.[87] In addition, the coastal fort at South Shields was turned into a huge supply base. Initially, to the pair of existing granaries were added at least thirteen more, and others were built later, bringing the total to twenty-three. The capacity was about 3,200 tonnes, sufficient to feed 15,000 men for six months; interestingly, the grain included much bread wheat, probably shipped in from the Continent.[88] There were also new works, including the rebuilding of a granary at Corbridge, suggesting that the Dere Street was amongst the lines of supply.

The Severan campaigns in Scotland were apparently to bring peace to Britannia for nearly a century. About the same time, the province was divided into two, Britannia Inferior (which included York and Lincoln) and Britannia Superior, administered from London. More significantly, in 212 (or 214) Caracalla proclaimed an edict granting citizenship to all freeborn. Soldiers were also now allowed to marry, which in the long term was to tie them ever more closely to their bases. These were fundamental social changes which in time helped to create the very different world of the later empire.

What is remarkable, however, is that Britain largely escaped the disastrous consequences of a period between AD 244 and 284 which brought more than fifty rulers, of one sort or another, to prominence – and usually to a rapid death. Coupled with invasions, wars, folk movements and soaring inflation, parts of the empire, not least Gaul, were plunged into chaos and anarchy. It is not easy to measure the effect of those events upon Britain; but the Channel will have helped to isolate the province, and the northern tribesmen, so far as we know, stayed quiescent. There is evidence, both epigraphic and archaeological, of routine repair work at a number of military bases, and there was work, too, on some of the roads. One is nevertheless left with the impression that the island's standing garrison must have been much reduced by the requirement for soldiers elsewhere. Some forts seem to have been completely evacuated, while others may have been manned by quite small forces, which could be supplemented as necessary. Indeed, one estimate considers that there may have been fewer than 20,000 troops in Britain by about AD 300.[89]

During the third century, there were also significant changes in the deployment and nature of some military bases, especially in southern Britain. In the second century the military presence in the south had been very limited. There was a fort of 4 hectares in London; very probably one of the later second century at Brancaster in north Norfolk; a base covering about 1 hectare for the British fleet, the Classis Britannica, at Dover; and possible forts for the fleet at Lympne and Reculver (both in Kent), both of which have yielded suitably stamped tiles (also found in abundance at Dover). The fleet was of particular importance. Although also employed in building work (including Hadrian's Wall) and iron-working, its principal peacetime role was to suppress piracy, an endemic feature of the ancient world. Its main base was at Boulogne, where there was a town of 60 hectares, including a 12 hectare fort on the hill overlooking the harbour;

this has also yielded CL.BR tiles, as well as inscriptions which amply confirm the fleet's presence.[90]

Although the Classis Britannica is not directly attested after the 240s, its continued existence can hardly be doubted, although probably on a reduced scale.[91] This may be the explanation for the abandonment of the base at Dover in the early third century, and for a decrease of accommodation in the fort at Boulogne. But there are no records of naval engagements before 286, when M. Aurelius Mausaeus Carausius, who came from the coastal lands of Belgium, was given a naval command and charged with suppressing raids by the Saxons and Franks on the shores of northern Gaul. Accused by the government of personal profiteering, but presumably backed by the legions in Britain, he established himself as emperor of Britain and northern Gaul, with an eye on the throne in Rome itself. But two years earlier, a soldier of low social rank from Dalmatia (modern Yugoslavia) had become emperor: Gaius Aurelius Valerius Diocletian. This was to be a further watershed in the history of the empire, since Diocletian was a ruler of genius with capabilities that have been justly compared with those of Augustus himself. In 293 he set up a tetrarchy of rulers, two senior (Augusti) and two junior (Caesars). Diocletian himself oversaw the East, aided by Galerius, while Maximian and his junior, Constantius Chlorus, administered the West.

21 Antoninianus of Carausius, about AD 292, possibly struck at Colchester. It shows Carausius with the emperors Diocletian and Maximian; with the inscription CARAUSIUS ET FRATRES SUI ('Carausius and his brothers'), this is an attempt to legitimise his usurpation. British Museum.

In Britain and Gaul, Carausius was able to enjoy just seven years of rule. In 293 Constantius took Boulogne, and soon afterwards Carausius was murdered by his finance minister, Allectus. Interestingly, recent work at Peter's Hill, to the south of St Paul's Cathedral in the City of London, has demonstrated the existence of what may be a palace, built, on dendro-chronological evidence, in 293–4: Allectus must have been responsible.[92] Three years later, Constantius invaded Britain, and Allectus was defeated in a battle near Silchester and slain. Now reforms could be put into effect, amongst them a further division of Britannia into provinces, described in the Verona List of AD 314 as Prima, Secunda, Maxima Caesariensis and Flavia Caesariensis. Across the empire as a whole, relative stability was achieved, inflation was checked, and the beginnings of change were brought to the army, with the creation of *duces*, whose role was quite separate from civilian administration. Later, Constantine I was to extend this by introducing a new distinction between *limitanei*, who guarded the frontiers, and *comitatenses*, mobile field armies of higher-grade troops. Although the old regimental titles were often retained, the once fundamental division between legionaries and auxiliaries had gone: a new type of army was needed to respond to the quite different world of the late empire, where threats could arise at any time, in any place.

The disposition and appearance of some third-century military bases in Britain (and elsewhere) to some extent anticipated these developments. In the course of the century, the south-eastern coast was provided with a series of forts which the *Notitia Dignitatum*, a document apparently of early fifth-century date, describes as the frontier of the *litus Saxonicum*, the Saxon Shore. Typological and archaeological considerations imply that the system was put in place gradually during the third century, although with a spurt in the 270s and 280s. The earliest forts are probably Brancaster and Reculver, which are laid out, so far as we know, on fairly traditional lines. But their later successors, such as Burgh Castle, Richborough and Lympne, have massive high walls and external towers, and in some instances have lost the rectangularity of plan which so characterises earlier military architecture: they were as much places to be defended as bases from which to attack.[93]

The chronology of these forts is controversial, but Probus, emperor from 276 to 282, was surely responsible for some. It was he who completed the massive walls of Rome, begun by his predecessor Aurelian, and he is credited with much work on town walls in Gaul.[94] Coin finds suggest that Carausius may have constructed Portchester (Hampshire), while the strangely ovoid plan, and a coin apparently from beneath one of the towers, point to a date in the 330s for Pevensey (Sussex). In short, these coastal defences seem to have been built up relatively gradually, although most belong to the later third century – a period when many towns in Britain were likewise provided with strong masonry walls.[95]

Very little is known of the internal arrangements of the Saxon Shore forts. Stone-built headquarters buildings have been identified, with greater or lesser certainty, at four of the ten forts (Brancaster, Reculver, Richborough and Lympne), as well as a few other substantial structures, such as baths. But large-scale work at Burgh Castle and Portchester has failed to reveal any proper barracks (but plenty of evidence for occupation, including finds suggestive of the presence of women and children); it all hints at a significant departure from the rigorous standards of before.

What, then, was the purpose of the Saxon Shore *limes*? Five of the forts had good harbours, and there seems little doubt that detachments of the Classis Britannica (whatever that was now called) were based there, alongside, or as part of, the units stationed there. Contact by sea with the other forts would have been easy, since all have suitable beaches, and regular patrol of the waters between Britain and the Continent was doubtless desirable: hence the existence of a comparable series of fortified coastal sites stretching from Belgium down into Brittany. Given, however, both the likely diminution in the size of the available forces and the plurality of forts, it is by no means impossible that vexillations were moved as the need arose: hence the apparent lack of permanence in the accommodation within these massively constructed military bases.

Some forts in the north-west of England were also reoccupied in the mid- to late third century. At Watercrook near Kendal, for example, one of the guard-chambers yielded an occupation layer containing four coins of the period 268–73; the room does not seem to have been used after the 220s, and the whole fort may have been empty during this period.[96] Similarly, at

Lancaster in about 262–6 'the bath-house and basilica which had collapsed through old age' were restored from ground level;[97] again this follows a period of little or no military activity. Interestingly, a *numerus Barcariorum* – unit of boatmen – may have been stationed here, and may have been involved in naval patrols; still more significantly, sometime after 326 Lancaster was provided with defences of the Saxon Shore type, one of very few sites in the north to be remodelled in this way. The others include Cardiff and Caer Gybi (Anglesey), and it may be that, in combination with other coastal forts known to be in occupation at this time, such as Ravenglass and Maryport, both in Cumbria, particular attention was also being paid to surveillance of the western seaways.

But with these words we have come firmly into the problems of the fourth century, which will be the subject of the final chapter. Sketching out some of the evidence – and problems – relating to the military history and archaeology of Roman Britain is a task made difficult by the limited, prejudiced and inaccurate nature of the written sources; by the scarcity and complexity of the epigraphic evidence; and by the profound problems of using archaeological data, which is both anonymous and very rarely easy to relate to known (or perceived) historical 'events'. It is with these caveats in mind that we shall conclude this chapter, and turn our attention to the civilian population.

FURTHER READING

We have tended in this chapter to follow a fairly conventional approach of the sort excellently exemplified by, among others, I.A. Richmond, *Roman Britain* (2nd edn, 1963), S.S. Frere, *Britannia* (3rd edn, 1987) and P. Salway, *Roman Britain* (1981). It is, however, only fair to say that there are moves away from these attempts to write a 'narrative history' from the snippets of information in the ancient sources and the archaeological evidence. Martin Millett's *The Romanization of Britain* (1990) is particularly interesting in this respect; see also Richard Reece's review of Salway in *Archaeological Journal* 139 (1982), 453f., and W.S. Hanson, *Agricola and the Conquest of the North* (1987). G. Wester (ed.), *Fortress into City* (1988) contains excellent essays on the military origins of six towns, and there are some exemplary recent monographs on fortresses and forts, amongst them Manning 1981 and 1989 on Usk, Pitts and St Joseph 1985 on Inchtuthil, Bidwell 1979 on Exeter, Frere and Wilkes 1989 on Strageath, and Zienkiewicz 1986 on Caerleon. The Carlisle material is gradually being published, with now M.R. McCarthy, *Roman Waterlogged Remains at Castle Street* (1991), while S. Johnson's *Hadrian's Wall* (1989) is readable and up to date, building upon standard works, particularly D. Breeze and B. Dobson, *Hadrian's Wall* (3rd edn, 1987). Vindolanda lacks a recent all-embracing publication, but the reader is referred to Birley 1977, Bidwell 1985 and the reports on the tablets by Bowman, Thomas and Adams listed in the Bibliography. The most recent work on the Antonine Wall is splendidly summarised in the fourth edition of A.S. Robertson, *The Antonine Wall* (1990), while Wales is very well discussed in B.C. Burnham and J.L. Davies (eds), *Conquest, Co-existence and Change. Recent Work in Roman Wales* (1990). P.A. Holder's *The Roman Army in Britain* (1982) remains very useful, and there are some important essays in V.A. Maxfield and M.J. Dobson (eds), *Roman Frontier Studies* (1991). V.A. Maxfield (ed.), *The Saxon Shore* (1989) is similarly a volume of great value.

3

THE ROMANISATION OF TOWN AND COUNTRY

W ithout doubt Britain ... was a land that the state could ill afford to lose, so plentiful are its harvests, so numerous are the pasturelands in which it rejoices, so many are the metals of which seams run through it, so much wealth comes from its taxes, so many ports encircle.

22 Bronze statuette of Venus, found at Verulamium. Some classical deities retained their original identity, as this example from a major Roman town shows, while others became conflated with local divinities. H. 20 cm. Verulamium Museum.

The sentiments are those of Eumenius in a panegyric[1] lauding the achievements of the emperor Constantius in recovering Britain in 296. Eumenius lived at Autun (ancient Augustodunum) in Gaul, where Constantius had appointed him to the headship of a school, after service as the emperor's imperial secretary. Even though the literary device of the panegyric arouses disbelief, he ought to have known something of adjacent Britannia, and his view may well have been that of many educated Romans. Indeed, for Haverfield at least, the province in the late third century was on the threshold of a golden age, symbolised in a material sense by, for example, traces of about 1,000 mosaics, mainly from fourth-century villas.[2]

This, then, is one view of Roman Britain: that it was a prosperous place with many of the characteristics and amenities of the Mediterranean world – roads, baths, theatres, comfortably appointed town and country houses and a concomitant level of material goods. Against this must be set the sentiment that 'Romanisation' was a façade, restricted to a privileged few, and even then in a modified and diluted form. It is an intriguing and important debate, which will be touched on frequently in these pages. But it is as well to start with some discussion of the size and nature of the population. Estimating figures is fraught with difficulties for any part of the empire. There were very large cities such as Rome, Carthage, Alexandria and Ephesus, all with populations of several hundred thousand and, in the case of Rome, about one million. But the latest calculation for a major provincial capital such as Iol Caesarea (modern Cherchel), from which

Caesarea Mauretanensis (central-western Algeria and eastern Morocco) was governed, favours as few as 20,000, even though the defences enclose as many as 870 hectares.[3] This would be in accord with estimates of about 3,000–5,000 for the generally much smaller principal towns of Roman Britain, with perhaps 15,000 for larger places like Verulamium, Colchester and Cirencester; a total of about 120,000 might be indicated for the twenty-five places that belong in this category. In addition, there were some eighty so-called 'small towns'; a recent study of that at Neatham (Hampshire), which covers 14 hectares, has suggested a figure between 2,270 and 3,972,[4] and it may be that as many as 200,000 overall lived in such settlements. When added to the army (about 60,000 in its heyday) and people in attached settlements or *vici* (40,000 is one guess), we arrive at a total of 420,000 for the more urbanised and military component in the population.

The bulk of the population lived, however, in rural sites, although these were of varying sizes and occur in varying densities. In the fertile flat-lands of the Solway Firth, for example, aerial photography indicates that the average site covered about 1,500 square metres, with a density of one site for every 3.6 square kilometres.[5] We cannot assume that all were in occupation at the same time, but the impression is of a fairly dense rural population. In the Lincolnshire silt fens, the figure (for the late second century) is much higher, one site per square kilometre,[6] while in the nearby Nene valley the ratio is in places as great as four or five sites per square kilometre.[7] Given a land mass for England and Wales of 143,738 sq. km (some of it, of course, wholly unsuited for settlement), we might guess at a rural population of 2 million or more, and a total figure therefore of about 2.5 million. This would be comparable with estimates of 1.75–2.25 million worked out from the Domesday Book of 1086, and is in harmonious relationship with a calculation of 7.5 million for the much more densely settled country of Italy.[8]

There is of course much that is fanciful in these sums, and they cannot be pressed too hard. Moreover, they may conceal significant fluctuations during the Roman period, with hints of a peak in the second century and a gradual decline thereafter. But they do emphasise the fact that, as elsewhere in the Roman empire, most people were the descendants of the pre-Roman Iron-Age families, living in rural surroundings in a relatively unchanged way. They continued to pay some form of taxes, as they had doubtless done before the conquest, to whoever had then wielded local power; and they carried on speaking their Celtic tongues with little or no concession to the Latin that was the official language of their new masters. Even in so heavily urbanised an area as North Africa, Punic was a *lingua franca* down into the fourth century, and Berber and Libyan dialects survived too.[9] This reflects a Roman attitude that was concerned above all with the élite members of society, and their education in Roman ways so that they could undertake the duties of administration and patronage. Hence Tacitus' celebrated remarks about the resultant enthusiasm for Latin, the toga and the baths, promoted by Agricola: but it was a very limited segment of society to which he was referring.[10]

We shall say something shortly of the evolution of towns and the Romanised country estates that are conventionally termed villas. But it is appropriate to begin with some comments about the much more numerous settlements of the humblest classes. In Northumberland and Cumbria a great deal has been learnt about such sites in recent years. There is a certain diversity of plan – circular and rectangular, enclosed and unenclosed – but also many consistent features, of which three stand out. One is the longevity of such sites, many of which originated in pre-Roman times and in all probability carried on long after the final withdrawal of the Roman army. This is underlined by as many as a dozen phases of rebuilding at sites like Burradon and Hartburn, emphasising the immutability of the indigenous tradition.[11] Secondly, the dominant architectural form is the round house, built in either timber or stone and rarely in groups of more than two or three: these, then, were family residences, although some may have been extended units, as was common in Celtic society. Lastly, the surviving material culture was almost always poor, with no coins, little metalwork and very few pots of Roman type. The inhabitants of some sites, like the farmsteads at Silloth and Penrith,[12] did acquire more (including Gaulish samian ware and also *mortaria*); but there is little evidence for any real cultural integration with the world of Rome, even though aerial photography around forts such as Old Carlisle appears to show farmsteads which are linked into the local road system.[13] This fits with evidence from animal bone studies which suggest that livestock, especially cattle, was driven to forts on the hoof.[14]

Indeed, animal bones, seeds, field systems and finds such as rotary querns indicate that in northern England a mixed agricultural economy was practised at many sites, especially in lower-lying terrain. Fields, enclosures and trackways are amply documented in areas of long-standing pasture, such as the Lune valley of northern Lancashire, as are upland communities where environmental considerations dictate a pastoralist emphasis in the economy. The analysis of pollen-bearing deposits is here beginning to prove rewarding. There are hints of an intensification in forest clearance during the Roman period, to create either pastureland or arable, pointing to a gradual rise both in settlement density and, it would seem, in the size of the population. Even so, there is at present little evidence to show that the presence of the Roman army necessarily stimulated production or change.[15]

The northern rural sites, a very few villas apart, also show little archaeological sign of a social hierarchy. There are some sites, such as Ewe Close in Cumbria,[16] which grew to a larger than average size, but no clear pattern can yet be seen in their distribution. It may be, of course, that distinctions in rank (assuming that they existed) were manifested in ways that are now archaeologically undetectable, such as the elaboration of buildings above

ground level; even apparently simple wooden round houses may once have been highly decorated, as a symbol of social status. On the other hand, items of quality metalwork, a customary expression of rank in the Celtic world, are also rare in the northern part of the Roman province, although they are common in southern Scotland, as are architecturally imposing duns and brochs.[17] It could be, therefore, that these material differences between Roman and non-Roman Britain reflect the imposition of a continuous army of occupation, an environment in which local aristocracies were slow to flourish. Later, as conditions stabilised and the size of the garrison declined, matters may have begun to change. This may be the significance of the creation in the third century of the *civitas* (self-governing community of non-citizens) of the Carvetii, focused on Carlisle and the Eden valley to the south; and of inscriptions attesting tribal sub-groups of *pagi*.[18] One, found near Vindolanda, reads 'to the goddess Sattada the assembly (*curia*) of the Textoverdi willingly and deservedly fulfilled the vow'.[19] However inconclusive the archaeological evidence, the epigraphy does imply the gradual emergence of local leaders.

Much of Wales, the south-eastern corner excepted, presents a not dissimilar picture, with large numbers of stone-built enclosed homesteads.[20] The tradition is that of the Iron Age, and many sites can probably trace their origins to that period. At Walesland Rath in Pembrokeshire, for

23 Aerial photograph of the 'native' settlement at Ewe Close, Cumbria. The stone walls of the houses, byres and yards, which cover some 0.6 hectares, can be clearly made out.

example, a small enclosure of just 0.2 hectares was first built in the third century BC, with two or three circular wooden houses.[21] The surviving material culture was poor, even though it included some wooden artefacts of a sort that normally would have disappeared. The excavator postulated a break in occupation in the first century AD: with so few finds this must be open to question, but what is not in doubt is that in the second century AD two new circular wooden houses were constructed, together with a rectangular building in drystone footings. The latter may indicate some impact of 'Romanised' ideas; however, just twenty-two sherds of samian pottery made in Gaul and fewer than 200 sherds of coarse ware (spanning three centuries) were found in this large-scale excavation, eloquent testimony, it would seem, of the inhabitants' isolation from 'Roman' markets. It is not irrelevant here to recall the abundant evidence from Roman North Africa for a two-tier market system, one geared to the towns and the other to periodic rural gatherings, where the goods exchanged may have had little to do with Romanised artefacts. Open-air Celtic festivals, well known from medieval Ireland, could reflect a similar system.[22]

Walesland Rath represents a common class of settlement in Wales. But, even outside the south-eastern part of the Principality (where, as we shall see, more Romanised farms are common), there are hints of sites of higher status. Fifty kilometres to the east is Carmarthen (Roman Moridunum), the apparent centre for the local tribe of the Demetae; two sites within a 25-kilometre radius of the town, namely Cwmbrwyn and Trelissey, are manifestly more Romanised, with mortared stone walls and, at Cwmbrwyn, a hypocaust.[23] These surely housed some of the local aristocracy, who played an important role in social, political and economic terms in the town. Equally, in north-west Wales, and especially on Anglesey, there are some larger and richer sites. Ty Mawr, which has some fifty buildings, and Din Lligwy, which has yielded a silver ingot, coins and much Roman pottery, might be taken to epitomise these. Din Lligwy, with its four late Roman rectangular buildings and two circular structures, all set within a strongly constructed enclosure, certainly had a well-to-do owner, profiting perhaps from Anglesey's rich soils and the nearby market of the military base at Segontium, modern Caernarvon.[24]

A third major area of upland is the south-western peninsula of Devon and Cornwall. This was the territory of the Dumnonii, administered from the town of Isca Dumnoniorum, present-day Exeter. Originally a legionary fortress, by about AD 75 the last troops had gone.[25] Unlike in northern England and Wales, the withdrawal represented, so far as we know, the end of a permanent military presence in the south-west, but, in contrast to many other parts of the province, it made little practical difference to the patterns of rural settlement. The majority of the population lived, as they had in the Iron Age, in small enclosed homesteads, known as rounds, more than 1,500 of which have survived, especially in west Cornwall. Few have been extensively examined, but the presumption is that many represent family groups, some perhaps of extended type. Thus at Tregurthy, not far from St Austell Bay, there were four or five oval stone-built structures within an enclosure of 0.2 hectares, the same size as Walesland Rath. This settlement was inhabited between the third and sixth centuries (when it was receiving imported pottery, African Red Slipware made in what is today Tunisia); it is one of a number of late Roman sites which may have exploited the Cornish tin deposits after the decline of the Spanish industry – the main source of tin in the empire – from the mid-third century.[26]

Yet, as in many other upland areas, the surviving material culture is generally poor, so much so that Cornwall was long thought to have remained outside the Roman province. There are exceptions, like the finds from Carvossa, near Probus, a sub-rectangular enclosure of 2.3 hectares which lies in the Truro area, only a few kilometres from the Fal estuary. This region was densely settled in Roman times, and Carvossa is extra-ordinary for its rich array of high-quality glass, brooches and pottery, dating to the first century AD.[27] Similarly rich in first-century amphorae, metalwork and other finds is Caerloggas (St Mawgan in Pyder), an enclosure of about 1 hectare, and both must be regarded as residences of local notables, who perhaps profited from treaties with the Roman authorities.[28] But one suspects that, for the region as a whole, the Roman interlude was largely an irrelevance, except for a small aristocracy who exercised their power at Isca.

Thus far, we have surveyed the principal upland regions of England and Wales and found them largely wanting of traces of Romanised culture. The doubtless complex social systems mainly escape elucidation in archae-ological terms, but it may be that these people eschewed the display of rank and importance in ways recognisable either to the Roman world or, for that matter, to us. Again, North Africa may offer a parallel in that a provincial capital such as Iol Caesarea could be surrounded by a belt, 15 kilometres in radius, of villas, beyond which lay upland tribal territories; an inscription recording the boundary between the lands of a retired army veteran and the tribe of the Tabianenses would seem to underline the distinction.[29] On the other hand, we have perhaps identified a sufficiency of sites with a greater preponderance of 'Roman' objects to suggest in many areas some hints of incipient social divisions, as measured by material culture.

Even so, most of the north and west remained under military control for the whole of the Roman period, and it is therefore interesting to find amongst the Vindolanda tablets the reference, already noted, to Annius Equester, apparently based at Luguvalium (Carlisle) and described as being 'centurion in charge of the region' (regio).[30] Such posts are not commonly mentioned and the duties are far from clear, although the evidence from Egyptian papyri suggests that they included policing. In the third century two officers of this sort are known from Ribchester, in the Ribble valley of Lancashire; they are described as being both commanders of the fort and in charge of the *regio*. It is just possible that these appointments related to Sarmatian cavalry veterans, who had been given lands there a half-century or more earlier, in AD 175; but this is highly hypothetical.[31]

Another class of official who may have been involved in organising the policing and tax-collection of the unromanised rural population was the *beneficiarius consularis*.[32] He was attached to the governor's staff, but inscriptions show that he could be based anywhere in the province, and especially in the areas controlled by the army. Interestingly, the tablet from Vindolanda containing a report on the unit's strength shows that sixteen men were on detachment to the governor, and it is not impossible that some were involved in administration of rural areas.[33]

What, then, was the effect of the army in the militarised areas of the north and west? Around most of the forts there grew up communities of *vicani*, namely people resident in a *vicus*.[34] This is not a term without its difficulties, for it can apply variously to a village, a part of a city or, as in this case, to extramural settlements around a fort.[35] In the civilian sphere, the people of a *vicus* were answerable to the authority (*respublica*) that administered the area in which it lay – normally in Britain a *civitas* capital. Indeed, some of the *vici* in north-eastern Britain will have lain in the lands of the Brigantes, whose capital was at Aldborough (Isurium Brigantum). But many more were in territory without any *civitas*, certainly during the earlier Roman period, and we should therefore assume that these *vici* were governed by military authority. As we have seen, an altar from near Vindolanda records an assembly of the Textoverdi, which shows that local councils could, and did, exist, and magistrates are also known; but their main role seems to have been primarily religious, rather than administrative.

The *vici* of the north and west still remain archaeologically little known, although the current programme of work outside the west gate of Vindolanda is helping to remedy the situation.[36] What is clear is that they grew up mainly in a haphazard and piecemeal way, as traders and camp-followers flocked to take advantage of a permanent garrison with ready money in the pocket. They were certainly of mixed origin, for analysis of inscriptions from the frontier region suggests that about half bore Celtic names from areas of north-west Europe, about a third names typical of Italy and other western regions of the empire, while the remainder derived from the East.[37] Although soldiers below the rank of centurion were not permitted to marry (until the Edict of Septimius Severus revoked the law in AD 197), women are nevertheless relatively frequently attested on inscriptions. They range from the high-born to slaves, and many no doubt had informal liaisons with soldiers.[38]

The houses in the *vici* comprised in the main long and narrow 'strip buildings', where production of one sort or another was often combined with residential functions. In addition, there was a bath-house (built and used by the garrison, as a Vindolanda tablet indicates),[39] and temples – again constructed at the expense of one or more soldiers, normally high-ranking officers. At many sites, especially those listed in the ancient road itineraries, there will also have been a *mansio*, or official inn, although these have not proved easy to identify in the archaeological record: a comfortably appointed courtyard building with its own bath-house at Vindolanda is possibly an exception.

Many of the *vici* will have developed a market role, as some of the Vindolanda letters imply, and it has been suggested that the *mansiones* may here have played a part. When the *annona militaris*, a tax in kind, was introduced, perhaps in the early third century, the *mansio* often became an official centre for collection and storage of these goods, and it may be that such buildings were already associated with marketing. Certainly, there is some evidence from elsewhere in the empire to suggest that there was official encouragement for *vici* to develop this sort of role.[40]

That the *vici* also absorbed some of the garrisons' earnings is evident from the rich array of monuments, buildings, sculpture and portable goods that they yield. Still more of the wealth will have been channelled south and eastwards, to places engaged in supplying the army with the vast range of goods that it required. Little, on the other hand, found its way into the rural *pagi*, as we have seen. Thus, while there is some evidence pointing to an expansion of the rural population in the north and west (arguably the result of the *pax romana*), botanical studies suggest a depression of agricultural production during the Roman period.[41] This is manifested both by an increase in depleted soils and by a sharp rise in the growing of rye and oats – both crops typical of the poor farmer working bad soils mainly in a manual way. The stimulus for rural populations over large parts of the north and west 'to become different without knowing it', as Cassius Dio puts it, was almost entirely lacking.[42]

This somewhat negative picture changes remarkably as one moves south and east into what is conventionally, if not altogether accurately, called the 'lowland zone'. It has been one of the revelations of recent decades to learn of the density and variety of settlement that is encountered over very large parts of the landscape. This has become particularly clear in areas susceptible to aerial survey, such as the Thames and the Nene valleys, especially when combined with field survey and excavation. What is revealed are myriad farms, larger settlements, roads and trackways, together with complex field systems, reflecting a highly organised and managed landscape. There is also a clear hierarchy of sites, much more so than in the north and west. At the top are the twenty or so planned towns, which were to be the centres of adminstration and religious, economic and cultural foci for the new province. It was also envisaged that local aristocrats would undertake many of the administrative duties, including tax col-lection, and pay for many of the amenities that were required to grace the Graeco-Roman city. As had happened in other parts of the empire, members of the élite would compete amongst themselves to gain social and political advantage and advance their standing and power within the community.

The number of planned towns (which ultimately included four *coloniae*, three founded for retired legionary veterans) may seem small, especially when compared with areas such as Italy, with about 430 towns, North Africa (about 500) or the sixty or so of the Three Gauls. However, in Britain the conspicuously affluent may not have been particularly numerous (or, it is sometimes argued, especially keen to display their wealth in Roman ways) and, the few late Iron-Age *oppida* apart, the country lacked any real urban infrastructure. Certainly, compared with most other western provinces, there are very few inscriptions advertising individual munificent gestures such as building baths or paving the streets, either in the first century or later: Marcus Ulpius Ianuarius, *aedile* (junior magistrate) of the *vicus* of Petuaria (Brough-on-Humber), who in about AD 140 paid for the erection of a stage in the theatre, stands out as a notable exception.[43] It may well be that aristocratic Britons were less seduced by Rome's conventions than their colleagues abroad; but it is more likely that a dearth of real wealth – unless our epigraphic evidence is very deficient – was the root cause behind so manifest a lack of written self-advertisement.[44]

More numerous than the planned towns (in order of rank: *coloniae, municipia* and *civitas* capitals), are the so-called 'small towns' or 'townships'. Here we are referring to the eighty or so sites with some urban characteristics but which normally lack a formal foundation charter, the rigid grid planning of the main centres and most of the public buildings, especially the forum and basilica.[45] *Mansiones* have been identified at some of these settlements, as well as bath-houses and temples; but few substantial private houses are known and, while about half these sites were ultimately to receive defensive walls, it would seem that imposing buildings were something of a rarity. The main exceptions were small towns like Bath, Springhead (Kent), Harlow (Essex) and Frilford (Oxfordshire), where major sanctuaries grew up – usually in places that seem already to have been venerated in the late Iron Age. Here it is reasonable to suppose that religious events were combined with periodic fairs and other events, especially at sites like Frilford where there was also an amphitheatre.[46]

One conspicuous feature of many of these small towns is the considerable evidence for production, whether of pottery, metalwork, leather, salt or other commodities. Even a great religious site such as Nettleton Scrubb in Wiltshire (where Apollo Cunomaglos was worshipped with Silvanus, Mercury, Diana, Rosmerta and other deities) had its commercial side: here was an iron foundry, bronze and pewter works and even a water-powered mill, a rare discovery in Britain.[47] Admittedly, much of this industrial activity belongs, it would seem, to the fourth century, when the appeal of the pagan cults may have been declining (or so it has been argued); but it is likely always to have played some part in the settlement's economy, and is to some extent echoed by signs of productive activities at other temple-dominated settlements such as Bath and Springhead, where pilgrims provided a steady stream of customers.[48]

Amongst the most successful small towns was that at Water Newton (Cambridgeshire), which is known to have been a *vicus* called Durobrivae. Its origins are not entirely clear but, like a third or more of the 'townships' (and at least forty per cent of the 'high-status' towns), it may already have been settled in the Iron Age. As in many of the indigenous centres, there was an early phase of military occupation (in this case both an auxiliary fort and the legionary fortress at nearby Longthorpe), which will have concentrated additional wealth in the area. But other features also encouraged the emergence of a town. One critical factor was the construction, soon after the conquest, of a major northern route, the Ermine Street, which formed the principal street of the settlement. Many of the minor towns grew up along the main roads, and often became hubs in the local and regional systems of communications. At least four other roads converged upon Durobrivae and its environs, influenced no doubt by the crossing, presumably by bridge, of the River Nene, just to the north of the town.

The Nene valley itself was a source of considerable bounty. Its good agricultural land apart, there was an abundance of clay suitable for the manufacture of pottery and tiles; considerable deposits of iron ore and, nearby, a variety of good building stone. Moreover, to the east lay the vast

24 'Colour-coated' pottery beaker made in the Nene valley and found at Stonea, Cambridgeshire. The applied decoration consists of rows of very stylised phalli, symbols thought to attract good luck. H. 11.5 cm. British Museum.

expanse of fertile Fenland which, as we shall see, was greatly developed in Roman times and provided both produce and a ready market.

Our limited knowledge of the development of Durobrivae suggests that its growth began in the early years of the second century. The area that was later to be enclosed by walls covered 18 hectares, and aerial photographs show a medley of mainly irregular side streets, numerous strip houses and two large courtyard buildings. Beyond the defences grew up large suburbs on both sides of the Nene, covering 100 hectares or more. Excavation has demonstrated an emphatic industrial base for these suburbs, especially potting and ironworking, industries which *inter alia* expanded enormously during the third and fourth centuries. The profits that accrued are dramatically illustrated by a number of richly appointed suburban houses (villas) which lie only a few minutes' walk from the walls of Durobrivae.[49]

Another town on the Ermine Street was at Braughing, in Hertfordshire. Once a nationally eminent Iron-Age centre, as we have seen, especially in the time of the emperor Augustus, it too was likely to have been the recipient of a temporary Roman garrison in the Claudian period. Thereafter it prospered, and in one area of the site there are hints of some regular grid planning of streets and of substantial 'Romanised' buildings, one possibly a *mansio*. But the overall impression is of a dispersed settlement, with a modest bath-house down by the river, 200 metres or so from the apparent main centre, and with no walls – a symbol, normally speaking, of a settlement's wealth and status. Indeed, excavations by the Ermine Street suggest a huddle of modest stalls and dwellings flanking the road, where the inhabitants produced trinkets in bronze, bone, iron and doubtless other materials to sell to passers-by. That there were more affluent burghers is suggested by the rich contents of some of the graves, but their houses have so far largely eluded identification.[50]

At Ancaster in Lincolnshire, an inscription records how one Trenico (clearly a native name) erected an arch in honour of the god Viridius, a munificent personal gesture that is wholly classical in tone. The settlement was a large one, covering 25 hectares or so (although fewer than 4 hectares were enclosed when defences were constructed in the first half of the third century), and appears to have been a centre for the making of stone sculpture. But there is little else to suggest that Ancaster was anything more than a small town of no particular consequence, and Trenico's generosity stands out as being exceptional in Britain's impoverished epigraphic record.[51]

Another small town of considerable interest is Godmanchester which, like Durobrivae, lies on the western margins of the Cambridgeshire Fens. A place with a long sequence of prehistoric occupation, it was the site of an early Roman fort, which is overlain by a larger military establishment, possibly built in the aftermath of the Boudiccan revolt. As in the north and west, the military occupation created a focus of civilian settlement which, once the army had moved on, evolved into a small township.[52] But the process of transition from fort to town is likely to have been complex and variable, and much influenced by local considerations. Godmanchester, for instance, lies just to the south of the crossing of the Great Ouse, and was a significant hub (as at Durobrivae) in the road network. Major pre-Roman monuments may also point to an existing local political infrastructure, capable of developing a 'township'. Land allotment and building was soon under way, especially in the Flavian period of the later first century, around the main cross-roads. In the early second century, a complex identified as a *mansio* was established, along with small-scale industry. But the most dramatic changes came in the early third century, when a gravelled *piazza* was laid out, surrounded by a timber arcade. By this time the *mansio* had been built in stone as a courtyard house, with an adjoining bath-house, possible granaries and a structure interpreted as a stable. In addition there was a masonry 'basilica', 24 x 12.9 m, of official appearance, and three temples are also known.

Although Godmanchester has only been summarily published,[53] and the conclusions about its development must be correspondingly provisional, its emergence as an apparent official centre is of great interest. It may well have become a collecting centre for the *annona militaris*, the tax in kind that was possibly introduced around AD 200. Further sustained by flourishing industry and, in the later third century, provided with stone fortifications enclosing about 11 hectares, its prosperity and local importance is not in doubt. Kenchester, in Herefordshire, may have had a not dissimilar history, to judge from signs of some quite elaborate architectural elements, and a milestone of AD 283–4, set up by the canton of the Dobunni *(res publica civitatis Dobunnorum)*.[54]

We shall have more to say about the small towns in our final chapter; but enough has been said here to demonstrate their diversity, their generally *ad hoc* development and their role as local centres of production. The last is a matter of some importance, especially concerning their relationship with officially promoted, carefully planned towns and cities. The commercial aspect of ancient cities has been much debated over recent years: were they primarily prestige centres of munificent display by the patricians, and thus parasitical upon the countryside, or did they have a more productive side? Inevitably, there is no simple answer, and the matter is further clouded by the desire of Roman aristocrats to disguise their commercial activities (as they were legally obliged to do). Yet cities such as Corinth had their industrial quarter (as did Camulodunum, as we saw earlier), and at Pompeii, Herculaneum, and even in the heart of Rome itself, upper-class houses existed cheek by jowl with shops and other commercial premises. Respectable wealth in antiquity certainly lay in the land and its produce; but commerce did take place – and on a large scale – within the urban context, and doubtless filled the aristocratic pockets through rents and other means.[55]

25 Detail of joists and a sill from the warehouse excavated at Southwark in 1988 (see also Fig. 1), showing dovetail joints and mortice holes for the wall uprights.

It is thus not surprising to find that in Britain the early urban houses tend to combine the functions of residence, production centre and shop. Moreover, while often dismissed as architecturally unprepossessing (partly because they are usually built in wood), this is slightly to distort the picture. At Watling Court in London, for example, one structure had at least eleven rooms, one with a mosaic, and a floor area of nearly 300 square metres, while an adjoining, incompletely excavated building had at least three tessellated floors.[56] These are much smaller and less elaborate than contemporary upper-class atrium-peristyle houses in Pompeii, which average seventeen rooms and about 800 square metres;[57] but it is a perfectly reasonable residence for someone fairly high on the social scale (especially if the building had two floors, as seems to have been the case at Watling Court), exploiting commercial possibilities in a city much given over, on Tacitus' evidence, to trade.[58] To this, indeed, we can now add the abundant and striking evidence for a series of massive wooden wharves along parts of the north bank of the Thames, with storage buildings behind, and even the well-preserved remains of a timber warehouse, recessed into the foreshore at Southwark.[59] Here presumably were put the perishable goods requiring a cool environment that became ever more popular amongst those who espoused a more Roman way of life. The amphorae that contained wine, oil, fish sauce and other luxuries (at least in a northern environment) are an equally tangible reminder of this commerce; traders, whether foreign or British, cannot have failed to recognise the chance of profit, and aristocrats will have been quick to take due advantage.[60]

It may of course be that London was something of a special case, since the main impetus for its development probably came from the officially encouraged establishment of a *conventus civium Romanorum*, an association of Roman citizens, in this instance mainly *negotiatores*, traders.[61] However, it is clear from the discovery in London of the tomb of Gaius Julius Alpinus Classicianus, the procurator who was sent to Britain in the aftermath of the Boudiccan rebellion and died in post, that London had by then become the provincial capital.[62] This explains its rapid development over the following thirty or forty years or so, when building projects included the first ('proto') forum and basilica, the probable governor's palace (*praetorium*), 33 baths at Huggin Hill and Cheapside and – about AD 100 – a fort and, in all probability, the adjacent amphitheatre.[63] Indeed, a tombstone from Ludgate Hill, which probably dates to the late first century and was set up by Anencletus, 'slave of the province', suggests that the provincial council was already meeting in London.[64] Composed of delegates from cities and tribes within the province, its main purpose was to promote the cult of the Roman emperor, especially through games and festivals; it was not, therefore, a legislative body, although it served as a useful instrument of Romanisation: it is also known to have reported directly to the emperor (especially in the first century AD) about the behaviour of governors and other high officials. This underlines how necessary it was for the aristocracy to maintain some sort of town residence, so that they could exercise and extend their power and influence: hence the evolution of ever grander private buildings, culminating in the splendid town houses of late Roman times that are so conspicuous a feature of the aerial photographs of towns like Silchester, Wroxeter, Verulamium and elsewhere (although not, as we have seen, so much in the minor towns).

Some of the other 'administrative towns' also burgeoned quickly, especially in areas which had been receptive to Roman influence before the conquest. Amongst them are Canterbury and Verulamium, where the known forum was dedicated in AD 79 but overlies a still older masonry structure, possibly an earlier forum.[65] Similarly, in the territory of the client king Tiberius Claudius Cogidumnus (whose title may have been *rex magnus*, great king, and who was also, according to Tacitus, 'presented with certain states'),[66] towns developed precociously. Silchester and Winchester almost certainly lay within his realm, the former at least being a major Iron-Age *oppidum* with a street grid and numerous imported goods. Recent excavations have shown that the masonry basilica was preceded by a wooden precursor, built about AD 80, and that this in turn had superseded a public-looking structure, also in wood, constructed about AD 55–60. Given that it has also been established that the first amphitheatre was put up in the same period, between about AD 55 and 75, it is clear that there was considerable private investment from early on – for it was the wealthy élite who had perforce to pay for the work.[67]

Winchester is less well documented for this early period, but more is known about Chichester.[68] Although called Noviomagus Reg(i)norum, meaning 'new place' or 'new market', it lay within the dykes that enclosed the late Iron-Age *oppidum* of Cogidumnus and, as we saw in chapter 2, may have been the landing place of the Roman invasion fleet. Certainly Cogidumnus would have assured a friendly welcome, and there is known to have been a military presence both at Chichester and at nearby Fishbourne, where a highly classical 'villa' – surely a royal palace of Cogidumnus or his family – was later to be constructed. Moreover, the epigraphic record from Chichester also indicates rapid Romanisation, especially a dedication of AD 57–8 to Nero and the much discussed inscription recording the erection of a temple to Neptune and Minerva 'by the authority of Tiberius Claudius Cogidumnus' and built by 'the guild (*collegium*) of smiths ... from their own resources'.[69] The site for the temple was presented by a man whose name is now, alas, lost, although he calls himself 'son of Pudentinus' and was presumably one of the local aristocracy.

At London, Chichester, Verulamium and elsewhere, the archaeological evidence points to a rapid development of industrial activity, most visibly in metalworking and pottery production but doubtless not confined to these. Thus, a recently excavated building of early second-century date at Verulamium, measuring 14 x 24 metres and comprising at least seventeen rooms, yielded abundant evidence for productive activities. Some rooms had ovens and furnaces, two possessed raised floors for storage, probably of grain (perhaps for brewing), and in one was a barrel and press. The presence of slag shows that metalworking was practised, and dyeing is also a possibility.[70] Canterbury, too, where the theatre (one of just five known in Britain, although there were assuredly more) was built in the late first century, shows a not dissimilar picture of industrial activity.[71] Paying for the amenities normal in a Graeco-Roman town, namely fora, basilicas, temples, markets, theatres, amphitheatres, baths and the like, took time – as much as a century and a half in some cities in the much richer North African provinces[72] – and had to come largely from the private purse: hence, perhaps, the loans, the recall of which was to encourage Boudicca's followers to rebellion in AD 60–61. The incentive to develop profitable industries, especially in Roman-style goods, must have been considerable.

As in the minor towns, the army inevitably played some part in creating these new urban centres, even though its precise role has been the subject of some dispute. All four of the *coloniae*, the highest-ranking cities, grew out of legionary fortresses, although York (Eboracum) was not promoted to colonial status until much later on, probably in Severan times (and certainly by AD 237). One of the other three, Colchester (Colonia Victricensis, *c.* AD 49), while extended to the east, nevertheless retained much of its basic military layout, often converting part or all of the barracks into rather plain domestic housing. A rather similar process may have taken place at Gloucester (Colonia Nervia Glevensium, AD 97), and at both Lincoln (Lindum Colonia, *c.* AD 90) and Gloucester the forum and basilica overlay the legionary headquarters building.[73]

Exeter also originated as a legionary fortress, and extensive excavation

has shown a complex sequence in the town's central area.[74] Here lay the fortress baths, partly demolished when the military moved away in about AD 70–80. A temporary wooden basilica then appears to have been put up, while the permanent civic centre was under construction in the 80s and, perhaps, the 90s. A new site was found for the public baths, the aqueduct for which has been dated through dendrochronology to AD 100–101, the felling date of the foundation timbers. The legionary defences were for a time retained, but of those who came to populate what became the administrative centre of the Dumnonii, Isca Dumnoniorum, little is known. The epigraphic record is scant, reflecting perhaps the backwardness of the region, and few traces of their houses have yet been uncovered. Here, we might suspect, was a town which needed some official encouragement of the sort that Tacitus attributes to Agricola, precisely at this time.[75] Similarly, at Wroxeter in Shropshire (likewise of legionary origin), the great inscription of AD 129–30 from the gateway to the forum, dedicated to the emperor Hadrian by the *civitas* of the Cornovii, may also indicate external munificence.[76] Hadrian, who greatly embellished the architecture of the empire – Athens is a conspicuous example – had visited Britain in AD 122, and it is by no means impossible that he provided imperial funds for a splendid forum: certainly Wroxeter lay in an area that was then scarcely Romanised, and it is hard to envisage much significant private patronage at the time.[77]

The burden of these remarks, therefore, is that the army promoted urbanisation almost by accident, for the sites of its bases were chosen above all for political or military reasons – either in centres of existing power (e.g.

26 Part of the Ditches villa, set within a late Iron-Age defended enclosure at North Cerney, Gloucestershire. In origin, the villa dates to about AD 60, and was later enlarged.

27 Detail of the cellar at
The Ditches.

Colchester) or in places such as Exeter where strategic considerations were
paramount. Sometimes the two factors combined. Thus at Cirencester,
later to become the largest city in Roman Britain after London, the initial
occupation took the form of an auxiliary fort, placed on low-lying ground
beside the River Churn.[78] Founded in the AD 50s, the new army base soon
attracted camp-followers: amongst them may have been one Philus, of the
Sequani tribe from the Besançon area of France, whose tombstone records
that he lived until he was 45 years of age.[79] However, some five kilometres
to the north lay the *oppidum* of Bagendon–North Cerney. The original
nucleus was probably at the site today known as The Ditches, an enclosure
of 4 hectares occupied from the late first century BC. A 'high status' place,
it has yielded some fine jewellery and other metalwork, and gold and
silver coins were minted there. Bagendon itself, with its well-known dyke
systems, appears, however, to belong entirely to the post-conquest period,
and limited excavations have revealed a rich array of imported goods as
well as abundant signs of production, especially ironworking and the
minting of Dobunnic coins. It is tempting to interpret the whole vast
complex as the settlement of a Celtic aristocrat and his followers (*clientes*).[80]

What is fascinating about the Bagendon complex is that its heyday was
remarkably brief. Around AD 60 it entered sharp decline, and one can
hardly doubt that the population was shifting down into the *vicus* that was
burgeoning around the junction of two main roads, the Ermin Street and
the Fosse Way, to the north of the fort. Coercion is not impossible – feelings
must have run high in the army after the near disaster of Boudicca's

rebellion – but there is no tangible evidence of this. However, at The Ditches (where the defences were by then lapsing into desuetude) a rectangular building, 6.8 x 24 m, with masonry footings and six rooms was constructed in the central part of the enclosure at about this time. Later enlarged to about 15 x 30 m, with the addition of front and rear corridors, projecting rooms at either side, and a cellar, it took on the plan of a typical so-called 'winged-corridor villa'. But, more importantly, it seems likely that here was a country residence, built in as Romanised a way as was possible in the Cotswolds of the mid-first century AD, of a British aristocrat whose family had long ruled the Bagendon complex.[81]

During the same period, Cirencester saw the transition from military to civilian rule. The army seems to have evacuated the fort around the mid-70s, and the site was partially cleared to make way for the new *civitas* capital Corinium Dobunnorum. The streets were orientated with the Fosse Way and Ermin Street, an integration which reflects the importance of the new system of communications. Before long the forum and basilica – a massive structure 100 metres in length – were under construction, as were an amphitheatre, a market and, in all probability, a theatre.[82] Given the modest size of the villa at The Ditches (surely owned by one of the new town's decurions, with his obligations as a member of the council, the *ordo*, to promote civic development), it is hard to see how all this work was financed: there must surely have been some level of external subsidy.

Early military occupation has also been demonstrated at several other *civitas* capitals, such as Leicester, Dorchester (Dorset) and Brough-on-Humber, and may yet be found at sites like Caistor-by-Norwich, the centre of the Iceni. However, we may suspect that an army presence was not the only factor that helped to promote these places as administrative and cultural centres. Equally important will have been both a central position in the new system of communications and the proximity of local *equites*, capable of assuming novel municipal duties. Indeed, it is probably the lack of such people that explains the negligible urbanisation of such large parts of the north and west.

Villas are another hallmark of Romanisation, with an overall distribution that closely reflects that of the major and minor towns. The term 'villa' is somewhat problematic, in that it is a Mediterranean concept which was adapted to the predominantly Celtic world of northern Europe. It is perhaps best defined as any sort of Romanised complex on a rural estate, although there are occasional hints of the divisions recommended by Columella into a *villa urbana* (town-style residence), *villa rustica* (the productive part of the farm: *rusticus* means bailiff), and *villa fructuaria*, the storage area.[83] Similarly, it was also recognised in antiquity that country dwellings could be ranked by wealth and ostentation: hence Varro's distinction between the *villa*, the *casa* and the lowest form of rural building, the *tugurium* (hut).[84]

Romanised 'villas' seem to have been sufficiently rare in Britain – only a thousand or so are known – as to imply that all were owned by people of relatively high social standing. As in the Mediterranean, they were also places where status could be expressed through elaborate and imposing architecture. Although the ground plans of many British villas may suggest comparatively modest structures (some have been disparagingly dismissed as cottages), the reality was often probably rather different. Thus when the fallen façade of the supposedly simple aisled 'barn' at Meonstoke v (Hampshire) was recently lifted, it turned out to be an ornate and elegant building, with clerestory windows, Ionic capitals and a striking arrange ment of contrastingly coloured materials; it had even been designed down 37 to the last detail in various units of Roman feet (the *pes Monetalis*, equivalent to 29.6 cm).[85]

The Meonstoke building, admittedly, was put up in the early fourth century, but there is no reason to suppose that architectural pretensions, largely undetectable at ground level, were not introduced much sooner. An early villa such as The Ditches, which had footings nearly a metre thick, will surely have appeared sophisticated and imposing, and it has been interestingly argued that the Celtic nobles rapidly exploited these architectural possibilities of enhancing their social position – especially once those traditional modes of display, weapons and armour, had been vitiated by the disarming of the tribes in AD 47; that, in effect, they sought to establish their power base in the countryside rather than in the incipient towns, and that the early villas were architectural statements about status rather than centres of productive farming estates.[86]

In reality, as we have seen, it was crucial that they were involved also in urban life, as decurions and magistrates, and the more important will surely have had more than one residence: Pliny the Younger, for example, owned a grand house in Rome and five estates in Italy.[87] Indeed, there are a number of early villas in Britain which were probably built by local leaders. We have already alluded to Fishbourne, arguably erected by Cogidumnus or a kinsman, not least since it lies in close proximity to Chichester and within the system of late Iron-Age dykes to the north.[88] Both the so-called 'proto-palace' of about AD 65 and the 'palace' that succeeded it a decade or so later were highly classical in most respects, symbolised, *inter alia*, by a great Corinthian capital from the earlier complex. Foreign craftsmen were surely employed (Roman feet were used to lay out the building), as they must have been at nearby Hayling Island, where a late Iron-Age temple was converted into a magnificent masonry-built sanctuary of Gallic type at about the same time.[89] Taken together, the contemporary processes of municipalising Chichester, remodelling Hayling and building Fishbourne show strong Romanisation at work in this client kingdom or – for we do not know when Cogidumnus died – early *civitas*.

Other villas were put up not long after the conquest, although they cannot be said to be numerous. Some, like those at Eastbourne, Folkestone and Mersea (Essex), lie close to navigable waters, and it has been suggested that they may have been built by foreign traders.[90] But merchants did not in general enjoy much status in antiquity, and were not unduly wealthy; it is much more likely that they were the country houses of native aristocrats. Similarly, at Eccles in the Medway valley of Kent, a remarkable building of about AD 55–65 has been excavated; of linear plan (although with a detached bath-house), it had a range of twelve rooms over a length of 75 metres (253 *pedes Monetales*), linked by a corridor. At least five rooms had mosaic floors, and there was what may have been a long ornamental pool in front. The layout cannot be readily paralleled outside northern Europe, and the view that it was occupied by a Celtic extended family has decided attractions.[91]

Like The Ditches, other villas seem to have grown up within the context of major Iron-Age sites. That at Tidbury Ring (Hampshire), a still conspicuous hillfort, is known only from aerial photography, and its date is uncertain; but Ditchley and Shakenoak (Oxfordshire) lie within the Grim's Ditch complex, while in the environs of Verulamium a number of early villas appear to have developed within the context of late Iron-Age settlement.[92] The best studied is at Gorhambury, less than 2 kilometres from the town centre.[93] It appears to relate to the Devil's Dyke–New Dyke–White Dyke system, and originated as a rectangular enclosure with an internal area of about 3.25 hectares. Constructed in Verulamium's '*oppidum* phase', around the beginning of the first century AD, it comprised a number of timber buildings, including an incompletely preserved large rectangular house, a granary and, in the eastern enclosure, an aisled barn of well-known Romano-British type. Although a masonry villa was not constructed until about AD 100 (possibly due to the Boudiccan sack of Verulamium, which seems to have affected Gorhambury too), its superimposition upon the Iron-Age residence implies a striking continuity of role. Similarly, the aisled barn was also repeatedly rebuilt on the same site, and there are abundant signs that the separation between workers and master was established early in the site's history and maintained down into the fourth century. Gorhambury therefore provides a remarkable instance of what could be regarded as a late Iron-Age form of villa (perhaps one of several in the Verulamium region), which helps to explain the town's rapid development and also its early award of municipal status.

The majority of these early villas lie in the south-east and show a marked tendency towards a simple rectilinear plan, perhaps reflecting something of the family social structure. Fishbourne and nearby Southwick stand out as exceptions, with a courtyard arrangement which is much more reminiscent of the classical world.[94] But there are also outliers to the main distribution, such as Mileoak, near the small town of Towcester in Northamptonshire.[95] Built between AD 65 and 75 on a site with late Iron-Age occupation, it comprised a substantial stone house, about 40 x 16 m, with twelve rooms (one with a mosaic), a hypocaust, a cellar and corridors on both long sides. Wall plaster decorated with imitation marbling further points to its Romanised character.

That most of the these villas belonged to indigenous aristocrats seems, therefore, fairly probable: Fingringhoe, with its three houses, built close to a Claudian military supply base near Colchester, is likely to be a rare instance where the owner was probably not British. Moreover, a number of these sites seem to show a close topographical relationship with the richly furnished aristocratic 'barrow burials' that are so conspicuous a feature of the early Romano-British landscape in the south-east. Mersea Island in Essex provides two notable examples, while a fine mirror of Iron-Age type and a bronze patera and ewer found near an apparently early and grand villa at Rivenhall, in the same county, are also likely to have come from one of these monumental tombs.[96]

Although attempts have been made to trace the origins of these tumuli to the Continent, and even Italy itself, it seems much more likely that they were inspired by the barrows of the prehistoric past which even today survive in considerable numbers in some parts of the British countryside.[97] The superimposition of Romano-British shrines upon such barrows, as at Stanwick in Northamptonshire, suggests that these Bronze-Age and Neolithic monuments were highly venerated, and it has been plausibly suggested that the aristocracy of early Roman Britain may have sought to stress their long lineage (real or imagined) by imitating these evocative monumental images of the past. As burials like that at Lexden near Colchester show, this was a tradition initiated in the late Iron Age (Lexden contained many fine Roman objects, including a silver medallion of the emperor Augustus),[98] while a barrow cemetery like that at the Bartlow 'Hills' (i.e. tumuli) remains imposing down to this day. Here there were originally eight great mounds, the largest of which still stands to a height of nearly 14 metres.[99] Excavated early in the last century, they yielded a fine array of Roman objects (including a patera and ewer, and other objects associated with drinking and feasting), dating to the period between about AD 75 and the mid- to late second century. Three generations of Trinovantian nobles may be represented, and it would be not at all surprising to find that the little-known nearby villa at Ashdon was both contemporary and grand in the Roman manner.[100]

The emergence of these early villas has often been linked to supposed improvements in crops and agricultural technology, introduced into Britain as a direct consequence of the Roman conquest; this, the argument runs, enabled the accumulation of wealth necessary to pay for the building of the Romanised country estates. Recent research rather contradicts this view, however. Palaeobotanical studies, in particular, suggest that there was notable intensification in agriculture well before the conquest (especially of spelt wheat and hulled six-row barley), in common with large parts of northern Europe. Indeed, modern experiment at the Butser Iron-Age farm centre has shown that very considerable surpluses could be grown. Innovations were introduced into Roman Britain, especially bread wheat (*Triticum aestivum*, today, together with rice, the most important component

28 A group of iron
agricultural implements
from various sites,
including sickles, a
pruning knife, a hoe, a
spade-sheath and a plough
coulter. British Museum.

in the world's diet); but, as we shall see in our final chapter, these belong
mainly to the late Roman period.[101]

Wealth *was* present in parts of late Iron-Age Britain, as the astonishing
quantity of gold and silver in the Snettisham treasure aptly reminds us,
and the spread of villas must therefore be seen mainly as a reflection of the
social aspirations of the owners, not as novel forms of investment in
agricultural production. That said, the range of architecture is such as
to point to considerable variation in individual fortunes. A significant
proportion of villas do show a progressive elaboration of building during
the Roman period, and the site at Rockbourne in Hampshire, which eventu-

ally had some forty rooms, may be taken as an example;[102] but the pattern is by no means even, doubtless reflecting the normal vicissitudes of family life. For instance, at Piddington in Northamptonshire,[103] there were initially wooden round houses and then a masonry villa from the early second century. However, a disastrous fire occurred in the Antonine period, setting back the owner's fortunes for a considerable time; when building work was resumed in the late third century, it was soon interrupted, so that large heaps of mosaic tesserae were left piled up in the courtyard. Despite the fact that Britain in the early fourth century was relatively prosperous, the owner of the villa at Piddington seems never to have properly recovered from this setback (whatever brought it about), and the buildings were given over to bread-making, corn-drying, metalworking and the manufacture of tiles, some of which were laid out to dry on tessellated floors. Stamped tiles may indicate that one Tiberius Claudius Severus was master at this time; perhaps he had bought up the estate cheaply, and lived on some other villa, leaving his affairs in the hands of a bailiff.[104]

Equally, at Barton Court Farm in Oxfordshire, the admirably complete examination of a hectare or more of the site revealed a sequence of buildings from late Iron-Age times, culminating in a relatively modest eight-roomed masonry house, constructed in the late third century.[105] Within a surrounding enclosure was a two-roomed 'cottage', two corn-driers, wells and paddocks, and a sensitive analysis of the archaeological and scientific data permits a convincing reconstruction of the size and layout of the estate. From these it is calculated that around 160 hectares were farmed, about forty per cent of them arable, the rest supporting some 75–100 cattle and several hundred sheep. A permanent staff of no more than ten would have been required, probably increased at busy times of the year by help from tenants and *clientes* – those with obligations to the villa owner. There would seem, therefore, to be a close correlation between the modest size of the house and the size of the estate, and a not especially wealthy resident owner (whose local town was the similarly modest place at Dorchester-on-Thames) may here be suspected.

The illuminatingly large scale of the Barton Court Farm excavation is being increasingly repeated at other villa sites, always with intriguing results. Pride of place must go to the project, initiated in 1984 and completed in 1991, of investigating the near entirety of the estate of a villa situated in the Nene valley, at Stanwick (Northamptonshire).[106] We have already referred to the shrine erected around a Bronze-Age barrow, where some 500 coins of first- or early second-century date and vast quantities of oyster shells from the environs bear witness to ritual offerings and feasting. But this was just one component in a densely occupied landscape, where the villa estate seems to have extended over 20 hectares or more.

The evolution of the settlement is complex. There was a very substantial, village-like Iron-Age settlement of wooden round houses, together with four-post granaries. In the second century all of this was swept away, and

the site was laid out as a series of enclosures and trackways, focusing upon a villa. While the buildings (or at least their footings) were now constructed in stone, they included both rectangular and circular structures; it is a pattern that persists right through the Roman period and is a striking illustration of the conservative architectural tradition of the estate workers. The same cannot be said for the villa owner, for reused in the foundations of the fourth-century house were numerous sculpted stones, one showing a Roman riding down a barbarian, together with column drums and part of what may be some sort of honorific inscription.[107] Sculpture is not common in Roman Britain, especially in civilian contexts, and its presence at Stanwick (and the chosen symbolism) point to an owner who was thoroughly at home with the Roman genre.

One intriguing and elaborate building, of late Antonine date, comprises a walled court, entered by a gate, with turret-like structures at the sides, and two conjoined rooms opposite. There are hints that it may have been laid out in *pedes Monetales*, since the overall dimensions are very nearly 90 Roman feet square, while the court is close to 60 x 70 Roman feet. Given that the building also occupies a central position on the estate, it is very plausibly seen as an administrative centre, quite possibly a bailiff's office, where workers and tenants were received and wages paid.

Given the number of buildings, the owner of Stanwick must have farmed

29 The remains of what may have been the surround of a donkey mill at the villa complex at Stanwick, Northamptonshire. The stones are worn, as though by the constant tread of animals.

30 High-level view of the villa at Redlands Farm, near Stanwick, Northamptonshire. Also visible is a round house (top left) and part of the leat for the mill that preceded the villa.

a very large estate. However, the density of villas in its vicinity is considerable, including the recently excavated example at Redlands Farm, only 1,500 metres away.[108] Originating as a mill, it was converted in the second century into a 'winged corridor house' of 12 x 22 metres with six rooms, and was surrounded by yards, a barn and two stone-built round houses. A collapsed section of wall showed that it once stood at least 6.6 metres high, with indications that there was more than one storey. A mosaic and other tessellated floors, together with a hypocaust, were added in the later Roman period and, while never one of the grandest houses, its successive proprietors were evidently relatively well-to-do.

It would be fascinating to know more of the pattern of land ownership and how it may have changed, especially in terms of Stanwick and Redlands; but the archaeological evidence is largely mute. Virtually no written evidence survives,[109] and even imperial holdings are poorly documented.[110] Inscriptions like a fragmentary one from nearby Sawtry (Cambridgeshire)[111] hint at a boundary between public and private estates, while some large tracts of land, such as the Cambridgeshire and Lincolnshire Fens, may have been state controlled, as we shall see later. But the evidence on the ground alone does not permit any real light to be shed on the relationship, tenurial or otherwise, between two adjacent villas such as Stanwick and Redlands.

That said, study of villa building-plans has thrown up some interesting hypotheses about the make-up of the social group that owned them. Some, such as Beadlam in Yorkshire or Gayton Thorpe in Norfolk, appear to demonstrate a duality of residences, perhaps implying some form of joint proprietorship between two families. Others possess a large, centrally placed hall surrounded by multiple units of accommodation, and have been interpreted as representative of a rather different sort of social unit, quite possibly an extended family. Both types of layout can only be paralleled in other provinces of northern Europe and, however speculative these modern views of their social function, would seem to reflect a peculiarly Celtic adaptation of Roman architecture to suit local needs.[112]

Total excavation of the site at Whitton, on the Glamorgan lowlands of south Wales, yielded a not dissimilar story.[113] Founded around the time of the conquest, and provided with a bank and ditch enclosing about one-third of a hectare, it manifests considerable conservatism throughout its 300 or so years' existence. Rectangular stone structures, replacing circular timber houses, do appear in the second century, while by the late third century there were three ranges of buildings with masonry foundations. However, the hypocausts in the main residence were never fired, wall plaster was sparsely employed and there were no tessellated floors, leading to the conclusion that here, despite some architectural concessions, Romanisation was something of a veneer. The point is of interest, since the Glamorgan plain is the one area of Wales where villas do occur in some numbers. This was in the canton of the Silures, once one of Rome's fiercest enemies but whose *civitas* capital, Venta Silurum (Caerwent), was to become a prosperous and civilised town.[114] Great villas like Llantwit Major and Ely presumably belonged to richer decurions, and one wonders how a site such as Whitton related to them: was it the residence of a free owner, or a tenant, or perhaps a bailiff – and did, indeed, its status change? Alas, we cannot say.

The complex mix between the conservative indigenous tradition and the influx of Romanisation is one of the most fascinating aspects of rural studies of Roman Britain. Even a sumptuous villa such as that at Bancroft, near Milton Keynes (Buckinghamshire), had masonry round houses on the estate,[115] while at Great Doddington (Northamptonshire) aerial photographs suggest that similar circular structures shared an intimate architectural relationship with the main house.[116] Moreover, detailed landscape studies around villas such as Maddle Farm (Berkshire) and Wharram Percy and Wharram le Street (Yorkshire) suggest considerable continuity from Iron-Age times: here, in effect, the villa estates were not superimposed upon the landscape, but grew out of it.[117]

In many areas of Britain there were few or no villas, especially where the army remained in control and urbanisation was minimal. In the north-east, conventional thinking argues that the apparently rare examples were built mainly by retired soldiers. Dalton Parlours near Wetherby, finely

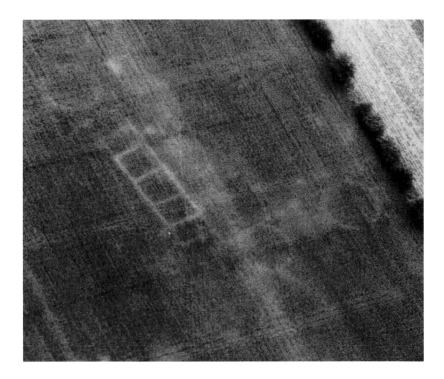

31 Aerial photograph of a combination of circular and rectangular houses in a villa at Great Doddington, Northamptonshire. They appear to be grouped around a court.

situated overlooking the Vale of York, has been regarded as being in that category although, since it originated as a prosperous Iron-Age and early Roman settlement, a British owner is just as plausible.[118] From about AD 200 it was laid out as a somewhat higgledy-piggledy arrangement of aisled buildings, baths and other structures, with hypocausts and, eventually, mosaics – a rustic architectural compromise which finds its parallel in some of the grander, if parochial, north-eastern houses of more recent centuries.

More puzzling is the archaeological picture derived from nearly two centuries of investigation into the rural sites of the Cotswolds. In the late Roman period, gracious country houses like the well-known Chedworth villa were ubiquitous, as indeed they are today: for this is favoured, fertile and attractive countryside. What is strange is that very few seem to have been built much before the late third century, despite the emergence of Circencester, Gloucester and Bath as early and significant town centres: the villa at The Ditches – which was abandoned by the late second century – is here a conspicuous exception. By way of explanation, a case has been put forward that much of the land of the Dobunni was taken into imperial control soon after the conquest, thus stifling the development of private estates.[119] At Claydon Pike, for example, a substantial site on low-lying land in the upper Thames valley near Lechlade in Gloucestershire, large-scale excavations have revealed a highly unusual complex, laid out early in the second century. Carefully organised into what appear to be residential, administrative and storage areas, and well provided with roads, it has been interpreted as a tax-collection centre; indeed, there are finds which may point to some form of military presence.[120]

Future work will doubtless show whether this seemingly anomalous picture of rapidly developing towns, but rather diluted Romanisation in the countryside – at least until the third century – is an archaeological reality. There are, however, other areas in the southern part of the province where villas are either absent or uncommon, one of them being Norfolk, the territory of the Iceni. Although a region of considerable wealth, as discoveries of hoards of gold and silver constantly remind us,[121] the *civitas* capital, Venta Icenorum (Caistor-by-Norwich), was a modest place, and villas of any period are conspicuously infrequent. Some of this must be consequent upon the aftermath of two unsuccessful uprisings, when the aristocracy was presumably decimated; but we might also detect a certain reluctance to adopt the full trappings of Romanisation.[122]

The adjoining Fenland, part of which also fell within Icenian territory, is similarly devoid of villas, except around its fringes.[123] Although all too easily dismissed as a hostile and marginal environment, in antiquity the diversity and bounty of suitably managed marshland was well recognised and highly valued. When in the course of the first century the Fens began to dry out, through natural changes in the levels of either the land or the sea, colonisation soon followed, reaching a peak between about AD 125 and 150. The settlements range from modest farmsteads to what might be defined as small villages and, while little studied through excavation, seem to belong mainly to a peasant level of development. Enclosed paddocks surround many of the sites, reflecting an emphasis upon a stock economy, especially the raising of sheep for wool, and evidence for the manufacture of salt, crucial *inter alia* as a meat preservative, is ubiquitous.[124]

As striking as the sheer density of Romano-British settlement in the Fens is the appearance of great waterways and drove-roads, laid out in long straight stretches. They would seem to reflect a form of landscape management that is entirely alien to indigenous traditions, but well paralleled in other parts of the ancient world, such as the Tavoliere of Apulia, in south-eastern Italy.[125] Indeed, military involvement is by no means impossible; the army was certainly at times involved in digging canals in other provinces, and an inscription from Goldcliff, a few kilometres from the fortress of Caerleon, implies that the IInd Augustan legion was involved in the reclamation of the Wentlooge Levels, some 325 square kilometres of low-lying terrain bordering the River Severn.[126]

It is likely that both the Wentlooge Levels and the Fens were lands in public or imperial ownership, administered by procurators and settled by tenant farmers (*coloni*). In the case of the Fens, this is based on good historical grounds, in that Prasutagus, the last king of the Iceni, in his will left part of the royal estates to the emperor Nero; other lands were surely confiscated after Boudicca's rebellion. Coin hoards suggest that a substantial part of the Fens lay within the realm of the Iceni, and it is plausible to see them as a Roman acquisition by inheritance or seizure. Moreover, at Stonea, an outcrop of higher ground in the central Fenland, a somewhat curious settlement is best interpreted as a *forum*, a term which in this sense means a newly founded market and administrative centre. Laid out with a regular arrangement of streets, the site's most remarkable feature was a central stone-built complex, incorporating what appears to have been a large and elaborate tower; it is unique in the northern provinces, and finds its only real parallel at Le Mura di Santo Stefano, just outside the city of Rome itself. One can easily imagine the symbolic significance of this great building, rising probably to several storeys, in the flat Fenland landscape.[127]

The Roman settlement at Stonea originated in the Hadrianic period, precisely when the main development of the Fens was getting under way. Indeed, it is not impossible that Hadrian himself took an interest in the region, since he is well known for promoting the cultivation of more marginal land, especially in Greece, Egypt, North Africa and Italy. We might therefore suggest that Stonea was intended to fulfil an administrative role for the surrounding state-owned territory, with the tower complex as the official centre. Indeed, in front of it was a piazza, measuring some 35 x 45 metres, which perhaps served as a public square and where, periodically, markets were held and taxes collected. A contemporary foundation in the Dutch lowlands, Forum Hadriani, near Arentsburg, may offer a remarkable parallel for the type of settlement. Both have somewhat eccentric features – Stonea its tower and Forum Hadriani a fort-shaped plan – and they were also both important pre-Roman centres for, respectively, the western Iceni and the Canninefates.[128]

The inference is that Stonea, like its Dutch counterpart (if that analogy is correct), was intended to become an urban centre; but, in the event, this was not to be. While Forum Hadriani was to be subsequently promoted to municipal status, Stonea failed to attract settlement. There may have been thirty or more houses, and the inhabitants seem to have been not unprosperous; but a large-scale investigation yielded no evidence at all for productive activities, agricultural or industrial, and the impression is of a community that never thrived – unlike so many other 'townships', not least Fen-edge places like Durobrivae, Godmanchester and Cambridge. The order, around AD 200, to demolish the tower complex must mark the official abandonment of the site (although it remained a focus of settlement), and very probably drastic changes in the administration of the region. Indeed, it is by no means impossible that this devolved upon Durobrivae, for at least one large building within the town has an official appearance, while the enormous and palatial complex of third-century date at nearby Castor, the so-called *praetorium*, also hints at a public role.[129]

It may of course be that, in inferring direct state control of the Fens, we are misrepresenting a more subtle and diverse system of land tenure. Indeed, it is sometimes maintained that the absence of carefully surveyed, regular field systems, resembling the centuriated landscapes of parts of

Italy, southern Gaul and North Africa, is a powerful argument against identifying the region as an imperial holding. In reality, by the time Britain was conquered, centuriation was largely a thing of the past, and the very few suggested examples from the province carry little conviction.[130] There are in the Fens some areas with hints of a more regular layout of ditches, especially to the north of Christchurch (Cambridgeshire) and at nearby Flaggrass (March). There is also the remarkable site at Rookery Farm, near Spalding in Lincolnshire, with its own approach road and an enclosure measuring approximately 200 x 250 Roman feet (c. 58 x 75 m); indeed, so different is it from the normal pattern, that it is tempting to think that this might have been laid out by a retired army veteran.[131] Despite this, the great majority of the settlements and field systems appear to represent little more than *ad hoc* development, by a population that must surely have been mainly of indigenous origin. Villas, as such, were never to appear within the Fenland proper, despite its vast extent of over 4,000 square kilometres, and the hypothesis that most of the inhabitants were lowly tenant farmers remains the most plausible interpretation of a landscape that is at once very 'visible', especially in aerial photography, and at the same time full of unresolved enigmas.

32 Aerial view of Rookery Farm, near Spalding, Lincolnshire, showing a Roman road and, in the foreground, a Roman farmstead (perhaps second century AD). The dark sinuous lines mark the courses of pre-Roman streams.

There are other areas of lowland Britain, for instance the great iron-producing region of the Weald and the fertile chalklands of Cranborne Chase, which have been similarly claimed as imperial holdings; for they, likewise, manifest little evidence of Romanised, villa-like buildings. However, in order to be certain, less ambiguous testimony is required, such as the well-known inscription from Combe Down, on the outskirts of Bath. Reused as the cover for a burial, found close to a substantial courtyard building, it records how Naevius, a freedman and assistant to the procurators, 'restored from ground level the ruined *principia*'.[132] If the adjacent building is indeed the *principia*, it may therefore have been the headquarters for an imperial estate, perhaps connected with the quarrying of local stone. A lead sealing of the provinces of upper Britain, used for official packages, adds credence to the idea.[133]

The identification of ancient systems of land tenure is therefore fraught with difficulties, and the recent intensification of landscape studies in fact shows an immensely complex mosaic of settlements and field systems. In the Retford area of Nottinghamshire, for example, aerial photography has revealed a striking arrangement of rectangular fields, laid out in long, roughly parallel east–west swathes and associated with a series of small farmsteads. One has been excavated, at Dunston's Clump, yielding a sequence of structures dating from the first to third centuries AD, set within an enclosure of about 40 by 50 metres. A substantial wooden house inside an internal yard was replaced, first by a number of stock pens and then by at least three post-built structures. A second adjacent enclosure, which has not been investigated, makes it difficult to interpret these findings in detail, for the two complexes are surely related; indeed, given the sparsity of

refuse from the excavated enclosure (a mere two boxes of finds), it is not impossible that it was devoted entirely to agricultural activities.[134]

Dunston's Clump lies in a region where villas are notably scarce; but even in the more Romanised areas of the south, non-villa settlements customarily make up eighty to ninety per cent of the landscape – although, as stressed above, this says nothing about the ownership of the land. As in the Fenland, there are occasional larger sites which might be classed as villages; but most are relatively small, reflecting perhaps a modest social unit, such as an extended family. Certainly, there were local hierarchies, with a site such as Maxey, near Peterborough, towards the very bottom of the pack.[135] This must be the implication of the few round houses and the low level of material culture that an extensive excavation has revealed. Doubtless, there were many more such sites, even in the most favoured lowland regions, where perspectives remained wholly parochial and to whose inhabitants Romanisation was a more or less complete irrelevance. The gap between those who shared in, and promoted, the new order, and those who perceived it as a modest realignment of their affairs, must have been considerable. Whilst the local squirearchy may have changed their way of life – quickly or slowly, according to will and circumstance – the faces (and family) remained largely the same. What the archaeological evidence really seems to tell us is that in Britain, as in many other provinces, there was a deep rurally-based conservatism, which was only slowly modified with time. It is the nature of these changes that we shall explore in our final chapter; but first we must turn our attention to the subject of Romano-British architecture and art.

FURTHER READING

A most perceptive recent study of the subject is M. Millett, *The Romanization of Britain* (1990), which has many novel and interesting perspectives. More specific works on the towns include: J.S. Wacher, *The Towns of Roman Britain* (1975 but currently being revised), B.C. Burnham and J.S. Wacher, *The 'Small Towns' of Roman Britain* (1990) and G. Webster (ed.), *Fortress into City* (1988); there is also a series of fine monographs on individual sites, too numerous to list here, although G.C. Boon, *Silchester: the Roman town of Calleva* (1974) remains a classic, as is S.S. Frere, *Verulamium Excavations*, vol.II (1983). On the countryside, R. Hingley adopts an interesting approach in his *Rural Settlement in Roman Britain* (1989), which should be read in conjunction with the essays by D. Miles and M.K. Jones in M. Todd (ed.), *Research on Roman Britain 1960–89* (1989). For villas, there is much of importance in M. Todd (ed.), *Studies in the Romano-British Villa* (1978) and in K. Branigan and D. Miles (eds), *Villa Economies* (1989), especially the essay by Mark Gregson. Major villa excavations include Winterton (Stead 1976), Gadebridge (Neal 1974), Gorhambury (Neal *et al.* 1990), Barton Court Farm (Miles 1986), Whitton (Jarrett and Wrathmell 1981), Lullingstone (Meates 1979, 1987) and now S. Wrathmell and A. Nicholson (eds), *Dalton Parlours. Iron Age Settlement and Roman Villa* (1990). The relationship between military and civilian worlds is explored in T.F.C. Blagg and A.C. King (eds), *Military and Civilian in Roman Britain* (1984), and C.S. Sommer, *The Military Vici in Roman Britain* (1984) provides a useful account. Finally, mention should be made of Alan Sutton's excellent series on the peoples of Roman Britain, e.g. Branigan 1985 and Todd 1991.

4

ARCHITECTURE
AND ART

S ince therefore so great a profession as this is adorned by, and abounds in, varied and numerous accomplishments, I think that only these persons can forthwith justly claim to be architects who from boyhood have mounted by the steps of these studies and, being trained generally in the knowledge of arts and the sciences, have reached the temple of architecture at the top. (Vitruvius, *De Architectura*, I, 1, 11.)

The principles of classical art and architecture have influenced European visual perceptions throughout the medieval and modern periods, and therefore remain so familiar to us that it is hard to imagine the change in artistic vocabulary which they imposed upon many of the societies which were incorporated into the Roman empire. Alien Mediterranean styles and techniques were transplanted into northern countries. Though the impact of Graeco-Roman canons of art was modified in Britain by the vitality of the native tradition, the visual effect of Roman buildings and engineering must have been spectacular: the Roman conquest would have transformed the appearance of the country as much as, or more than, the industrial revolution of the nineteenth century.[1]

It is a truism that Roman architecture and art owed much to Greek prototypes, and indeed many Roman architects, engineers, artists and craftsmen were of Greek origin. Etruscan influence was also of great importance, especially in engineering, but it would be wrong to underestimate the extent of the distinctively Roman contribution in these fields. Many innovative architectural techniques originated in Etruria, in Greek-speaking lands or further east, but were fully exploited and developed only within the efficient machine of Roman imperial organisation.

The use of columns in building design was an established tradition in the Mediterranean which the Romans merely continued and developed.

However, the employment of arches, vaults and domes, foreshadowing medieval architecture, was above all a Roman achievement, as was construction using mortar, concrete and fired bricks. Specialised structures were designed and standardised in response to the needs of the Roman way of life, including roads, bridges, aqueducts and piped water supplies, sewers and sophisticated heating systems. Whether buildings were of traditional timber construction, stone or brick-built, a wide repertoire of embellishments could be applied to them internally and externally. Decorative finishes included terracotta, stucco and plaster, fresco wall-paintings, veneer, inlay, mosaic and other colourful composite wall and floor surfaces.

All these things were new to a remote northern province like Britain. The establishment of Roman administration and culture required the introduction of the appropriate specialised buildings, and though there is some overlap, four major categories can be discerned – military, public/administrative, religious and domestic.

Military architecture has already been discussed, but its importance in the provinces was such that it must be touched upon again here. The design of the Roman fort epitomises certain aspects of the Roman achievement. A fort may be compared to a small town, complete with administrative centre, living accommodation and facilities for bathing and the storage and preparation of food. All this was laid out in a planned grid of streets and enclosed within a defensive wall, a tried and tested layout which was followed with only minor variations all over the empire. The natural, organic growth of unplanned settlements (vici) around permanent military bases would have served only to emphasise the regularity and uncompromising functionalism of the forts. Military architecture was not concerned with aesthetics: the brutal symmetry of a site like Housesteads, with its rigid lines of barracks and castellated walls hacked out of the wild countryside, was a wholly appropriate symbol of the harsher side of Roman domination embodied in the army and its formidable efficiency.

If the architecture of the military bases emphasised the arrogant power of Rome, that of the towns was more complex in its message, for it served as a significant element in the more subtle and persuasive process of Romanisation. Towns occupied a central position in Graeco-Roman ideals of a civilised way of life, and their physical construction and appearance and the amenities which they were expected to provide were all integral parts of the concept. The civic centre of a Roman town, the forum, consisted of a market square with one side occupied by the 'town hall', the basilica. The commercial and administrative elements in the life of the settlement thus came to a common focus where the town's main streets met. The basilica was a long rectangular building, often with an apse at one or both ends, or side aisles supported on columns and providing a higher nave with a clerestory for lighting. There were naturally many variant forms. The basilica was a public meeting-place for a range of purposes, including the administration of law, and usually provided accommodation for municipal offices: Vitruvius remarks that basilicas 'should be placed adjoining the forum in as warm a position as possible, so that in the winter businessmen may meet without being troubled by the weather', possibly a more difficult requirement in Britain than in the Mediterranean.[2] The long classical tradition of this type of building was wholly secular, but it was widely adopted in late antiquity as the favoured form for Christian churches.

Although Britain has no surviving buildings to compare with the magnificent restored late Roman basilica at Trier, whose stark and dignified lines provide such a memorable foil for the adjacent eighteenth-century palace, remains of the forum and basilica have been identified at many Romano-British towns, and even the most modest town would have possessed these essential public structures. At Silchester the basilica was some 82 metres long: it was apsidal at both ends, and the main entrance would have been in the long side facing into the forum. Within was a single side aisle, with Corinthian columns rising to a height of about 8.5 metres. Open colonnades surrounded all four sides of the forum. Fragments of large-scale statuary, marble wall veneer and painted plaster testify to the elegance of the basilica's interior.[3] We cannot know in detail how an Iron-Age tribal king might have expressed his authority in terms of the appearance and furnishings of his surroundings, but we can be sure that it would have been different from the polished brightness of a Roman basilica, with its lofty columns, hard concrete, plaster and marble, and life-size bronze statues. Even when built on a modest scale, as at Caerwent, the basic plan, which in essence resembles that of the *principia* of a fort, is unchanged. It has been suggested that military architects may in fact have designed many of the early Romano-British fora.

The earliest forum and basilica in London was also of moderate size, but by the second century, when the town's pre-eminent position had probably been formally recognised, it possessed a huge basilica, around 150 metres in length.[4] This would have reflected London's status as administrative centre not just for an area but for the whole province. Since the forum accommodated a town's major agglomeration of traders as well as the administrative centre, it would have been familiar not only to the town-dwellers themselves but to country people from the surrounding area who came in to buy and sell goods. Formal, rectilinear structures, brick and concrete, colonnaded porticoes, would thus have become familiar sights to most Roman Britons and would have been a subtle influence in making them aware of their membership of the empire.

There were other public buildings which symbolised adoption of the Roman way of life. The custom of visiting the baths, a practice which involved leisure, business and social contacts and the pursuit of health and fitness as well as merely keeping clean, was a quintessential element of Roman culture. Some public baths, such as the baths of Caracalla and of

33 Excavations in progress on the Huggin Hill baths in London, revealing heated rooms. The baths were in use from the later first century AD to the late second century.

Diocletian in Rome and the Barbarathermen in Trier, were buildings of exceptional size and magnificence, while bath-suites in some private houses could be quite small and simple, but the principles remained the same. Remains of bath-houses have been found at numerous Romano-British sites: town baths include those at Silchester and Leicester, a very large complex at Wroxeter, and of course Bath, which is a special case; military bath-houses are known at many forts, for example at Housesteads and Caerleon; and private baths have been investigated at many villa sites.[5]

Roman baths were of essentially the same type as Turkish baths. The precise number and layout of the rooms, and even their exact names and functions, were variable, but a typical arrangement would include a hall or courtyard for exercise (*palaestra*), an anteroom where the bathers undressed and and left their clothing (*apodyterium*), a cold room (*frigidarium*), warm room (*tepidarium*), and hot room (*caldarium*), plus hot and cold plunge baths. In some cases there was a room of intense dry heat (*laconicum*) as well as the steamier *caldarium*. The sequence of cold to hot rooms, exercise, massage, rest and immersion in hot or cold water, would be up to the individual. Both men and women visited the baths, but it was not considered acceptable for them to do so together, so some large public establishments had two suites of rooms, with separate entrances; in smaller baths, different hours were set aside for the sexes.

Organised communal bathing in purpose-built accommodation would have been completely new to the Celtic population, and no doubt their initial reaction to the idea would have been cautious, to say the least. In due course it would have become an effective means of Romanisation, since it is a highly agreeable experience, and once tried, is liable to become a habit.

Baths demanded specialised techniques of building and engineering, the existence of an effective method of heating and a reliable and abundant water supply. Timber construction would have been unsuitable to withstand the damp heat generated, so brick and concrete were used, the hot rooms generally being roofed with a concrete vault and finished on the interior with plaster rendering. Public latrines were often associated with bath buildings, and the used water could be employed for flushing them. The necessary heating was achieved by means of a hypocaust system: the floors of the rooms were raised on brick or stone pillars, and the heat from the furnace circulated under the floors, eventually escaping upwards through the hollow flue-tiles which lined the walls. The result was an evenly distributed high temperature such as would be difficult or impossible to achieve with fixed hearths or portable braziers. Though this system was devised for use in bath-houses, it was also widely employed in homes, a welcome luxury in the British climate.

The many remains of bath-houses in Britain bear witness to their integration into Romano-British life. Evidence for another characteristic feature of classical culture, the theatre, is far scantier. The theatre grew up in Greece

34 An ivory mount from Caerleon, Gwent, carved in the form of a tragic mask. It may have been used, with other ivory panels, to decorate a small box. H. 10.8 cm. Caerleon Museum.

as part of the religious festivals in honour of Dionysos, but by the time of the Roman empire many changes and developments had taken place, and though a religious element was certainly still present, entertainment had probably become the primary purpose of plays, dance, mime and musical performances.

The theatre at Verulamium, a modest building by Continental standards, was fully excavated in 1933–4.[6] Two theatres are known at Colchester, one within the town, the other in the temple complex at Gosbecks.[7] There are traces of a theatre at Canterbury, and an inscription from Brough-on-Humber testifies to the existence of one there, though the site has not been located. The inscription records the construction of a new stage at the expense of the aedile, one M. Ulpius Ianuarius, in the second century.[8]

The distinctive appearance of a Greek or Roman theatre is still familiar, since a great many survive in fine condition in various areas of the classical world. The rising tiers of seats look down on a circular or semicircular area (the orchestra) and the stage. In Roman theatres, the orchestra was not a full circle, and the stage was larger and more elaborate than that of a Greek theatre; behind it was an imposing architectural backdrop with columns and niches. It is interesting to note that at Verulamium the earliest phase of the theatre had a circular orchestra and a correspondingly large arc of seating, later modified by the enlargement of the stage to produce a plan of the more typical Roman design. The connection is not with Greek theatres of a much earlier date but probably with similar small theatres in Roman Gaul, and the original plan may have reflected the use of the building: the larger orchestra implies activities which were concentrated in that area rather than on the stage. The Gosbecks temple, though built to a more standard plan from the start, also has some anomalous features in the stage area, and the excavator has suggested that its principal use might have been for religious rites connected with the adjacent temple rather than for plays.

No doubt future work will bring to light additional theatres in Britain,

35 Aerial view of the amphitheatre outside the legionary fortress at Caerleon, Gwent. Long axis 81.4 m.

but it is unlikely that we shall ever be able to infer a great deal about their popularity or the kind of entertainment which took place in them. Cultured and literary performances were not the only ones enacted in theatres; cruder entertainments not far removed from those of the amphitheatre were also possible. Amphitheatres were designed for spectacles such as gladiatorial combat and wild-beast shows. Scenes from such events were familiar to Roman Britons, for they were part of the standard repertoire of decorative art on pottery, glass, mosaics and the like. Several small amphitheatres have long been known in Britain, for instance outside towns such as Silchester and Cirencester and at the legionary fortresses of Caerleon and Chester,[9] but they are all modest in scale compared with the enormous examples which survive elsewhere in the western Roman world, epitomised by the Colosseum in Rome. They are as distinctive in form as the theatres, the seating rising in tiers around an oval arena. In February 1988 excavation near the Guildhall in London revealed a small segment of the entrance to the amphitheatre, and no doubt there are other such discoveries still to be made.[10] Representations of chariot-racing also occur widely in Roman Britain, but as yet no circus, the appropriate building for this dangerous and popular Roman sport, has been found. However, a permanent structure was probably not essential for racing.

The buildings we have considered so far are all strictly practical. The monumental arch was equally typical of Roman architecture, but was non-functional and symbolic, a decorative gateway erected to commemorate some noteworthy event. Foundations for monumental arches have been found in Verulamium, and sculptured elements from the upper part of a

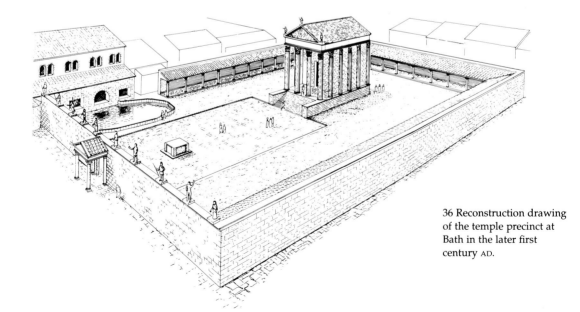

36 Reconstruction drawing of the temple precinct at Bath in the later first century AD.

large arch in London have been sufficient to provide a basis for a reconstruction of its appearance, though its position in the town, like that of
many of Roman London's public buildings, remains unknown.[11]

Religious buildings underwent architectural change and development
as a result of the Roman occupation. Some temples of traditionally classical
style were built, but more common were temples of the distinctive hybrid
Romano-Celtic form which was also widespread on the Continent. Though
Roman temples were not all built to the same design, certain features
derived and adapted from Greek traditions can be considered typical;
namely, a building set on a high rectangular podium, its columned entrance
porch reached by a flight of steps, and behind this, the enclosed cella, the
room which contained the cult-image of the deity. Engaged half-columns
sometimes adorned the cella walls and recalled the older tradition of the
peripteral temple (surrounded by free-standing columns). The overall effect
of such a building, well demonstrated by a surviving example such as the
Maison Carrée at Nîmes, gives an impression of commanding height even
when the building is of no great size.

Probably the best-known classical temple in Britain is that of Sulis
Minerva at Bath.[12] Though none of it survives above ground, the elevation
of its façade, with lofty columns and an elaborately sculptured pediment,
had been reconstructed substantially correctly by Samuel Lysons before
the end of the eighteenth century. The evidence for this important building
is extremely difficult to interpret, owing to the adaptations which the
temple itself and its surroundings underwent in the Roman period and,
even more, to the extensive disturbances caused by the post-medieval
development of the city of Bath. In brief, the temple of Sulis Minerva as
first designed in the late first century AD was a building of some 9 x 14
metres, constructed on a podium and containing a square or almost square
cella; the prostyle porch was supported by four Corinthian columns over
8 metres high, and featured a very remarkable sculptured pediment.

The paved precinct or *temenos* surrounding the temple included the
sacred spring itself. This had been enclosed within a polygonal reservoir,
and was linked with the bathing complex which adjoined the temple area.
In front of the temple, and lined up with the spring, there was originally
a large altar. From the late second or early third century, various modi-
fications were carried out to the temple and other features in the precinct.
The spring was enclosed within a vaulted building, with an entrance
opposite the altar, and an ambulatory was constructed around the temple,
together with two square chambers flanking the front steps. From the very
fragmentary remains it is not possible to envisage the remodelled elevation
of the temple with any certainty, but in plan it would appear to have
progressed from a purely classical design to one which approximates more
closely to the concentric Romano-Celtic form.

These changes to the temple and its surroundings may express changes
in ritual and belief. It is arguable that an architectural adaptation from

purely Roman to Romano-Celtic could reflect a corresponding religious shift, a diminution of classical ritual and a greater emphasis on the native element which had been present in the cult all along, but such a thesis is incapable of proof. What is certain is that in its early phases, within a generation of the conquest, the temple of Sulis Minerva was a striking example of Mediterranean architecture in Britain. In the words of its most recent excavator, '... a tetrastyle Corinthian temple set simply in a spacious precinct embracing the sacred spring and overlooking a great thermal bathing establishment, would have been a source of wonder in the province at this early date.'[13]

Another major example of Roman temple architecture has left even scantier remains than the temple of Sulis. Nearly seventy years ago, Wheeler surmised that the traces of a massive podium underlying Colchester Castle belonged to the temple of the deified Claudius mentioned by Tacitus in his account of the Boudiccan rebellion. Further investigation over the years has tended to confirm his identification. The podium is all that is left of the building, but it is of impressive dimensions, 32 x 23.5 m, and is constructed in such a way as to save building stone by incorporating large sand-filled vaults in the non-loadbearing areas. The position of these provides the only indication we have of the superstructure. This is thought to have had a porch with an octastyle (eight-columned) façade, probably of the Corinthian order, and a cella with freestanding columns along the side walls. The back wall may have been a solid one joining the cella and the ends of the side colonnades. No evidence of the pediment survives, nor of the inscription which was doubtless carved upon the frieze.[14]

There are traces of other classical temples in Britain, for example at Verulamium, and we can certainly infer the existence of such buildings in the fora of major towns: it is unthinkable, for instance, that there would not have been temples of purely Mediterranean form in London. Nevertheless, however many unidentified or uncertainly identified classical temples there may have been, we can be sure that the majority of shrines were temples of the Romano-Celtic type. Typically, these have a ground-plan of two concentric squares or polygons, representing a cella surrounded by an ambulatory.

There has been much recent work on Romano-Celtic temples both in Britain and on the Continent.[15] This has tended to emphasise the continuity of sacred sites from the Iron Age into the Roman period, and also the importance of examining not only the temple buildings themselves but also the ancillary structures present within the temple precinct or *temenos*. It is reasonable to postulate a degree of architectural continuity as well, and to attribute the distinctive characteristics of Romano-Celtic temples to the Iron-Age shrines which were their predecessors: thus at Hayling Island, the Roman-period cella, in the form of a round tower-like building with a rectangular porch set within a square precinct, was preceded by a circular Iron-Age shrine of unknown height.[16]

The great difficulty lies in reconstructing the appearance of Romano-Celtic temples from their ground-plans alone. In the case of classical temples, we are guided by examples which are still standing, by ancient pictorial representations, and by written precepts and descriptions. In the case of Romano-Celtic temples, great stress has been laid on the few Continental examples where the cella still stands in ruins, but it would be foolhardy to assume that all the many shrines known from their foundations alone would have had similar elevations. There is general consensus that the typical plan implies a cella rising to upper-storey height, lit by clerestory windows above a roofed ambulatory. Whether the latter was an open colonnade or an enclosed passageway is seldom certain.

Many models and reconstruction drawings of Romano-Celtic temples have been devised. All are to some extent conjectural, but it seems reasonable to infer that the continuity and fusion of Celtic and Roman traditions present in the actual religious beliefs and rituals (see chapter 6) found corresponding physical embodiment in the architecture. Existing Celtic shrines were developed in a number of ways: by enlarging them; rebuilding in whole or in part; using more durable materials; adding or incorporating classical details such as columns and porches. The wholly classical basilica or bath-house served a purpose which had not been envisaged in Britain before the conquest. By contrast, the hybrid architecture of the Romano-Celtic temple expresses an unbroken tradition.

One cult, that of Mithras, made use of places of worship which were distinctive and quite unlike both the temple types we have discussed. Like Christian churches, mithraea were designed for congregational worship, in which the devotees enter the dwelling of the deity instead of remaining at the altar placed before it. As the cult was exclusive, the number of Mithraists was not large, and the temples are quite small rectangular structures with raised benches along either side of a central aisle. They are always dark, and usually semi-subterranean, to simulate the surroundings of the cave which is central to the mythology of the faith. Mithraea also often have pits in the porch area which have been interpreted as having something to do with the ordeals undergone by initiates at various stages in their membership of the cult. There is really no certain evidence on this point, but the pits have been noted at more than one site, for example in the mithraea at Carrawburgh and Rudchester (Northumberland).[17]

Christian churches had no fixed architectural form during the period of oppression, and may often have been temporary house-chapels in the homes of Christians. When churches began to be openly designed and built, the secular design of the basilica was adopted, rather than that of the pagan temple, no doubt to dissociate the faithful from a tradition felt to be evil, but also because space was required to accommodate a congregation within the building. Probably the best-known putative Romano-British church is that at Silchester, and though real doubts have been expressed about this identification of what is basically a very small (c. 13 x 9 m)

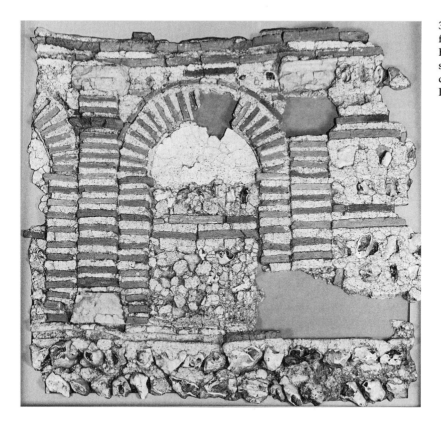

37 Part of the fallen façade from Meonstoke, Hampshire, lifted in 1989, showing the elaborate detail. See also Colour Plate V.

apsidal building, it does possess features which are strongly suggestive of a developed Christian church, notably a transept at the apse end. There are numerous other possible or probable Christian churches in the province, but as yet not one can be identified with absolute certainty (see chapter 7).[18]

Of course, it is often difficult to infer the function of a building from the partial remains which come down to us. A case in point is the important building from Meonstoke (Hampshire), where the survival of the fallen upper portion of the gable end as well as the ground-plan has provided a rare opportunity to reconstruct the actual appearance of a Romano-British building in the countryside. Excavation of the Meonstoke façade required considerable skill and ingenuity, and its results were something of a revelation. The building was an aisled basilica with a clerestory, and the end

38 Fragment of wall plaster from a villa at Hucclecote, Gloucestershire, with a drawing of a building not unlike that from Meonstoke incised on it. H. 9 cm. British Museum.

v elevation was embellished with highly detailed architectural ornament, using the colours, shapes and textures of flint, brick, stone and pink and white mortar to produce a complex and carefully calculated decorative effect more reminiscent of the domestic architecture of a great late Victorian city such as Cardiff than of classical purity or Iron-Age rural simplicity. Buildings of similar appearance can be found illustrated on late Roman mosaics and other pictorial sources from widely separated provinces. This structure, whatever its precise use, emphasises the integration of British taste and style into that of the empire as a whole.[19]

Domestic or private architecture encompassed virtually the whole range from rural dwellings in the Iron-Age tradition to the characteristically Mediterranean courtyard house, though with the exception of the villa estates, the most Romanised styles of building were to be found mainly in the towns. The simplest houses consisted of rectangular rooms opening into one another. Living quarters in central urban locations were often no more than rooms behind the open-fronted shops. One refinement to such a dwelling is the addition of a corridor so that rooms need no longer be intercommunicating. Another is the addition of an upper storey. Plans incorporating one or more corridors, projecting wings, and more complex layouts leading to the completely enclosed central courtyard are all known in excavated Romano-British town sites, but while these features can be identified from the foundations, the presence or absence of upper storeys can be very difficult to establish with any confidence. There are no known indications of the four- or five-storey blocks of flats which were built in Roman towns such as Ostia, but such buildings could well have existed in London and perhaps some other important centres.[20]

Amongst the wealthier members of Roman society, gardens also played a part in the planning of the domestic environment. Wall-paintings, from Pompeii and elsewhere, and written references demonstrate that the decorative potential of a garden was fully appreciated and exploited. We cannot doubt that the Roman Britons who aspired to Mediterranean elegance in their houses and furnishings would also have followed classical models in their gardens. Unfortunately, archaeological methods can only rarely recover details of a garden, so there is little evidence on the matter from Britain.[21] An exception is Fishbourne, where skilled excavation techniques revealed that the first-century palace boasted large formal gardens with colonnades, broad paths and an elaborate pattern of ornamental hedges. A sophisticated system for water drainage may also have supplied a series of fountains. The species of plants which were grown cannot now be established, so we do not know whether to envisage a green vista of lawns and trees, or colourful flower-beds; it has been plausibly surmised, however, that the formal lines and curves of the bedding-trenches detected in excavation contained neatly clipped box hedges. The general effect was undoubtedly impressive and appropriate as a setting for the building in its most palatial phase.[22]

On a more homely level, there could also be space for gardens in towns, and owners of houses which possessed a courtyard or even an open forecourt could plant trees, shrubs and perhaps a selection of kitchen-garden plants. The choice was vastly augmented after Britain became a province of the empire: the influence of Roman cuisine brought with it the fruit, vegetables and seasonings required, and many food plants which seem so basic to European diet that we might presume them to be native were in fact Roman introductions. The list includes cabbage, broad bean, pea, parsnip, radish, celery, carrot, turnip, lamb's lettuce (corn salad), chervil, coriander, dill, grape-vine, fig, walnut, Spanish chestnut and improved varieties of apple, mulberry, plum, damson and cherry. Roses, lilies and violets may also have been cultivated here for the first time in the Roman period. In terms of everyday life, such introductions are no less important than most manufactured items.[23]

As we have seen, Roman architectural design, materials and techniques created the appearance of the towns and transformed that of much of the countryside. Within these buildings, whether public or private, the influence of classical art was also to be seen, though in certain areas of artistic endeavour it was modified by the powerful Celtic traditions.

In antiquity, as in more recent periods, portable easel paintings were regarded as the epitome of artistic achievement. It is one of the frustrations of studying Roman art that these do not survive. The paintings which we are able to judge are those which were more intimately connected with the architecture, namely the fresco wall-paintings which adorned so many houses and other buildings. While some of these are very competently executed, they are unlikely ever to be in the same class as the best of the portable paintings. Wall-paintings have been most minutely studied where they are best preserved, in the cities destroyed by Vesuvius, but tantalisingly fragmentary traces are also found throughout Roman Britain.[24] Most of them are executed in the true fresco technique, in which the pigments are applied to fresh, damp plaster and thus become absorbed and incorporated into the material. The colour cannot flake away like a surface layer of paint, and the potential for the survival of the designs is therefore theoretically good. In practice, however, the destruction of buildings or their slow disintegration and collapse leaves ceiling and wall surfaces shattered and chaotically intermingled. The excavation of such fragments and the reassembly of what amounts to a large incomplete jigsaw puzzle with no key is more than merely difficult and time-consuming; it requires an amount of space which few museums, archaeological units or universities are able to provide. It is therefore not surprising that in spite of the frequent occurrence of painted wall plaster on Romano-British sites, few large areas have ever been restored and interpreted.

Painted interior plaster is recorded from town and villa sites all over Britain, and was often noted by nineteenth-century excavators. It was a wholly classical concept of interior decoration, and did not exist in Britain before the conquest. Its ubiquity is therefore of considerable interest. Painted walls were more widespread than the patterned mosaic floors which are so much better known; houses which boast mosaic floors in only one or two rooms will sometimes have had painted plaster throughout.

As far as we can judge, the design conventions which are seen in the well-preserved paintings of the Vesuvian cities applied equally in Britain, and it is difficult to detect any native elements. Ceilings were usually decorated with an all-over geometric pattern based on circles, squares or octagons, producing an effect resembling coffering. The background colour was often white, but the strong red ochre which was very popular for walls was sometimes extended to the ceiling. Walls were typically divided into three decorative zones, a dado at the bottom, a fairly deep frieze below the ceiling, and a large field between them which was further subdivided into panels. These conventions facilitated the difficult technique of painting in fresco, since the lines between the necessarily limited areas of plaster which could be treated at one time were neatly disguised in the layout of the pattern.

The most basic designs simply used large blocks and lines of colour, perhaps with panels of stylised imitation marble inlay, or architectural motifs such as painted columns. The next level of pictorial complexity featured wreaths, swags and scrolls with foliate and floral elements, and IV the inclusion of motifs such as panther heads and birds. This artistic vocabulary is universal in the Roman world, seen at its best in sculpture such as the Ara Pacis Augustae in Rome but appearing in a multitude of other guises, down to the ornament on small items such as relief-decorated silver, glass and pottery tableware. Motifs like the theatrical mask in a panel from a house in Leicester, though ultimately of religious and symbolic significance, are simply standard elements in the range of Roman visual motifs: it would seem that the Roman custom of decorating the walls of rooms in this way was carried out in entirely Roman terms.

Other wall-paintings were more elaborate pictorial compositions, landscapes and mythological scenes with human and animal figures. In these, too, the impression of a strictly classical range of themes is upheld. From the Flavian period at Fishbourne there are fragments of pastoral scenes which would not be out of place at Pompeii. Several later villa contexts have produced fragments of scenes with human figures: a head tentatively identified as Narcissus from Tarrant Hinton (Dorset); a Cupid from Southwell (Nottinghamshire) and an incomplete scene with a seated figure, thought perhaps to be Achilles at the court of Lycomedes, from Kingscote (Gloucestershire). From Colchester comes a panel with part of a gladiatorial scene. It is possible that future discoveries will modify the impression, but so far it appears that wall-painting in Roman Britain was a major vehicle for familiarising provincials with Roman style and subject-matter in art.

It is hardly possible that all these paintings were carried out by Continental craftsmen. Though some of the earliest work, and particularly that which adorned public buildings, would certainly have been executed by artists from elsewhere in the empire, British workers must have entered the trade and eventually set up their own workshops. The nature of the craft is such that it cannot be very centralised – work has to be carried out on the spot. In learning the technique, British apprentices must also have learnt the artistic repertoire, and evidently felt little or no need to add elements from their own Celtic background. There are occasional hints of Romano-British independence: a few fragments of wall-painting are known which imitate mosaic (e.g. at Sparsholt, Hampshire), and these have not so far been paralleled in any other province. Panels of this sort may have been visual links between the tessellated floor and the painted wall. Where enough survives to show it, there is evidence of floor, walls and ceiling being conceived as a single design, motifs from one area being repeated in another.

Floors smoothly surfaced in stone, tile or concrete formed a counterpart to the walls with their plastered finish, and were equally expressive of civilised life throughout the Roman empire. Plain tessellated floors composed of large mosaic cubes in a single colour, and *opus signinum*, mortar containing crushed brick, were far more common than patterned mosaics, yet even so, hundreds of the latter have been recorded from Roman Britain.[25] In the eighteenth century and earlier, the discovery of mosaic pavements was usually noted, even though in some cases they were re-buried, and all too often suffered damage. Those which have been preserved, either in museums or *in situ* at excavated Romano-British sites, represent a branch of provincial Roman art which vividly illustrates the complex balance of foreign and native elements.

The mosaic cubes were most commonly around 10–12 mm square and made of local materials – chalk, limestone, sandstone, shale, fired clay and occasionally glass. The majority of Romano-British pavements therefore achieve their effects with comparatively few colours and a bold, linear style: the subtleties of painterly shading are not available with a palette of half-a-dozen colours and units around 1 centimetre square. The tesserae could be laid directly into the prepared mortar on the site, and this method would have been used for the plain tessellated borders which usually surround the more intricately patterned 'carpets', but there were also methods which enabled more complex work to be prefabricated in the workshop and brought to the site in panels. Designs could be laid on coarse cloth with adhesive and then reversed onto the waiting mortar bed; once the cubes had set firmly into the mortar, the scrim could be soaked and peeled off.[26]

Even though this limited degree of off-site preparation was possible, it would have been essential to have many mosaic workshops in all parts of the country. A few large firms located in major towns could not have served the needs of the whole province, and stylistic analysis supports the logical conclusion that this was a decentralised industry employing much local labour. The fine mosaic pictures (*emblemata*) composed of minuscule tesserae 2–3 mm in size, in scores of subtly graded shades of colour, have not yet been discovered in Britain.

Because mosaics from different areas, even from different Roman provinces, can display striking similiarities not only in the conventional ornaments which were part of the stock-in-trade of Roman art, but also in the figural scenes, it used to be surmised that mosaicists worked from 'pattern books' which were widely copied and transmitted within the craft. Clients would, it was thought, select a design from a range of drawings presented for their inspection, rather as a modern householder picks a carpet or wallpaper from a portfolio of samples. This theory runs counter not only to the nature of skilled manual work, but also to what we know of the patron-craftsman relationship in antiquity. For the dissemination of the decorative motifs, no drawings would be needed; they would be in the minds and hands of the mosaicists, and as apprentices became masters, set up their own workshops or moved to other areas, the motifs would spread. If a client wished to check on such details in advance, no doubt a sketch or a quick demonstration in tesserae would suffice. For the scenes with figures, we must remind ourselves that famous paintings and statues were widely copied and reproduced in antiquity just as they are today. Copies of sculpture survive in every possible size and quality, down to the low-relief figure-types on lamps and moulded pottery, but the portable paintings and illustrated manuscripts which would have made many two-dimensional works of art familiar all over the empire are no longer extant. The owner of the villa at Low Ham (Somerset) who wanted scenes from Virgil's *Aeneid* on his floor is far more likely to have shown the mosaicist the pictures in his treasured manuscript of the epic than he is to have found them in the craftsman's 'pattern book'.[27] The work was commissioned, and we must assume that the buyer selected the subject. At the same time, we must bear in mind that a commissioned design would be seen and admired by the owner's friends, who might take it as a model, and request a similar pattern from the same firm of mosaicists (no doubt to the original owner's irritation). A local repertoire might thus be built up. This evidently happened in the case of the distinctive British fourth-century mosaics featuring Orpheus as the lord of the animals.

The site of the palace at Fishbourne is one of the few where reliably dated first-century mosaics have been found in Britain. During the heyday of the building in the Flavian period, many floors were finished with geometric patterns executed in black and white tesserae alone, an austere and effective style which is also found on the Continent, including Italy, at that period. Though the materials are local, those who designed and laid the floors very probably came from abroad. Other mosaics at Fishbourne, more colourful and less elegant, can be dated to the second and third centuries, as can a number of examples from town sites.

The majority of surviving Romano-British mosaics are from the late Roman period, especially from the villas which flourished in the country-side in the fourth century. They have been exhaustively studied, and scholars have been able to identify different schools of mosaicists serving the needs of the wealthy villa-owners in different regions of the country. The earliest of these, designated the 'Central Southern Group', was responsible for the fine series of floors at Bignor (Sussex): two successive work-shops flourished at Cirencester (the Corinian schools); and Dorchester, Brough-on-Humber – or possibly Aldborough or York – and Water Newton were the centres of other workshops.[28] We know nothing of contemporary names for these firms, but there is one example of a probable mosaicist's signature, the abbreviation TER, probably for Tertius, on a floor at Bignor.

Further research may augment and refine the classification and chron-ology of these industries, but for our purposes their precise definition and dating may be of less importance than some general observations. By the fourth century, if not much earlier, the craftsmen were surely all British, yet the repertoire of subjects in the mosaics remained strictly and uniformly classical: the villa-owners, whether themselves of British or Continental background, used the interior decoration of their houses to emphasise their pretensions as persons of culture, steeped in the traditional mythology and literature of the Mediterranean world. A mosaic floor was one of the symbols of *romanitas*, and doubtless Celtic design elements would have been inappropriate, undermining the impression of cosmopolitan polish which the householder wished to convey.

The list of mythological themes so far identified on Romano-British mosaics is extensive, and includes not only the major deities of the Roman world – Jupiter, Bacchus, Neptune, Venus, Mercury – and such standard figures as Cupids, the Seasons and the Winds, masks and the like, but also much more obscure mythological and legendary scenes which appear to indicate familiarity with literary sources.[29] At Brading on the Isle of Wight a series of motifs includes representations of an astronomer identified by some as Anaximander, Lycurgus and the nymph Ambrosia, and Ceres (Demeter) imparting the knowledge of agriculture to Triptolemus: at Lenthay Green (Dorset) a clumsily drawn group depicts the musical contest between Apollo and the ill-fated satyr Marsyas: an elaborate scene at East Coker (Somerset), now unfortunately known only from an eighteenth-century drawing, has been interpreted as the discovery of Ariadne on Naxos by Bacchus:[30] Europa and the Bull occur at three sites, Lullingstone (Kent), Broad Street (London) and Keynsham (Somerset): the scenes from the *Aeneid* at Low Ham have already been mentioned. The execution does not always reflect the range and sophistication of the choice of subjects. The svelte Venus who appears twice on the Low Ham Virgil pavement has
_{TITLE}
_{PAGE} little in common with the wild-maned, pear-shaped Venus of Rudston (Yorkshire).

The theme of Orpheus and the animals is widespread in the art of the late Roman period, reflecting the increasing popularity of mystical religious cults and perhaps also the fact that the imagery of Orpheus, like that of certain other figures of pagan iconography, for example Hercules, could be interpreted in Christian terms. The ten or eleven fourth-century Orpheus mosaics so far known in Britain are unlike those from other provinces, and are highly distinctive in their form and layout. Orpheus is depicted playing

39 Part of a chariot-racing scene from a large mosaic found at Horkstow, Humberside, in 1796. The theme is a Roman one, the execution Romano-British. Hull Museum.

his lyre in the centre of a wheel-pattern of charmed animals; the more elaborate pavements, like that from Barton Court Farm, Cirencester, have more than one circular frieze. The masterpiece of the genre is at Woodchester (Gloucestershire), a superb floor known since the seventeenth century and still *in situ*, though sadly damaged. With an overall size of nearly 14 metres square, it is the largest mosaic extant north of the Alps. At the centre, now lost, was an octagonal 'pool' design with fishes and a star or rosette; Orpheus himself occupied the first circle. A frieze of birds and rings of conventional ornament divide this from the main circle of wild animals. The whole of animal creation, the earth, sky and sea, is thus represented. The outermost border is a richly detailed acanthus scroll, and the whole design is set within an extraordinarily complex pattern of geometric panels. Like the majority of the British Orpheus mosaics, Woodchester is the work of one of the Cirencester firms, though stylistic links with mosaics from the Trier region can also be seen.[31]

A few fourth-century mosaics incorporate overt Christian symbolism even though their basic imagery remains firmly rooted in the established pagan tradition. Pre-eminent among these is the pavement from Hinton St Mary (Dorset), which bears a portrait of Christ set before the chi-rho monogram in its central medallion. Like the closely related floor from Frampton (Dorset), it can be attributed to the school of mosaicists based at Dorchester.

Wall-paintings and mosaic floors bring together two strands of classical influence in the everyday surroundings of Romano-British citizens, combining the effect of a totally new approach to architecture with an artistic vocabulary based in the traditions of the Mediterranean world. Their

40 The Christian mosaic floor from Hinton St Mary, Dorset, during excavation. The head of Christ is in the central position in the main room, while Bellerophon, mounted on Pegasus and vanquishing the Chimaera, is the main motif in the smaller adjoining room. The decorative elements all belong to the established pagan tradition, but can all be interpreted in Christian terms. British Museum.

importance was immense, bringing literally into the home the sensation of belonging to a world empire which linked the remote island of Britain with lands as distant as Egypt and Greece.

Mosaics and wall-paintings may both be perceived as deriving from painting as a fine art, but though they were undoubtedly expressions of Roman aesthetic values, they were intimately linked with the structure of buildings and therefore effectively part of the architecture, and were carried out for the most part by local labour. The other major area of fine art is sculpture, and here we can assume that, in some instances at least, we are dealing with imported work from the hands of metropolitan artists. Any division of the subject can seem arbitrary, but a good case can be made for treating life-size or colossal statuary alongside architecture while consigning smaller statuettes to a place amongst the minor arts and personal possessions (chapter 5). Large statues could indeed have taken their place in the embellishment of wealthy private dwellings, but they were also a prominent feature of public buildings and spaces, just as they are today, and images of gods and rulers can thus be regarded as an integral element in the Graeco-Roman urban environment.

It is a recurring theme that many concepts were introduced for the first time under the Roman occupation of Britain, but the Celts were already highly skilled artists, and we should reflect before declaring that large statues and portrait sculpture were completely new to them; carving in wood rarely survives, and might conceivably have included such sculpture. We can be certain, however, that life-size or larger statues of people and animals in stone and bronze were first seen here in Roman times. In the Mediterranean, such work had ancient traditions in Greece and Etruria, and the advanced technology required for the casting of large figures in bronze had been perfected.

Complete full-scale bronzes seldom survive, and in Britain the evidence for them usually consists of small fragments. The heads of two imperial statues, one of Claudius, from Saxmundham (Suffolk), and the other with the unmistakable features of Hadrian, found in the Thames in London, are two pieces of evidence for the presence of good-quality official sculpture in the province. The Hadrian is over life-size, and the complete figure would have been around 2.25 metres tall. Mounted as it would have been on a pedestal or even a column, this would have been an imposing statue, placed in some public space in London. A single bronze hand of about the same scale was also found in London, and it has been suggested that it is from the same imperial image, though it could equally well be a part of another statue. Like any important Roman city, London must have had a great many imperial images.

Large-scale work in marble was also imported, but the evidence is somewhat sparse; portrait busts such as the two famous second-century examples from the Lullingstone villa are personal imports by the family which owned them, not official sculpture, but pieces like the fine head of

41 The head of a colossal statue of Hadrian found in the Thames at London Bridge. British Museum.

42 *Right* Marble statuette of Luna from the Woodchester villa, Gloucestershire. H. 43.5 cm. British Museum.

Minerva from Bath (Roman Baths Museum) and the Serapis from the Walbrook mithraeum (Museum of London) give an idea of the statuary which might have adorned religious and official sites. However, much classical marble sculpture has entered the country in modern times, and care has to be taken in the interpretation of examples which do not come from formal archaeological excavation.

Some smaller imported marble sculpture of excellent quality is also known, such as the statuette of Luna from the Woodchester villa, but here we are moving into the area of private, rather than public, art. Nevertheless, such objects were an influence on, and an expression of, Romano-British taste, albeit at a fairly exalted social level.

There was much ambitious large-scale work in locally available stone, and though its style is often far from classical, sculpture of this kind still upheld a Graeco-Roman aesthetic. In the absence of suitable marble, Cotswold limestone was extensively used for sculpture, and one of the finest examples is the statue of Mercury from the temple at Uley. Only 74 small fragments of the body and of other figures in the group (a ram and a cockerel) survive, but the head is almost intact, and demonstrates that the quality of the work is outstanding. The sculptor possessed great skill in handling the material and had a sound understanding of classical visual ideals.[32]

Not all Romano-British sculpture is firmly rooted in this tradition, however, and this brings us to a point of central importance. As in so many other areas of Romano-British culture, there is a complex interaction between classical ideals and Celtic perceptions. At their finest, works which blend the two traditions successfully are immensely powerful images, as we see, for example, in the central element of the Bath temple pediment. We can appreciate the principles of classical art, for we have inherited them, and in any case, they are based on naturalism; Celtic ideals present more of a problem, since we do not possess the key to what was essentially a more oblique and allusive approach to visual imagery.

In trying to disentangle the Celtic and classical elements in any work of art, we must never forget that each piece is the product of the inner vision and the manual skills of one (or more than one) individual; where a statue or a painting conforms closely to a familiar Graeco-Roman ideal, and is executed with a confident feeling for the properties of the material, as in the case of the Uley Mercury, we can say that the artist had a Roman concept in mind, and possessed the technical skill to achieve it. Where the work does not conform to these ideals, it is not always easy to say why: in some cases, it may well be that the artist was deliberately following another ideal – dancing to a Celtic, rather than a Roman, tune – but in others, the explanation is perhaps quite simply a lack of technical expertise.

The point is worth stressing, because it is a contentious one. Critics imbued with the ideals of Graeco-Roman art have sometimes described typically Romano-British sculpture as crude and incompetent, while apologists for the Celtic point of view have retaliated by declaring that far from failing to achieve their objectives, these Celtic artists were deliberately and successfully following non-classical principles. It is relevant to point out that unskilled artists exist in all communities, and Roman Britain is hardly likely to have been an exception. Indeed, manifestly crude artistic work can be found in all parts of the Roman empire, including areas where the classical ideals were the only ones available. A statue such as the mother-goddess from Caerwent (Cardiff, National Museum of Wales) is far removed from naturalistic Roman work, but its impact and charm are not diminished if we admit that this is just as likely to be due to artistic limitation as to an ethnic predilection for unrealistic images.[33]

At the beginning of this chapter we observed that the Roman conquest transformed the physical appearance of Britain. The great majority of the rural population would have continued to live just as their ancestors had done, but the towns and roads, the buildings and sculpture in new forms and materials, some serving purposes undreamed of before the conquest, would have radically altered public perceptions of civilised living. The fact that a British peasant might still have experienced everyday living conditions similar to those of his Iron-Age predecessors (and indeed, his medieval descendants) would not prevent him assimilating some values which were specifically Roman, and current throughout the empire. And as we shall see in the next chapter, even those who could not aspire to marble statues and painted walls did become familiar with many everyday goods and utensils which were unknown before Britain was incorporated into the Roman world. Even on the humblest level, material culture was transformed.

FURTHER READING

The only book specifically devoted to architecture in Roman Britain is Guy de la Bédoyère, *The Buildings of Roman Britain* (1991), which has numerous interesting, if somewhat speculative, reconstructions, as does Stephen Johnson, *Hadrian's Wall* (1989). T.F.C. Blagg has published a number of important essays, including 'Roman civil and military architecture in the province of Britain', *World Archaeology* 12 (1980), 27–42; 'An examination of the connections between military and civilian architecture in Roman Britain', in Blagg and King (eds), *Military and Civilian in Roman Britain* (1984), 249–63; and 'Architectural munificence in Britain', *Britannia* 21 (1990), 13–32. F.A. Pritchard, 'Ornamental stonework from Roman London', *Britannia* 17 (1986), 169–90, is a useful study, while for particular buildings and structures see Frere 1983 (Verulamium); Hill, Millett and Blagg 1980 (the London arch); Cunliffe and Davenport 1985 (Bath), and King and Potter 1990 (the Meonstoke façade). Any study of Roman art in Britain must begin with J.M.C. Toynbee, *Art in Britain under the Romans* (1964), with now M. Henig (ed.), *A Handbook of Roman Art* (1983) as a useful background study. For sculpture see the *Corpus of Sculpture of the Roman World*, of which six fascicules have been issued for Britain; for mosaics, the three essays by Smith (1969, 1977 and 1984), and D.S. Neal, *Roman Mosaics in Britain* (1981); for wall-painting N. Davey and R. Ling, *Wall-Paintings in Roman Britain* (1982), R. Ling, 'The Kingscote wall-paintings', *Britannia* 12 (1981), 167–75; B.J. Philp, *The Roman House with Bacchic Murals at Dover* (1989); and now S.A. Mackenna and R. Ling, 'Wall-paintings from the Winchester Palace site, Southwark', *Britannia* 22 (1991), 159–72.

— 5 —

PERSONAL
POSSESSIONS

I n the upper rooms: kettle, bronze, 1; cup, tin, 1; saucepan, bronze, 1; small colander, bronze, 1; mixing bowls, 2; pruning knives, 3; dish, tin, 1; pitcher, bronze, 1; measure, bronze, 1; wooden measures, ironclad, 2; cloaks, gold-coloured, 3; large counterpane, linen, 1; cushions, green, 2; counterpane, coloured, 1; mattresses, stuffed, 2; bedcover, 1; couch, 1; chest, 1; small container, bronze, 1 ... (Part of a household inventory from Egypt, *c.* AD 200.)[1]

The physical remains of buildings, together with the ancient pictorial and documentary sources and archaeological evidence from other provinces, give us some idea of the environment which surrounded the inhabitants of Roman Britain and the ways in which it differed from that of their pre-conquest ancestors. Yet other aspects of material culture, the everyday as well as the luxurious and exotic, were just as important as the roads and bridges and buildings in identifying the society as a provincial Roman one. Archaeologists base much of their interpretation on the evidence provided by personal and household equipment, and a survey of the objects in everyday use is crucial in any attempt to gain an overall picture of the way of life and the changes brought about by Roman rule. The material culture of Roman Britain may be classified in several different ways, and here we shall survey it briefly and selectively on the basis of function and material, at the same time noting the distinctions between luxury goods and more commonplace items, and between imports and objects of British manu-facture.

Allowing for all the variables – region, social status and date within the period – the overwhelming impression is that the Roman conquest led to a vast increase in both the quantity and the range of goods available. Material culture became far richer and more diverse. This fact alone is

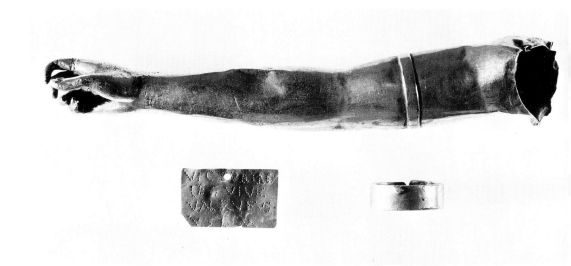

43 The arm of a silver
statuette of Victory found
at Tunshill, Lancashire. The
associated inscription
records its dedication by
one Valerius Rufus to the
Victory of the VIth legion.
L. 22 cm. British Museum.

significant in any speculation about the degree to which the British population accepted their new status as members of the Roman empire, since
the greater choice of goods would surely have been welcome to all who
could afford to buy them.

Painting and sculpture were important influences in familiarising people
with the images of Roman rulers and Roman deities and mythology as
well as the artistic ideals of that culture. Naturalistic sculpture was not
confined to life-size bronzes and marble statues adorning public and
religious buildings or the homes of the very wealthy. Small bronze statuettes
in household shrines and temples also disseminated those classical concepts and established the Romanised versions of native deities. This smaller-scale sculpture, partly functional (as a focus of religious observance)
and partly decorative, is a feature of Roman life throughout the empire.
Roman Britain has produced some fine examples. We have already alluded
42 to the large marble statuette of Luna from the Woodchester villa: from
another Gloucestershire villa, Spoonley Wood, there is a marble of similar
78 scale and almost equal quality depicting the god Bacchus with his panther,
leaning on a vine-entwined tree-trunk.[2] But the majority of the larger
statuettes, that is, figures over about one-third life-size, are of metal.

Sculpture in precious metal is naturally much rarer than bronze. Gold
was seldom used, not only for the obvious reasons of cost, but also because
the traditional techniques of working it were less well suited to the modelling of human figures. A gold bust such as that of the emperor Marcus
Aurelius at Avenches (Switzerland) is not only an intrinsically valuable
object but a technical and artistic *tour de force*.[3] There is, however, a surviving
fragment (the right arm) of a very important large silver statuette of Victory
from Britain.[4] It was found in a slate quarry at Tunshill, near Rochdale
(Lancashire), in 1793 and remained in private collections until 1983 when

44 Reconstruction of the probable original appearance of the silver statuette of Victory from Tunshill.

it was acquired by the British Museum. Found with the arm was a silver ring which fits it as a bracelet, and a small rectangular plaque with a punched inscription recording a dedication by Valerius Rufus to the Victory of the VIth legion. The obvious context for the statuette would be in the shrine of the VIth legion's fortress at York, and we can only guess at the sequence of events which might have resulted in a portion of it being concealed, probably as loot, many miles away. The Tunshill Victory is unlikely to have been a unique object in the province of Britain. Public temples in major towns as well as some other military shrines might have possessed equally splendid and valuable images, but it is hardly surprising that their survival, even in a fragmentary state, is rare.

Bronze statuettes on this scale are also fairly unusual. The splendid figure identified as Nero in the guise of Alexander the Great which is said to be from Barking Hall (or Baylham Mill), Suffolk, is a complex multi-piece casting richly embellished with silver, copper and niello inlay. Acquired by the British Museum in 1813, no date or other details are known of its discovery, and there must be a slight possibility that it was in fact brought to England in modern times by the noble family which owned it. However, we should not lightly assume that because it is a piece of the highest quality, it cannot have been imported into Britain in antiquity.[5]

A superb large bronze which is free from uncertainty about its provenance is the graceful Mercury from Gosbecks Farm, Colchester.[6] It is on a similar scale (50 cm high), and depicts the naked god alighting on a base which is now lost. Wings grow directly from his long, windblown hair. Both arms, and therefore any attributes which he held, are lost. The figure is finely proportioned and modelled, a wholly classical piece of sculpture worthy of any temple in the Roman empire.

The same can also be said of some smaller statuettes from Britain. The figure of an archer from Cheapside is one, an accomplished representation 45 of an athletic male figure, while the Mars from Earith (Cambridgeshire), in full, elaborate armour, is a good specimen of a standard image of the god.[7] The elegant Venus from Verulamium with her gracefully mobile pose and 22 floating drapery is closely similar, if slightly superior, to another from Augst in Switzerland, a telling example of the homogeneity of art and religion in the empire, notwithstanding the varying native cultures of the provinces.[8] More idiosyncratic is another small Mars, from Fossdyke 46 (Lincolnshire): he has coarse facial features and the musculature of a bodybuilder, and stands nude, apart from a lavishly crested Corinthian helmet, on an inscribed pedestal which records the names of the donors, together with that of the bronzesmith himself, Celatus, who likewise contributed towards the cost of the statuette by donating a pound of metal. We can assume, therefore, that the statuette was made in Britain for presentation at a local temple of Mars. While its exaggerated style precludes it from being classed as great art, it is a typical provincial Roman product without any obvious trace of native aesthetic standards.[9]

Even amongst the small metal statuettes, figures around 5–7.5 centimetres high, we still find some impressive examples of miniature sculpture, though the majority in Britain, as in all other areas of the empire, are relatively crude. These little figures of deities would in some cases have adorned private *lararia*, household shrines of a traditionally Roman kind, though others may be connected with temple sites. A silver statuette from

XI London Bridge of a pantheistic Harpocrates[10] reminds us of the religious diversity in the empire: the Egyptian god is represented in Roman guise with the wings and quiver of Cupid, and is accompanied by a dog, a tortoise and his own hawk. Some bronzes from the Thames are also classical in style and proportion, notably a standing Mercury and a figure of Apollo, sadly incomplete. Likewise a herm of Priapus from Pakenham (Suffolk)[11]

69 is wholly Mediterranean in concept, and, considering its small size (8.5 cm high), is modelled with consummate skill.

Partly by means of their artistic style and partly in their subjects, small bronze statuettes can express quite graphically that fusion of Roman and native elements which is so typical of Roman Britain. The statuettes of a

45 Bronze statuette of an archer, from Cheapside, London. H. 27 cm. British Museum.

mounted warrior-god, an equestrian Celtic Mars who seems to be indigenous to Britain, exemplify the fusion of subject-matter: the god is certainly of Celtic origin, but he is represented as a Roman cavalryman, his own armour and his mount's equipment appropriate to that role. The finest statuette of the type, from the Lincolnshire border near Brough 73 (Nottinghamshire),[12] adds yet another, unexpected, dimension to our knowledge, for the horse, clearly a trained parade-mount, is performing a collected, high-stepping amble which indicates a level of horsemanship approaching the standards of modern dressage. Like many of the other statuettes, this piece is probably a miniature copy of a much larger version, possibly a cult-statue at a temple.

Another typically Roman possession, which was first introduced into Britain as an exotic import even before the conquest itself, was silver plate.[13] Tableware made of precious metal was extremely highly prized in Roman society, and was regarded as a prime vehicle for the display of wealth and status. Gold table utensils would also have existed in substantial numbers amongst the very rich, but few examples have survived, and none is known

46 Bronze statuette of Mars from Fossdyke, Lincolnshire, with an inscription on the base recording the names of those who commissioned the piece as a votive gift and of the bronzesmith, who donated some of the metal. H. 27 cm. British Museum.

from Britain. From the empire as a whole, the quantity of silver tableware which has been preserved is surprisingly large. The expansion of the empire during its first century brought under Roman rule new sources of mineral wealth: Britain itself was one of the sources of silver, though a minor one compared with Spain.

Silver drinking-cups are amongst the earliest Roman imports to Britain. The rich graves of two Iron-Age aristocrats of the first century BC at Welwyn and Welwyn Garden City (Hertfordshire) contain not only wine-amphorae imported from the Continent but also the silver cups which at this date were considered appropriate for drinking the wine – a pair of them at the former site, and a single specimen at the latter.[14] The cups are deep ovoid vessels of classic Hellenistic/early Roman form, with small pedestal bases, handles and delicately chased decorative borders; they must be of Italian manufacture, though they could well have been imported by an indirect route, probably via Gaul. It is not difficult to imagine the British rulers who owned such pieces being enormously proud of them as symbols of wealth, power and cosmopolitan sophistication. Though Iron-Age craftsmen were unsurpassed in the working of gold and bronze, silver was used less often, and the shape and decoration of these cups would have appeared very foreign. The British nobleman of the first century BC probably could not aspire to the full matching set of table silver possessed by his Mediterranean counterpart, but he was clearly well aware of the prestige conferred by the ownership of such artefacts.

Full sets of silver plate in the Roman world included utensils for the service of food (*argentum escarium*) and for wine (*argentum potorium*), together with items which can broadly be described as furniture; in the well-to-do households which owned such material, other silver equipment, such as mirrors, would be included in an inventory, while items which we would regard as specifically for toilet purposes, such as bowls and jugs for hand-washing water, were also appropriate vessels at the dining table. Large treasures from the first century AD, like those from Boscoreale and the House of the Menander at Pompeii, and from Hildesheim, beyond the frontiers of the empire, give us a very clear idea of the unparalleled magnificence and sheer beauty of the silver tableware of the early imperial period; but Britain has not yet revealed anything of this quality from the early and middle empire. However, we must bear in mind that even a single fortuitous discovery can alter the picture quite dramatically, and we cannot know what future finds may reveal. In the present state of knowledge, the British evidence for the early and middle Roman period is centred on very few individual finds and small hoards of silverware.

One of these, found at Hockwold-cum-Wilton (Norfolk) in 1962, consists of the fragmentary and deliberately damaged remains of seven silver drinking-cups of early Roman type.[15] Originally they were thought to be examples of pre-conquest silver comparable with the wine-cups found in the Hertfordshire burials, but research following their conservation and restoration established that they do not correspond closely with the known Augustan types of silver cup. They are either somewhat later in date, perhaps mid- to late first century AD, or of provincial manufacture, or both. Although this hoard is unique for the period, it does demonstrate the presence of conventional Roman silver of good quality in the province. Such utensils would have been used and admired only in a very small section of society. Whereas the classical influence in architecture, religion and many everyday items would have become familiar to a wide cross-section of society, silverware remained the preserve of the rich.

The Backworth treasure was found around the beginning of the nineteenth century, and its precise findspot is not known.[16] It consists of coins, spoons and jewellery which had been placed in a deep silver pan and covered with a makeshift lid in the form of an old and damaged silver mirror. The handle of the Backworth skillet is elaborately decorated with leaf and flower scrolls picked out in gilding, and bears an inscription, also in gold letters, recording that the object was a gift to the mother-goddesses. The latest coin in the treasure dates the burial to about AD 139, a period confirmed by the jewellery and three small silver spoons. Since the inscription on the vessel is personalised, giving both the name of the donor (Fabius Dubitatus) and the divine recipients, it might be assumed that the object was manufactured in Britain. But it is possible that the inscription was an addition, and the donor, with his Roman name, may have been a recent incomer.

Scattered finds of silver spoons represent the domestic element in the silver of this period: we do not as yet have any large silver table utensils from second- to third-century Britain. The spoons are of standard Roman forms, and it is impossible to tell whether they were imported or made in the province, but they must represent only a tiny proportion of the silverware in use. We must be careful not to assume that because little survives, little existed. It may be that most silver hoards buried for safe-keeping in the earlier periods were in fact duly retrieved by their owners, and would later have been reworked into more fashionable and up-to-date forms.

The quantity of surviving silver in late Roman Britain presents a marked contrast to earlier centuries, a wealth of material indicating considerable use of luxury tableware in the country, and its widespread burial and non-recovery in the turbulent times of the late fourth century. Many of the late hoards consist solely or principally of spoons, but there is one large assemblage, the Mildenhall treasure, which contains a variety of table and display vessels,[17] and a unique set of early Christian liturgical silver from Water Newton (Cambridgeshire).[18] From Traprain Law, near Edinburgh, a large hoard of silver hidden in the fifth century includes important pieces of Roman tableware,[19] and the Thetford and Hoxne treasures consist of 87 silver tableware and gold jewellery.[20] XII

Well over 150 fourth-century spoons are now known from Britain. 86

The typical form is larger than a modern teaspoon (around 20 cm long overall) with an oval or pear-shaped bowl and a slender, pointed handle attached to the bowl by a decorative offset which may be developed into an openwork scroll or a stylised animal-head with chased detail. The bowl may be decorated or bear an inscription, and towards the end of the century Christian mottoes are often found. There was also a larger 'tablespoon' with a short coiled or recurved handle terminating in a bird's head. These, too, are sometimes inscribed. The prevalence of religious inscriptions, pagan at Thetford, Christian elsewhere, including Hoxne, implies a function beyond that of a straightforward domestic eating utensil; nevertheless, the primary purpose of the spoons was an everyday one. Christianity was not the only cult which involved a shared meal among the worshippers, and the development of religious connotations for an eating utensil made of precious metal is understandable.

IX   The Water Newton treasure is composed of objects which were evidently made specifically and solely for Christian ritual purposes, and the religious importance of the group is discussed in chapter 7. What we should note here is that their unusual forms and distinctive finish hint at Romano-British manufacture. The objects could well represent part of the domestic wealth of an influential family which, on conversion to the new religion, donated an altar set made from reused tableware to their local Christian community. Silver was recycled, and at any given time reused metal was probably a major resource.

More in the stylistic mainstream of late Roman silverware is the group from Mildenhall (Suffolk). The 'picture-plates' of the fourth century are salvers intended for display rather than use; they are decorated with elaborate pictorial decoration on popular mythological themes, executed in relief by chasing.[21] Some of the most flamboyant examples which survive are over 70 centimetres in diameter and weigh more than 10 kilos. The Mildenhall Great Dish is not quite so large, at 60.5 cm and a weight of 8.25 kg, but it is still of impressive size, and has the further distinction of being probably the most beautiful and technically accomplished example of its type from anywhere in the Roman empire. Its decoration is wholly pagan and incorporates the head of the sea-god Oceanus surrounded by a marine frieze and an outer zone depicting a Bacchic revel. Bacchus, Hercules, Silenus and Pan, together with dancing satyrs and Maenads, express the energy and excitement of the traditional pagan cult which was a focus of the anti-Christian party in the fourth century. This dish is the finest piece in a treasure which contains nearly thirty items of superb silverware, and it must have been made at one of the empire's leading workshops for the manufacture of decorative silver plate. Unfortunately, in our present state of knowledge we cannot even guess at the source.

The designs which were fashionable for tableware in non-precious metals were derived essentially from those current in the more expensive silver plate, and although the technology of bronze-working had been mastered

47 The Great Dish from the Mildenhall treasure, one of the finest extant examples of late Roman silver. The decoration features Oceanus in the centre, with Bacchus (centre top) and his companions forming the main frieze. Diam. 60.5 cm. British Museum.

48 *Left* The contents of a rich grave of the late first century AD at St Albans, Hertfordshire. The cremated remains were in the large glass jug, and there is other glassware, samian pottery, a very fine bronze bowl with handles, a set of strigils, glass gaming-counters, four oil-lamps and a folding iron tripod. Verulamium Museum.

49 *Right* The handle of a bronze skillet with tinned interior, from Prickwillow, Ely, Cambridgeshire. The highly decorated handle depicts marine creatures (the mythical beasts called *ketoi*), dolphins, a cupid and a shell, and an elaborate scroll of vine and ivy. The design is enhanced with copper and black niello inlay, and the craftsman has stamped his name, BODVOGENUS, on his work. British Museum.

in Britain long before the Roman period, the forms taken by domestic and religious bronze vessels after the conquest were distinctively classical. Many of the early Roman examples were probably made elsewhere in the empire; in most cases we are unable to distinguish between Continental and Romano-British products, a fact which in itself says much about the homogeneity of Roman material culture.

The finest first-century bronze jugs and bowls have been found in rich graves. A grave-group found in 1988 at St Albans serves as an example.[22] It contains a handsome shallow bronze bowl with handles, along with a wealth of other objects – glass, pottery, lamps and an iron tripod. Though the objects are all specifically Roman, many of them imported, the grave fits into a local series of rich burials going back to the pre-conquest period,

and it is tempting to see it as the interment of a local aristocrat who possessed and took pride in the material trappings of *romanitas*. The burial can be dated to the later first century AD.

Makers' names are sometimes found upon high-quality bronze tableware. One example from Britain is a large, shallow, handled bowl from Chatham (Kent) which bears the stamp of Africanus.[23] While this may indicate that the bronzesmith was of African nationality or descent, there is no way of knowing where he actually worked. Name-stamps may also appear on the decorated handles of metal 'saucepans'; a relief-decorated handle from Colchester has a stamp which may give the name Pomponius. Another example is a Celtic name (Gaulish or even British), BODVOGENVS, incorporated into the elaborate handle decoration of a deep 'saucepan' from Prickwillow, near Ely. The vessel is an outstanding example of the bronzesmith's art. The interior of the bowl is tin-plated, and the complex ornament of the handle is picked out with plating and inlay in niello and copper.[24] This form of enhancement of the decoration on metal vessels was a Roman introduction, but the technique of enamelling was already familiar in pre-Roman Britain. After the conquest, while enamelling on base-metal jewellery in a range of colours was common, it was also sometimes used to embellish small bronze containers. The Rudge cup, found in 1725 at Froxfield (Wiltshire), is such a vessel.[25] The pattern depicts a series of castellations, and around the rim of the cup are the names of five forts at the western end of Hadrian's Wall. There can be little doubt that the decorative design, stylised though it is, is meant to evoke a visual image of the wall itself. Presumably colourful enamelled cups like this were intended as souvenirs of some kind, and it seems likely that examples were also made with the names of other sites on the wall.

Possibly the most remarkable technical achievement in enamelling was the production of *millefiori*, incredibly tiny and intricate patterns formed from sections of coloured glass fused to the surface of a bronze object. Many examples of studs and brooches with *millefiori* have been found in Britain, but in 1990 a specimen of a much rarer type, a tiny bronze container (*pyxis*) enamelled in this technique, came to light at Elsenham in Essex.[26] Fewer than twenty of these little hexagonal boxes are known from the whole of the empire, but what makes the Elsenham box especially important is that it was found in a datable grave. The other grave-goods included samian and coarse pottery, glass, bronze and iron objects and gaming-counters. Three coins give us a date for the burial of around AD 150 and therefore provide the first sound chronological evidence for the manufacture of these enamelled boxes. The function of the Elsenham container and others of its kind is not known, though it may have been something as prosaic as an inkwell. It was certainly made on the Continent, probably in northern Gaul or the Rhineland.

A few cast-bronze vessels are made wholly or partially in the form of figures. Examples such as the sleeping slave boy from Aldborough are

50 An enlarged detail from a small bronze oil-flask found in a grave at Bayford, Kent. The vessel is decorated with three heads in high relief depicting youthful Africans. The facial features and the locks of hair are carefully observed. H. of head 3.2 cm. British Museum.

probably best regarded as statuettes which simply have an additional practical function; parallels are known in silver, though not yet from Britain.[27] A small bronze pot from the Bayford cemetery retains a symmetrical form but incorporates three heads of young black Africans, sensitively modelled in high relief.[28] The exotic beauty of this distinctive racial type clearly appealed to Hellenistic and Roman artists, since it is a recurring theme in the art of the time. Britons would have become aware of the existence of black people by way of Roman culture, and some of them undoubtedly reached the province during the centuries of Roman rule.

Other bronze table and cooking utensils include plain sheet-bronze bowls of kinds which were similar to those of earlier periods, and specialised types such as lamps. While there was a clear relationship between tableware made of bronze and the more expensive silver, it is seldom possible to perceive precise equivalents. The materials had separate, though linked, traditions. Romano-British pewter tableware was another category of metalwork combining a strong connection with silver with a unique tradition of its own.[29]

Pewter is an alloy of tin, generally containing varying proportions of lead. The raw materials were available in Britain, and the manufacture of pewter tableware took place on a large scale. Tin and tin-alloy vessels are far less common on the Continent, and some of the examples which have been found in France and the Netherlands may be imports from Britain. Pewter is unsuitable for working as sheet metal, but with its very low melting point it is particularly easy to cast, so all vessel forms, from large flat platters to bowls, spoons and jugs, were manufactured in moulds. Some of these, made of fine limestone, have been found. Limestone would not be a suitable material in which to cast other metals with much higher melting points.

Close dating of pewter production in Britain is difficult, but there is no doubt that the industry was at its height in the fourth century. Several large hoards of pewter tableware, such as those from Appleshaw and Icklingham

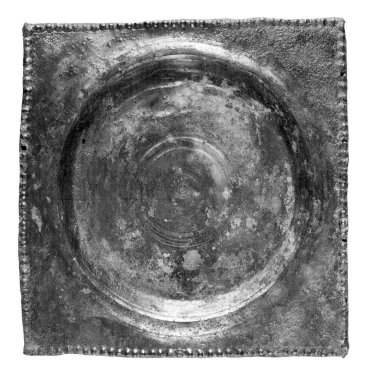

51 Serving-plate from a hoard of fourth-century pewter found at Icklingham, Suffolk. The form, and in particular the border of raised beads, can be found in silver tableware of the same period. 35 cm square. British Museum.

(both in Suffolk), can be assigned confidently to the late Roman era.[30] Many pewter vessels are decorated, some in clear imitation of silver, for example those with incised geometric patterns in the centre of large platters or cast copies of the raised beads which edged many fourth-century silver bowls. Christian motifs are found on quite a few, again emphasising the late date. The metal corrodes to an unattractive rough grey surface, but when new and well polished it would have appeared an acceptable substitute for silver.

Both before and after the Roman conquest, containers for the preparation and serving of food were normally made of earthenware, but there was another material, less valuable than metal but more highly prized than ceramic, which became truly familar only in the Roman period: glass.[31] Glass itself was by no means a recent invention, but the technique of glassblowing for the manufacture of hollow vessels had been developed only in the first century BC, making possible mass-production, with the effect that glass became cheaper and much more widely available. Some glassware was made in Britain.

Roman glass vessels are usually both beautiful and technically highly VII accomplished, whether they were intended as high-quality tableware or merely as packaging for some other commodity. Fragile, but easily recycled (unlike pottery), complete glass vessels survive principally from graves, in which they were placed with other grave-goods alongside inhumations or

52 Beaker of light green glass found in Colchester and decorated with a chariot-racing scene. The words in the upper zone of decoration are names of charioteers. First century AD. H. 8.3 cm. British Museum.

served as containers for cremated bones. Some large vessels were made as cinerary urns, but large cylindrical or square bottles with a single handle were also reused for the purpose.

To our eyes, the most elegant glass vessels are probably the fragile, thin-walled jugs and flagons like that from Bayford (Kent).[32] The natural pale green or bluish-green colour is the most usual, but an important first-century grave-group from Radnage (Buckinghamshire) contained a flagon in amber-coloured glass, together with a 'pillar-moulded' bowl – a shallow bowl with raised ribs on the exterior – in a deep cobalt blue marbled with white.[33] Such sophisticated glassware would have been imported, but must have been in more common use than its occasional survival suggests.

Some noteworthy mould-blown glass vessels have been found in Britain. One of these, from Colchester, is a cylindrical beaker in light-green glass which belongs to a class of cups, well known in the western provinces, decorated with scenes connected with the arena or the circus.[34] It has three zones of decoration, the lowest depicting four racing *quadrigae* (four-horse chariots), the middle frieze illustrating some of the features typical of the Roman race-track, and the rim bearing the names of the charioteers. The cup is in virtually perfect condition. By contrast, a drinking-cup from London in the shape of an African's head is badly damaged, but the complete form can be reconstructed.[35] It bears faint traces of the maker's name, C. Caesius Bugaddus, which was incorporated into the three-piece mould. Like the chariot-beaker, this is one of a known series, and another from the same mould has been found in Britain, at Caerleon.

Metal and glass vessels were superior possessions. For everyday table-ware and for most cooking purposes, ceramic vessels were the norm. Pottery may seem unduly important to archaeologists: many ancient cultures are characterised for us principally by the broken remains of their earthenware. Nevertheless, pottery vessels for the storage, preparation and serving of food and drink and for packaging and transport did play a major part in the everyday material culture of the past. Being relatively cheap and very fragile, pottery was broken, discarded and replaced regularly, just as it is in many households today, and changes of fashion were reflected comparatively quickly. In the Roman period, earthenware was used for most cooking purposes where we would tend to use metal utensils, as well as for tableware, and pottery was therefore more fully representative of material culture of all levels of society than the more expensive glass and metal vessels.

Since the pottery in use in Roman Britain included both imported and locally made wares, it might be imagined that Roman pottery from the Continent appeared in Britain only after the country became part of the empire, and that it represented the classical element, while pottery made in Britain was part of the native Celtic tradition. The real picture is much more complicated and reflects the intricate cross-fertilisation of Roman and northern European cultures which affected Britain long before the Claudian invasion. There was a pattern of increasingly close involvement with the Roman-influenced culture across the Channel which began even before the invasions of Julius Caesar, and became more intense afterwards.

The pre-Caesarian links are exemplified by the import in the first century BC of Italian wine, which was destined for consumption by a small group of wealthy aristocrats in southern Britain. Silver wine-cups from rich graves such as those at Welwyn and Welwyn Garden City were accessories for the drinking of wine; the range of native tableware did not include cups suitable for the purpose.[36] As we saw in chapter 1, the wine itself was transported in large earthenware amphorae. Throughout the Roman period, amphorae were used for the shipping not only of wine but of other comestibles such as fruit, olives and olive oil, and sauces such as *garum*. Perhaps even more than the elegant silver cups, the early appearance of these typically Mediterranean containers in the graves of wealthy British Celts symbolises the inexorable move towards involvement in the growing

Roman empire. Name-stamps on amphorae refer to the pottery manufacturer, who was often also the producer of the contents. The name of the shipper and the commodity carried also sometimes appear in painted inscriptions on the vessels.[37]

Other pre-conquest pottery imports included Arretine ware and *mortaria*. The former is a somewhat less luxurious ceramic equivalent of Roman table silver. Made near Arretium (Arezzo) in Tuscany, and at some other centres, Arretine ware, also known as *terra sigillata*, was the forerunner of the most distinctive class of imported earthenware in Roman Britain, samian ware manufactured in Gaul. The latter was a Roman introduction which would have been well within the reach of people who could not have afforded silver, and was in general use throughout the province. The fashion for earthenware with a glossy surface bearing figures of gods, humans, animals and other motifs in low relief had a long history in the Mediterranean world, and the technology used in its production was likewise derived from classical Greece and the potteries of the Hellenistic East. By the time Britain was part of the empire, the industries producing such wares were well established, and the production centres in Tuscany were already ceding their export markets to the growing workshops in southern Gaul.[38]

Gaulish samian ware embodies three major points of interest. First, like its Italian predecessor, samian was manufactured on a huge scale and marketed over a very wide area. Vessels were made in standardised shapes and sizes, the decorated forms being mould-made and the plain vessels precisely shaped with modelling tools or templates. Secondly, the mass-production methods and the name-stamps of potters, mould-makers and factory-owners often enable the archaeologist to date even small sherds quite closely. Finally, the manufacture of pottery in an industrialised Graeco-Roman tradition in the Celtic province of Gaul, and then its export throughout the western empire, is a typical example of cultural complexity and fusion in the Roman world.

Red-gloss pottery of this kind was made in many regions. There were numerous centres in the Gaulish provinces, a large local industry in Spain, and related wares were made in the eastern provinces of the empire. Even Britain had a small and short-lived production centre at Colchester.[39] The first-century factories in South Gaul, however, were remarkable for the scale and success of their operation. They were concentrated in the Toulouse area, the kilns at La Graufesenque, near Millau, being the most important. In the second century, potteries in the vicinity of Clermont-Ferrand, especially at Lezoux, came to great prominence, as did East Gaulish centres in the Rhine/Moselle area at Trier and Rheinzabern. Though the pre-eminence of the Gaulish industries waned and their products changed in the third century, the tradition of mass-produced red-gloss wares continued in the Mediterranean area, based on the workshops of North Africa which continued in production up to the time of the Arab conquests.[40]

Britain was a significant market for the South and Central Gaulish red wares of the first and second centuries, and a smaller amount of East Gaulish samian from the Rhineland was also imported. The presence of these wares in quantity on Romano-British sites is an important element in establishing the dating framework. In the first century in particular, samian is a very precise chronological indicator for excavators because fashions in decoration changed so rapidly and because potters' name-stamps, even though the detail of their use and significance is still not fully understood, are a valuable aid to dating and comparison between sites.[41]

The decoration of the moulded samian vessels is Roman, based ultimately on the mythology and the artistic repertoire of the classical world and more immediately on the Italian sigillata of Arretium. The slaves who worked in the Arretine potteries had Greek names, and the decoration of Arretine ware is typical of the art of the Augustan period with its conscious emulation of classical Greek ideals. The workshops of South and Central Gaul, on the other hand, were manned by native Gaulish artisans. While there is scarcely any sign of Celtic artistic preferences in their work, there is much stylisation and simplification of motifs, and some indications that the meaning and significance of figures and other decorative elements has not always been fully understood; but the ornamental motifs and their arrangement are firmly based on Roman taste.

53 Decorated samian bowl made in South Gaul in the late first century AD and found in Great St Helen's London. The moulded decoration includes the name of the potter's workshop, MERCATO. Diam. 24.4 cm. British Museum.

To the British customer, these shiny red pots with their exotic, detailed designs and miraculously crisp and precise shapes must at first have seemed wholly Roman, yet they were the creations of Gallo-Roman industry, as hybrid as anything made under Roman influence in Britain itself. The 'Roman' designs with which they were embellished were seen through the filter of other Celtic eyes, but they would still have played a significant part in making their purchasers familiar with Roman imagery. Most samian dishes, bowls and cups were plain forms, and the majority of the decorated examples were mould-made, but other techniques of decoration were also sometimes employed, for example incised patterns and trailed slip, the latter occasionally in elaborate designs.

Another class of pottery which is found in Britain and illustrates the links between native and classical cultures is Gallo-Belgic ware. This was made in Gaul in response to the influx of Arretine to the Gaulish provinces in the late first century BC. The range consists of cups and dishes closely modelled on plain Arretine forms, reproducing the intricately detailed profiles and frequently provided, like the Italian prototypes, with name-stamps. Red-surfaced Gallo-Belgic pottery (*terra rubra*) approximates to the colour of Arretine as well, but was later supplanted by a black-slipped variety (*terra nigra*).

The *mortarium*, a thick-walled mixing bowl with a grit-roughened interior, was an essential kitchen utensil in the Roman world. *Mortaria* were initially imported from Gaulish and even Italian sources before the conquest, but were subsequently manufactured in Britain, and the presence of these bowls indicates that food was being prepared which was based on Roman recipes and required some ingredients to be pounded, puréed or pulverised. Some were in use in south-east England a generation before

54 A pottery *mortarium* found in London. The gritted interior surface has been almost completely worn away by use, and the base of the bowl was finally broken through by wear before the vessel was discarded. British Museum.

the Claudian conquest, but their distribution was very limited and they were not imitated by local potters. Later they became standard kitchen equipment available from many British-based manufacturers. Name-stamps of the maker are sometimes found on the heavy curved rims, where they were highly visible.

Moving on to pottery imports which first appeared after the Claudian conquest, one class worth noting for technological reasons is pottery finished with a vitreous glaze. Brought in at first from sources in Central Gaul, some lead-glazed pottery was eventually produced in Britain, but it was never common.[42] The technology for making, applying and firing lead glazes presented no problems, so the small market must have been due either to the fact that the products were expensive or that their visual appeal was limited.

In the northern provinces, pottery finished with a glossy black or dark slip similar to the red samian slip became increasingly popular in the middle empire period; it is known to archaeologists as colour-coated ware. The imported specimens found in Britain are of Central Gaulish or Rhine-land manufacture, but they were very soon superseded by similar products made in Britain. Relief decoration in barbotine (trailing) and painted motifs using white or yellow slip occur on some of these, while others have simpler ornamentation of 'rouletting' (a regular notched, 'engine-turned' pattern) or other textured surfaces. Hunting scenes are the most typical themes on the barbotine beakers, hence the term 'hunt-cups' which is sometimes used to describe them.

The British versions of these vessels were made in more than one area, but initially the most important was the valley of the Nene in the Peterborough/Castor area. Stylistically, the trailed relief decoration is very like that found on the Continental examples and indeed on some samian ware which was ornamented in the same way. A wide range of human, animal and abstract motifs is depicted on British colour-coated wares, including Graeco-Roman deities and overtly Roman activities such as chariot-racing and gladiatorial combat. The appearance of phallic motifs and occasionally of very bawdy scenes is also a Roman tradition rather than a Celtic one. There is no doubt that the potters were Celts or Gauls, but we should view with caution the theory that curvilinear patterns and the stylisation of figures results from their aesthetic tastes. The contrast with the more finely detailed and static motifs seen in moulded samian vessels may be adequately accounted for by the differences of technique, and we should recall the fact that samian pots with barbotine decoration display the same stylistic features as the black wares made in the same way.

The overall picture is one of pottery manufacture in Britain responding to the stimulus of new styles and techniques coming in from abroad and imitating Roman fashions, but it is important to remember that the ancient native tradition of utilitarian earthenware made locally and used as an essential everyday material also survived and evolved under Roman rule. While Roman styles of tableware and cooking utensils rapidly became familiar to the native population, existing industries, far from being cut out, found opportunities for expansion under the new regime.

The classic example is that of black-burnished ware, a range of hand-made black cooking-pots and bowls originating as a pre-conquest industry in the tribal area of the Durotriges (Dorset). The abundance of this pottery on Roman military sites in the second century can only be due to the Durotrigian potters winning a contract to supply the army. Though the forms developed over time, the tradition remained an Iron-Age one, even to the technology, which made very limited use of the potter's wheel and none of purpose-built kilns. Despite the simple manufacturing techniques, black-burnished ware was practical, durable and probably good value for money, and the potters were obviously able to convince Roman quarter-masters that it was worth ordering it in large quantities.

Basic, functional kitchenwares were produced in most areas of the province, and there was a tendency in the late Roman period for such products to revert to Iron-Age traditions in technology and style. The variety of imported ceramics diminished, and some Romano-British industries developed fairly extensive distribution areas within the province. Though red tablewares continued to be manufactured in the traditional samian-making areas in Gaul, they changed in appearance and served only a local market, so that the vast Gaulish samian industry as such died out: in Britain, the gap which this left was filled by British products, from potteries in Oxfordshire, the New Forest, the Nene valley and elsewhere. Some of the late samian shapes, such as the hemispherical or segmental bowl with a horizontal flange placed well down the wall, are clearly reflected in the repertoire of these British manufacturers. The variety and choice of ceramics available, as well as the highly developed technology and extensive markets, demonstrate the results of generations of integrated provincial Roman culture.

One final point worth noting is that the trade in pottery between Britain and the Continent was not one-way. In addition to developing new pottery industries in response to imported Roman ceramics and continuing the existing Iron-Age traditions, some British-made pottery was exported to Gaul. The exports included black-burnished ware and colour-coated ware from the Nene valley and Oxfordshire. Pottery may, of course, be the only visible surviving evidence of trade in perishable goods, such as foods, which leave no archaeological trace in themselves. We have to bear in mind the possibility that these smaller pots were simply packaging, like amphorae, but only the fortuitous survival of organic remains which can be analysed will provide any proof. So far there is no certain evidence on this point.

The study of pottery is such an important field that we have been able to present only the merest overview of the subject. The great variety of other portable items known collectively to archaeologists as 'small finds' are likewise too diverse to be discussed fully in the scope of this book, so we are obliged to be selective. Tools and other artefacts made of metal survive in great numbers, enabling us to compare the equipment of the Roman period with that used before the conquest. We can establish which types continued unchanged, which exhibit an uninterrupted pattern of evolution and which were Roman innovations, initially completely foreign to the indigenous Britons. The patterns we perceive influence our theories about the extent to which life did or did not change for the inhabitants of Britain. Many other equally essential items are less well known to us because burial destroys them or damages them so severely that they cannot be usefully studied. Leather, wood and cloth were used for numerous purposes, and our very limited knowledge of artefacts made from these materials, both in the Iron Age and after the Roman conquest, deprives us of a vast body of evidence which would bear on the theme of Romanisation as well as on the more obvious area of technological history. Items of personal adornment were made in a wide range of materials, and form a particularly interesting class for study.

Some jewellery, such as brooches, hairpins, and sealstones set in rings had practical functions, but even the necklaces, bracelets and earrings worn by women may not have been perceived solely as adornment. Jewellery was frequently the vehicle for images of deities and other apotropaic devices, and the averting of evil would have been regarded as a genuine and serious function by the owner. Precious-metal jewellery has the additional aim of attracting attention to the wearer's wealth, status and taste, and the standard of design and craftsmanship reflects this. Carefully selected and used by individuals rather than by households or families, jewellery provides us with an insight into personal taste.

PLATE VIII A small bronze box from a second-century grave at Elsenham, Essex, with intricate and well-preserved *millefiori* enamel. The box, possibly an inkwell, belongs to a rare type made in northern France or the Rhineland. H. 4.6 cm. British Museum.

Once again, it is possible to trace two traditions, the native and the exotic. The existing native styles persisted especially in base-metal jewellery of a utilitarian nature, above all in brooches and other fasteners, while most luxury jewellery in gold and silver reflected classical preferences, and at least some of it would have been manufactured outside Britain. It is important to bear in mind that most of the technical traditions and skills for creating elaborate jewellery in gold were unquestionably available in Britain: magnificent pre-Roman objects such as the gold, silver and bronze torcs from Snettisham demonstrate this beyond any doubt.[43] But Celtic goldwork did not incorporate fine gold wire and intricately linked chains.

Necklaces and other ornaments made of fine chain reached their technical and artistic apogee in the Mediterranean world long before the time of the Roman empire, and chain necklaces, often with additional pendants, beads or decorative clasps, remained standard feminine adornments in the Roman world. They were new to Britain and belong to a truly universal Roman tradition: it is significant that Romano-Egyptian mummy-portraits can be used to illustrate Romano-British gold necklaces and earrings in use.

PLATE VII Cut-glass beaker found at Barnwell, Cambridgeshire. First century AD. H. 9 cm. British Museum.

PLATE IX The treasure of Christian silver plate from Water Newton, Cambridgeshire. This group is thought to constitute the earliest set of liturgical plate in the Roman empire. Fourth century AD. British Museum.

PLATE X A woman's leather shoe, one of a pair found in 1801 in a sarcophagus at Southfleet, Kent. Though now shrunken, faded and distorted, this shoe was once a very colourful and elaborate item, with leather in two colours, openwork and gold stitching. Probably third century AD. British Museum.

PLATE XI *Left* Silver and gold statuette of Harpocrates (Horus), son of Isis. The god is winged and wreathed, and accompanied by a dog, a tortoise and a hawk; he is thus a pantheistic figure, with attributes of other deities. H. 6.5 cm. British Museum.

PLATE XII *Above* The gold body-chain from the Hoxne, Suffolk, treasure, found with other gold jewellery, silver tableware and 15,000 coins dating to the early fifth century AD. The clasp at the back of the chain is set with a gold coin of the Emperor Gratian (AD 367–83). British Museum.

Necklaces composed of strings of small beads were also popular, and are massively under-represented in museum collections because it takes painstaking modern excavation methods to recognise and retrieve them. In recent years, some fine examples have been found in London, including a long string of tiny blue-glass beads, some incredibly delicate gold-glass beads which are thought to have been manufactured in the Black Sea or upper Danube region, and a necklace made of glass beads imitating amethyst, emerald and pearl.[44] Pearls were obtainable in Britain, and were

55 Funerary portrait of a woman, from Hawara, Egypt. The painting, on wood, dates from about the second century AD, and the jewellery depicted would have been familiar in any province of the Roman empire, including Britain. The lady wears pearl earrings, a gold hairpin and two necklaces, the longer one a string of red and green beads, probably gemstones, and the other with a pendant containing a green stone, probably emerald. British Museum.

probably extensively used in both necklaces and earrings, but they are fragile and decay easily, and rarely survive burial in a recognisable form.

Earrings themselves can be difficult objects to recognise as stray finds, especially when damaged, since many of them were simply rings of metal wire carrying a bead of hardstone, pearl or glass.[45] The beads are often lost through decay and breakage, and the slender wires corrode if they are of bronze. We are often left only with thin gold loops which tell us little about the original appearance of the jewel. But again, some of the more complex Roman types are attested in Britain.

Serpent jewellery had a long history in Hellenistic goldwork: parallel types in bracelets and rings used the sinuous form of a snake to create striking and beautiful ornaments. The choice of the reptile was not based solely on the suitability of its form: snakes were creatures of good omen in pre-Christian mythology; they were associated with the underworld and the spirits of the departed, and also with rebirth and healing, the latter quality specifically linked with the god Asclepius. There were also Bacchic and other cult associations. Naturalistic snake-bracelets familiar from other parts of the empire were known in Britain, but more common are highly stylised versions of the penannular snake-bracelet, such as those from Snettisham, with a simple broad hoop terminating in flattened snake-heads so simplified that only the traceable history of the type makes them recognisable.

56 *Left* A second-century gold finger-ring from the Backworth treasure, with two stylised snakes' heads. This design is common in Roman Britain. British Museum.

57 The Roman jeweller's hoard from Snettisham, Norfolk, consisting of silver jewellery, engraved gems ready for setting into rings, scrap silver, a burnishing tool and silver and bronze coinage. All the objects were concealed in the small pottery jar. The treasure was hidden around the middle of the second century AD. H. of pot 17.5 cm. British Museum.

The Snettisham Roman treasure is of immense importance because it is a closely dated assemblage of Roman silver jewellery and gems made in Britain.[46] The associated coins establish the date as Antonine, and the unmounted gems, unfinished and miscast jewellery, scrap silver and a burnishing tool establish the find as a workshop hoard. The types include Romano-British snake-rings and bracelets, ordinary gem-set rings and wheel-and-crescent necklaces. The silver was evidently obtained in an unofficial manner, from denarii, over a hundred of which are included in the cache. The designs are wholly Roman, and the use of silver sets the material above common, inexpensive ornaments in base metal but still within the reach of people who could not aspire to the luxury of gold jewellery.

The stock of engraved carnelian gems (110 unmounted stones) in the Snettisham treasure indicates that these, too, were being made in Britain. Semi-precious stones engraved with figures of deities and other motifs were part of the Graeco-Roman tradition in jewellery, and the most brilliant period of gem engraving was already over by the time Britain was part of the empire. The figures of Bonus Eventus, Ceres, Mars, Fortuna and others on the Snettisham gems are crude by comparison with these earlier masterpieces, but they are entirely Roman in concept, design and execution. As a simple measure of Romanisation, these tiny objects can scarcely be bettered. Gems engraved as intaglios were originally intended as seal-

147

stones, and many would have been used for that purpose. Cameos were purely decorative, and they are less common. Throughout the Roman world, the head of Medusa is a particularly frequent subject for large cameo hardstones.[47] The gaze of the Gorgon, with her snake-entangled locks, could turn to stone those who encountered her; her image was therefore a powerful charm against the evil eye. A ring set with a standard type of Medusa-head cameo comes from a South Wales hoard and is a universal Roman type.[48] Two jet necklace pendants from London carved as Medusa heads are especially interesting as another illustration of the full integration of Roman and British traditions. The type is as classical as can be; the material, and presumably the skilled craftsmanship, is native.[49]

Jet is found on the Yorkshire coast at Whitby. In Victorian times it was

58 A jet pendant found in London, carved as a cameo of Medusa: the snakes and wings in her hair are carefully depicted. The material and the craftsmanship are native, the theme purely classical. Probably third to fourth century. W. 4.3 cm. Museum of London.

extensively used because its black colour made it suitable as mourning jewellery, but that symbolism did not apply in the Roman period. The material is easily carved, takes a brilliant polish, and has electrostatic properties which would have enhanced its reputation as a magical sub-stance. Bracelets, rings, beads and hairpins were made from it as well as pendants, but the larger London Medusa head is probably the finest item to survive. Hairpins were also made of other local materials, including metal and bone. Wooden examples must also have been common, though they rarely survive.

We have moved from new types of feminine adornment in expensive materials to Roman ornaments made in Britain of local materials. With finger-rings we are in somewhat different territory. The wearing of rings was rare in pre-Roman Britain, so that its great popularity after the conquest reflects Roman custom, but the range of types in use over the centuries of Roman rule was very wide, and embraced everything from precious metal and gems to bone and jet, from the elaborate to the basic. Furthermore, unlike the ornaments we have been discussing, finger-rings were worn by men, women and children. Rings were thus one of the most universally adopted Roman fashions.

Gold or silver rings set with engraved gems have survived in considerable numbers, and the types are identical with those from the rest of the Roman world, though many were made in Britain. For example, the twenty-two rings from the Thetford treasure form a unparalleled group, [88] and though they follow the general tendency of late antique jewellery to be colourful and florid, with filigree and polychrome glass and hardstone settings, the precise designs have not been matched elsewhere. They must be of Gaulish or British manufacture, and the latter now seems more likely.

59 Two iron finger-rings set with fine-quality engraved jasper stones. That on the left, from Malton, North Yorkshire, bears a head of Hercules; the other, from Warlingham, Surrey, has a head of Helioserapis. British Museum.

Even when bronze ornaments were made as direct copies of more expensive gold and silver ones, it is important to remember that many of the techniques of manufacture had separate traditions. Some types of bronze jewellery are never found in silver or gold, and this is especially true of brooches, which were items of use as well as ornament. The fibula, or safety-pin type of brooch, worn in pairs to fasten clothing, was long established in the Celtic world, and its development in the Roman period is based on native rather than Mediterranean traditions. Enamelling, also an established Celtic technique, is frequently found as an integral part of the design in both fibulae and plate-brooches made of copper alloys. The typological development of fibulae and their relatively common occurrence gives them some potential as dating evidence for archaeologists.

Functionally lying between fibulae and plate-brooches (fasteners which have a decorative front and a straight hinged pin, capable of clasping only a thin, narrow span of cloth) is another uniquely British type, the dragonesque brooch.[50] With a flat front surface but a deeply curved and very simply hinged pin, these brooches can take in a thick fold of cloth in the same way as the normal fibula, and were worn in pairs, one on each shoulder, in the same way. These sinuous ornaments with two animal-headed terminals of some fantastic species are usually picked out in col-

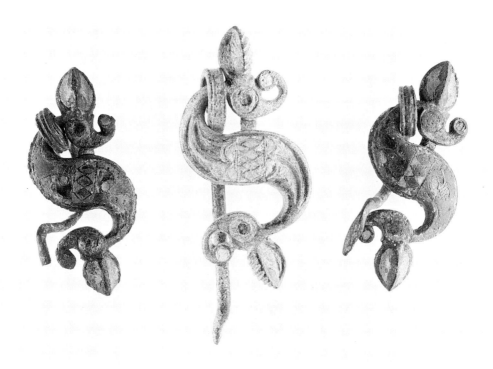

oured enamels. They are widely regarded as the epitome of Celtic design continuing in a Roman milieu, and it is easy, if simplistic, to draw comparisons with early medieval Celtic art. However we classify them, they are intriguing, beautiful, and full of the spirit of Britain as a Roman province. Other animal-brooches in bronze and enamel can appear to our eyes similar to some modern jewellery, but we should refrain from interpreting them simply as an ancient foreshadowing of Art Deco kitsch.[51] Many of the animals represented may have been chosen for their associations with various cults and deities. Such brooches have never yet been found in gold or silver, and enamelling on precious metal is extremely rare in the Romano-Celtic world.[52]

Jewellery is of course closely connected with clothing, but textiles are almost absent from the archaeological record. There is a certain amount of documentary evidence which hints at the importance of the things we have lost, and we know that cloth was comparatively expensive in antiquity and was highly prized. There are references on curse tablets from both Uley and Bath to thefts of cloth.[53] The price-edicts of Diocletian (AD 301) listed the *birrus britannicus*, the 'British cloak', a hooded, weatherproof garment which was evidently known throughout the empire. This was an important British product, probably little changed in style and material by the coming of Roman rule, which was sufficiently admired to be exported to other provinces, yet leaves no direct archaeological trace. Also from historical

60 Three dragonesque brooches. The matching pair (left and right) are from Faversham, Kent, and the single example from Norton, North Yorkshire. The decoration is in brightly coloured enamels. L. of centre brooch 7.3 cm. British Museum.

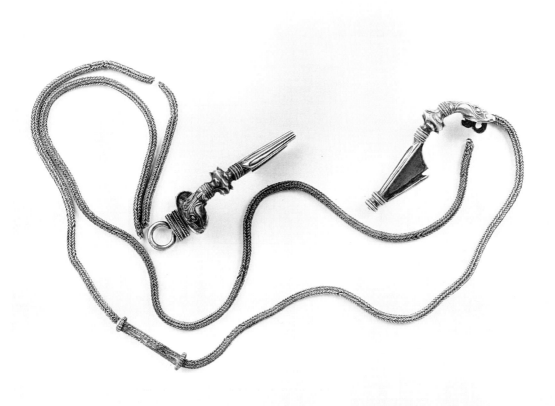

61 A matching pair of silver trumpet brooches with the silver chain which linked them in wear. Both brooches are somewhat damaged and incomplete, but the fine quality of the cast decoration can be seen. The set is from Chorley, Lancashire. British Museum.

sources, we know that woollen cloth with coloured checked or striped patterns was favoured by British Celts before the Roman invasions, and that the men of Celtic Europe wore trousers. Trousers require pattern-cutting and sewing skills which differ from those employed for draped Mediterranean garments.

We can assume that the preparation of wool and linen, and the crafts of spinning, bleaching and dyeing, weaving and sewing were very sophisticated in the Celtic north. In their separate tradition the same was true of the Mediterranean world. We have much indirect evidence, written and visual, of extremely intricate decorative weaving from the Greek and Roman world: in Egypt, where conditions are favourable for the survival of textiles, there are many actual examples of cloth with woven patterns of astonishing complexity and beauty. The combination of northern and southern European traditions in textile design, and the availability of very high-quality wool and linen in Britain, must have led to an excellent and much extended choice of fabrics and styles for clothing and for such purposes as upholstery and hangings.

Our evidence for all this splendour is confined to a few written sources, a number of stylised, not to say crude, representations of clothing and furniture in stone sculpture, some of the equipment for manufacturing textiles and a handful of pathetically rotted and discoloured scraps of woven fabrics. A great deal of imagination is required to envisage the impact on everyday life of a range of cloth and clothing which still included the practical and colourful plaids and duffel-coats and trews of the Iron-Age past, but which had been augmented, at least for the wealthier sections of society, by luxurious embroideries and fancy weaves of Graeco-Roman design, and of course by Roman garments.[54]

Though articles made of leather are found far more commonly than woven textiles, they are still too rare for us to make informed judgements about the balance between native tradition and Roman introductions. Leather had many uses in military equipment, including tents and boots and sandals. Even though fragments of robust hide and thick, often metal-studded shoe-soles survive from many sites, the full range of uses is not even hinted at. Shoes or parts of shoes are amongst the most frequent recognisable leather items to survive, but they are usually of fairly plain and practical types. A burial in a sarcophagus found in 1801 at Southfleet in Kent contained an exceptionally elegant pair of women's shoes made of thin and supple dark blue leather with hexagonal cut-out patterns outlined in gold thonging.[55] There must have been many uses in wealthier households for fine leather decorated with embossing, coloured stitching, cut-work and perhaps gilding and painting. At the other end of the scale, there would have been numerous uses for leather in industry and agriculture. We can only speculate on the extent to which some of these traditional uses continued unchanged from pre-Roman times.

The widespread use of wood for purposes ranging from large structures like buildings, vehicles and boats to household and industrial equipment and to small decorative items or personal adornment is perfectly obvious, but like textiles, because so little survives in good condition, it is all too easy to overlook its importance. In the absence of adequate concrete evidence we are forced to rely on imaginative speculation. We are only beginning to learn what some Romano-British buildings might have looked like, and it seems unlikely that any combination of fortunate circumstances will ever occur to reveal the elevation of a timber building. Yet such buildings would have been everywhere: would they have differed radically from their Iron-Age predecessors, or would they have preserved elements of British taste completely unknown to us? Probably both. And what of sculpture? In Gaul, waterlogged conditions have preserved collections of wooden *ex votos*, and though these were intended for religious, not decorative, purposes, they demonstrate that there were highly skilled wood-carvers in Romano-Gaulish society, and there is no reason to doubt that the same was true in Britain. Our judgements about Romano-British art, which are based on stone and metal objects, are at best partial: it may be that the finest and most typical work was in wood, a perishable material.

Wood may not seem an obvious material for jewellery, but as we noted above, carved bone and jet hairpins imply the existence of similar examples in wood. Wooden beads have been used in most cultures, and would probably have been popular both before and after the Roman conquest.

62 Detail of a bone hairpin from London, carved as the bust of a woman wearing an elaborate first-century hairstyle. H. of bust 5.5 cm. British Museum.

There may in fact have been very common types of ornament, especially those used by the less wealthy sections of society, which remain completely unknown to us. It follows that we cannot know whether such ornaments were traditional or Roman in design.

Within houses, wood was used for furniture.[56] We have very little idea what would have been in use in the pre-Roman Iron Age, even in the richest households. From the classical world, much is known about couches, chairs, tables and other domestic items, but it is not always easy to apply this knowledge to a province like Britain. The couches which were characteristic pieces of furniture in Roman houses were apparently in fairly common use in Britain, judging from the many funerary reliefs on which the deceased is depicted reclining upon one. They were living/dining-room furniture, but were also often used as beds. Turned and carved wood, veneers and inlay in wood and bone, ivory or metal, carved or cast embellishments; draperies, cushions and upholstery in textiles or leather, stuffed with wool, feathers, horsehair or straw – the list of techniques and materials which might have been used in the manufacture of these important everyday objects is long, but virtually the only evidence we have for their actual existence is a series of simple and often ambiguously carved stone bas-reliefs and a reference in one of the Vindolanda tablets. Representations such as the crude sandstone tombstone from Kirkby Thore (Cumbria) give some indication of the presence of the standard Roman couch with turned

63 Part of a woman's tombstone from Kirkby Thore, Cumbria, carved in red sandstone. The deceased, whose name is not preserved, is seen reclining on a couch and holding a cup. In front of the couch stands a small table. L. 76 cm. British Museum.

legs, mattress and cushions, and curved ends. In front of the couch is a small table for the funerary meal.[57]

Sculpture also provides the main evidence for the basketry or wicker-67 work chair, evidently used mainly by women, including mother-goddesses. Pipeclay figurines of mother-goddesses were made in Gaul, but tombstones such as that of Julia Velva from York are British, and also depict this type of seat.[58] Basketry was an ancient craft, and it may well be that furniture made in this technique, particularly the comfortable high-backed chair, spread from the Celtic provinces to other parts of the empire. Smaller objects in basketry, particularly containers, must have been very common, but we have no surviving examples from Britain.

Amongst smaller items of domestic equipment, lamps should be noted. Small oil-lamps, usually made of fired clay but sometimes of metal, had a long history in the Graeco-Roman world and were first introduced into Britain in the Roman period, though compared with their great abundance on many Continental sites, their use in Britain remained rather restricted. One factor which may have influenced this was that olive oil, the most suitable fuel, had to be imported and may have been substantially more expensive than it was in provinces which cultivated the olive: there could well have been a degree of reluctance to use the oil for any non-food purpose.

To some extent, the function of lamps dictates their form. They have to possess a suitable reservoir for oil and a nozzle of some kind to support the end of the wick. Even so, there was much variation in detail, and the typology of Roman lamps has been extensively studied by specialists, so that there is a vast literature on the subject.[59] Most pottery lamps were manufactured in two-part moulds, and some have manufacturers' names on the base; as in the case of the sigillata industry, the combination of known sources, makers' names and a well-defined sequence of typological development makes it possible to date many of them fairly closely and to study the distribution of types and the trading patterns which they reveal. Many forms have decorative motifs in low relief on the *discus*, the circular field on the top of the lamp. The subjects of these decorative motifs parallel to some extent the range seen in sigillata, though close comparisons are surprisingly rare: even if the lamps are made in Gaul or Britain, the designs are traditionally Roman, including Graeco-Roman deities and objects connected with their cults, Roman institutions such as gladiatorial combat and the circus, and erotic themes: there is absolutely no evidence of native Celtic elements appearing in these illustrations.

Lamps were distinctively Roman artefacts, unknown before the conquest, and the somewhat limited extent of their use and manufacture in Britain may be significant; however, we must be cautious in drawing this conclusion because we are unable to assess the way in which the other main method of artificial lighting was used. For all we know, Britain may have had a major industry in the production of tallow or beeswax candles which predated the conquest and flourished and expanded under Roman rule. The use of lamps may have seemed unnecessarily extravagant to the ordinary Roman Briton, and their rarity may reflect common-sense domestic economy rather than a resistance to Romanisation.

Simple domestic utensils such as spoons would often have been made of wood and bone rather than more expensive metal. Both bone and ivory

64 A terracotta oil-lamp of the first century AD, made in Gaul and found in Colchester. The discus depicts an oared sailing-ship; the steering-oar, the goose-head on the stern and the eye at the bow are all clearly indicated. L. 9.2 cm. British Museum.

were used for decorative purposes, and some of the finest small-scale carving from the ancient world is found in ivory plaques, probably intended as inlays for furniture and boxes. These were not wholly unknown in Britain: a fine ivory carving of a tragic mask from Caerleon is an exotic 34 import in several respects – the material, the subject, relating to the Graeco-

155

Roman drama, and the use, probably as a decorative panel on a piece of furniture or a casket made to contain valuable possessions.[60]

A few additional classes of object are worth selecting for discussion here, for example objects connected with writing. The comparatively robust wooden tablets which were covered with wax and written upon using a pointed stylus survive more easily than the thin, fragile wooden tablets like those from Vindolanda which were intended for documents in ink, but they are nevertheless rare finds. The styli themselves, made of bronze or iron, are fairly common, however, unlike the pens and brushes which must also have been used in great numbers. Inkpots of pottery and metal provide further evidence, but probably the most abundant and widespread indication of the presence of written communications are the decorative bronze seal-boxes, often with enamelled ornament. Brief inscriptions, often owners' names, scratched on articles such as pots and metal vessels, indicate that a basic level of literacy was widespread, but wood probably took

65 Enamelled seal-box from Reculver, Kent. L. 4.8 cm. British Museum.

the place of the stone or pottery fragments (*ostraca*) and the papyri which have survived in enormous quantities from Egypt and represent everything from legal documents, fragments of literature and petitions to private letters, notes and artists' sketches. We probably have little notion of the amount of written material which was in circulation in Britain once it had become part of the Roman world.

Most crafts and industries require specialised tools, and in many cases the function dictates the form to such an extent that ancient examples differ little from recent ones. This is particularly true of the iron tools used in agricultural work, carpentry and blacksmithing. Roman anvils, wood-

28

planes or shears are part of an unchanging material continuum which stretches from prehistory to the Industrial Revolution and beyond.[61]

The introduction of Roman medicine is demonstrated by finds such as surgical probes, scalpels and forceps and the oculists' stamps which were used to mark eye ointments. In terms of everyday custom and practice, pre-Roman beliefs about health, disease and healing would have changed little, and indeed native traditions may well have been broadly similar to those of the classical world, but the Roman genius for cunningly designed and accurately made tools, together with the experience of surgery gained in the military campaigns of a world empire, gave rise to sophisticated surgical instruments which were not equalled until modern times.[62]

It has not been possible in this chapter to do more than to highlight some of the interesting facets of material culture in Roman Britain. The view it presents is partial, being merely a sample of the great variety of artefacts which were in use, and including some pointers about the inferences we can draw from them about their owners and users. More specifically, the underlying theme of British and classical traditions is illuminated by some classes of artefact, but perhaps concealed by others, where the evidence is too sparse or patchy to help us. This problem of incomplete survival and skewed evidence, central to both historical and archaeological research, must always be borne in mind, but it should never make us underestimate the importance of the objects which were part of the physical environment of people in the past.

FURTHER READING

R.G. Collingwood and I.A. Richmond, *The Archaeology of Roman Britain* (1969) still remains very valuable, now usefully supplemented by Guy de la Bédoyère, *The Finds of Roman Britain* (1989). J.M.C. Toynbee, *Art in Britain under the Romans* (1964) remains fundamental, while the British Museum *Guide to the Antiquities of Roman Britain* (3rd edn, 1964) by John Brailsford has proved of enduring value. Most of the material discussed in this chapter is the subject of specialised monographs, listed in the Notes and Bibliography. More general syntheses are harder to find, but mention may be made here of the very valuable essays in D. Strong and D. Brown (eds), *Roman Crafts* (1976); W.H. Manning's important *Catalogue of the Romano-British Iron Tools, Fittings and Weapons in the British Museum* (1985); two comprehensive surveys of 'small finds': N. Crummy, *The Roman Small Finds from Excavations in Colchester* (1983) and L. Allason-Jones and R. Miket, *Catalogue of Small Finds from South Shields Roman Fort* (1984); and K. Greene's excellent *Roman Pottery* (1992). See also C.M. Johns, 'Research on Roman silver plate', *Journal of Roman Archaeology* 3 (1990), 28–43.

— 6 —

PAGAN GODS
AND GODDESSES

To them that ask thee, where hast thou seene the Gods, or how knowest thou certainly that there be Gods, that thou art so devout in their worship? I answer first of all, that even to the very eye, they are in some manner visible and apparent. Secondly, neither have I ever seene mine own soule, and yet I respect and honour it. So then for the gods, by the dayly experience that I have of their power and providence towards my selfe and others, I know certainly that they are, and therefore worship them. (Marcus Aurelius, *Meditations*, 12, xxi, trans. Casaubon, 1634.)

An understanding of religious belief and practice is of central importance in attempting to gain a balanced picture of any society, and Roman Britain is no exception. However, the study of religion at a period which is on the borderline between prehistory and history presents special problems. While it is clear that underlying Celtic and pre-Celtic beliefs and customs came to coexist with imported classical paganism, it is not easy to unravel the different strands. This is partly because Celtic and Graeco-Roman paganism were based on the same fundamental concerns and preoccupations, those which form the basis of religion and superstition in all pre-industrial societies, namely the reverence and awe felt towards natural forces and the need to ensure the health and increase of humans, animals and plants. It was the rise of Christianity, with its emphasis on personal salvation, its vigorous proselytising and its total rejection of traditional beliefs, which led to serious tensions between varying religious systems. By comparison, Celtic and Roman paganism differed only in superficial detail.[1]

Much has been written about the religion of the pre-Roman Celts, but the inferences which can be drawn from archaeology alone tend to be of the broadest and most general kind, often relating to a stratum of belief which is in any case likely to be of pre-Celtic origin. Written evidence does exist, but it emanates from contemporary or near-contemporary Greek or Roman authors, whose perceptions were naturally coloured by their own classical sensibilities. Julius Caesar's famous passage in which he lists the gods worshipped by the Gauls as Mercury, Mars, Apollo, Jupiter and Minerva is a case in point.[2] But though we may regret the inexactitude of Romans who translated the customs of other peoples into their own terms, there is a good deal of hidden truth in this approach. Moreover, much of the written evidence is from the Roman imperial period, when the complex process of assimilation of Celtic into Roman was well advanced.

Later written evidence has also been used in an attempt to illuminate the beliefs of the pagan Celts. Early medieval literature in Irish and Welsh has the advantage of stemming from within Celtic society. The superbly rich texture of these tales clearly contains much that is extremely ancient, and they have been referred to as a 'window on the Iron Age'.[3] But the prehistoric elements are glimpsed only through the accretions of later centuries, culminating in an overlay of Christian interpretation. The final picture is a bewildering one. Gems of medieval literature such as the *Four Branches of the Mabinogi* or the Ulster Cycle, with its accounts of the superhuman exploits of the hero Cuchulainn, will certainly deepen the reader's understanding of both the natural and the supernatural world seen through Celtic eyes; but their relevance to the interpretation of Celtic society during the period of Roman rule is debatable.

It is hardly surprising that most students of pagan Celtic religion stress its ambiguous and elusive nature.[4] These qualities are undoubtedly typical of the Celtic perception of life and death. It is also certain, however, that they are accentuated in our eyes by the patchy and unsatisfactory nature of the evidence. Our information about Roman religion is very much more extensive, and classical paganism consequently appears more orderly and comprehensible. Surviving written sources range from funerary and dedicatory inscriptions and calendars of festivals to legal and literary texts, while the archaeological evidence is replete with objects of ritual, places of worship and endless images of deities, generally represented in human form and with recognisable and predictable attributes. The names and myths of the major gods and goddesses of the Graeco-Roman pantheon have remained familiar throughout the succeeding history of western civilisation: they do not seem strange and remote to us, as do the dimly perceived gods of the Celts.

This apparent contrast is misleading, for Roman religion, too, was constantly growing, changing, and becoming ever more complex and many-layered. The influence of Greek culture had altered and augmented the prehistoric religious traditions of Italy, and while Graeco-Roman concepts affected the native cults of the Roman provinces, the inhabitants of the provinces in their turn made their own distinctive contributions. Furthermore, during the early empire and even before, Egyptian and other eastern cults were becoming increasingly popular in Rome. Their emphasis on personal and mystical experience marked a changing attitude towards religion, and thus ultimately provided part of the psychological basis for the rise of Christianity.

In the case of Roman Britain, another general point has to be borne in mind: the 'Romans' who settled in the new province, whether soldiers or civilians, were not all from Italy but from a variety of provinces, east and west. Some of these incomers might have seemed foreign and exotic to the native population: others were Celts from northern Europe whose language and religious observances would have differed little from those of the British.

For all these people, natives and settlers alike, the fundamental stratum of religious belief concerned fertility, and the most basic expression of this concept was the mother-goddess. The recurring cycle of the seasons, and the power for good and ill of the natural forces of sun, wind and rain, are all expressed in the mythology of the Earth Mother. The cult of the mother-goddess was universal among the Celts of Britain and the Continent, and in spite of the other aspects of fertility myth and ritual which had evolved in the lands of the Mediterranean, there too the principle of the Mother was still widely venerated in a multiplicity of forms. This complexity and underlying unity is perfectly expressed in a passage of Apuleius' novel *The Golden Ass*, written in the second century AD. The goddess Isis appears to the protagonist, Lucius, and explains who she is.

> You see me here, Lucius, in answer to your prayer. I am Nature, the universal Mother, mistress of all the elements, primordial child of time, sovereign of all things spiritual, queen of the dead, queen also of the immortals, the single manifestation of all gods and goddesses that are. My nod governs the shining heights of Heaven, the wholesome sea-breezes, the lamentable silences of the world below. Though I am worshipped in many aspects, known by countless names, and propitiated with all manner of different rites, yet the whole round earth venerates me. The primeval Phrygians call me Pessinuntica, Mother of the gods; the Athenians, sprung from their own soil, call me Cecropian Artemis; for the islanders of Cyprus I am Paphian Aphrodite; for the archers of Crete I am Dictynna; for the trilingual Sicilians, Stygian Proserpine; and for the Eleusinians their ancient Mother of the Corn. Some know me as Juno, some as Bellona of the Battles; others as Hecate, others again as Rhamnubia, but both races of Aethiopians, whose lands the morning sun first shines upon, and the Egyptians who excel in ancient learning and worship me with ceremonies proper to my godhead, call me by my true name, Queen Isis.[5]

Most goddesses in the Graeco-Roman pantheon had some maternal characteristics, and it would be possible to add to Isis' list of names. Furthermore, there would have been many deities in Celtic and other lands whose names are now lost to us, but who would have been of essentially the same nature. The interest of the passage above lies in the fact that the precise name and ritual is seen as superficial; the goddess is real, and different peoples have perceived different aspects of her.

In Gaul, the Rhineland and Britain, the Romans found the Mothers (the

66 A small stone altar dedicated to the mother-goddesses of Italy, Germany, Gaul and Britain. From Winchester. H. 51 cm. British Museum.

Matres or Matronae) widely worshipped, very often in a triple form, a detail which would itself have been quite familiar to them. Some classical deities, notably Hecate of the underworld, had triple manifestations. In Roman Britain, some fifty dedications to the Mothers are recorded in stone inscriptions, in addition to uninscribed sculpture and other objects, constituting ample evidence of the importance of the cult among native Celts and others. Typical of the altars is a small example from Winchester, dedicated by Antonius Lucretianus to the 'Italian, German, Gaulish and British Mothers'.[6] The practice of donating jewellery and other valuables as votives at a shrine is illustrated by the treasure found near Backworth (Tyne and Wear) in the early nineteenth century: contained within a handsome silver saucepan were second-century coins, as well as rings, necklaces and brooches of gold and silver. The handle of the vessel bears a dedication to the Matres by one Fabius Dubitatus, and a gold ring in the same hoard is also dedicated to the mother-goddesses.[7]

The finest stone sculptures representing the triad of Celtic Mothers come from the Rhineland, but the type is also familiar in Britain, as in a small limestone sculpture from Lincoln.[8] The dedicators are men, generally with Latin names and often associated with the military; it is therefore quite mistaken to imagine that the mother-goddess cult was a wholly feminine preserve, though of course, like most goddesses, they were invoked by women to give aid in specifically female concerns such as childbirth. This aspect may be most typically represented in the small pipeclay figurines

67 White pipeclay statuette of a mother-goddess, seated in a wickerwork chair and nursing an infant. This mould-made terracotta was manufactured in Gaul and found at Welwyn, Hertfordshire. H. 14.5 cm. British Museum.

68 A statuette of the Celtic horse-goddess Epona, holding grain and a yoke and accompanied by two very small horses. From Wiltshire. H. 7.5 cm. British Museum.

which depict a single mother-goddess sitting in a basketwork chair and nursing either one or two infants. These little statuettes were made in Gaul and imported into Britain; we may suppose that the goddess would have been known by a Celtic name, and that such figures were usually bought and dedicated by women. But for help in matters of female health, a woman could equally well have turned to many of the classical goddesses, such as Juno, Diana (who in spite of her virgin status had powers over childbirth) and Venus. Gallo-Roman pipeclay figurines of Venus are also very common. Venus was a goddess both of fertility and of erotic love, and both aspects would have been of interest to dedicators.

Though specifically Celtic names for the Matres are not recorded, there are some Celtic goddesses whose names have been preserved on altars and other dedications in other provinces. One of these is Nehalennia, to whom numerous inscriptions have been found in the Netherlands and who appears to have had special power over sea voyages. In sculpture, she is usually represented with a small dog on her lap (dogs were often associated with healing deities as well). Another is the Celtic horse-goddess, Epona. Though in the Graeco-Roman pantheon the sea-god Neptune was concerned to some extent with horses, no classical deity was responsible first and foremost for them and for people such as cavalry soldiers who spend their lives with them. Epona seems to have fulfilled a need, and statues, statuettes and dedications to her are found throughout the western empire, including Rome. Evidently her worship was adopted by the auxiliaries in the Roman cavalry and disseminated far beyond the area of her Celtic origin. Epona is depicted on horseback or sitting between two horses, generally with fruit, grain or other symbols of plenty on her lap. In Britain, she is very scantily represented in the archaeological record, but there is an attractive small bronze from Wiltshire, and a fine altar from Scotland.[9] The latter indicates Epona's acceptance among classical deities, since it is dedicated to her along with Mars, Minerva, the goddesses of the parade-ground, Hercules and Victory, a truly martial team.

In many cultures, a later development of the basic concept of fertility and health is symbolised by male rather than female manifestations. In the classical world, elaborate symbolism was attached to representations of the phallus and of ithyphallic gods. This included not only the obvious symbolism of virility and increase, but also protection from any powers which worked against this good, that is, power against the Evil Eye, and a role in overseeing the safety of boundaries, property and territory.[10] With very few exceptions, straightforward images of phallic gods in human form and the amuletic use of phallic ornaments were introduced into Britain and other Celtic areas after the Roman conquest. There is little doubt, however, that male fertility deities were already venerated; they were simply embodied in a different, less obviously representational manner. One relevant area appears to be the Celtic predilection for deities which were not merely associated with certain animals, like many Graeco-Roman gods, but were themselves of zoomorphic or semi-zoomorphic form: these were frequently horned or antlered gods of otherwise human shape. Many powerful male animals – boars, bulls, rams, stags, stallions – had a cult significance in Celtic society. There were part-animal gods in the Mediterranean world, such as the goat-horned and goat-legged Pan, a Greek fertility spirit who became universally known in the Roman empire. The Celtic horned god most often referred to by modern commentators was called Cernunnos. He has been equated with a horned deity often depicted sitting cross-legged and wearing a torc. It should perhaps be stressed that the name Cernunnos occurs only on a single incomplete inscription from Paris, and the god may have been known under many names.[11]

Images of horned gods occur in Roman Britain, and we can infer that they symbolise the male side of the basic fertility cult. Many of the stone reliefs are too simple to tell us much about the identity of the god, but occasionally links with classical deities are implied; for example, some Celtic images of Mercury replace the wings in his hair or his hat with small horns, attributes consistent with his powers in the classical world, where he was a guardian of property and promoter of fertility as well as a messenger god.

The Roman god Priapus, whose phallic image protected boundaries, ensured the success of gardens and other land and oversaw harbours, is only very rarely recorded in Britain, but we should bear in mind that he was often depicted in the form of very simple wooden statues which would be unlikely to have survived.[12] Another ancient Italian god of fertility and

69 Small bronze statuette of the god Priapus, bringer of good luck and fertility. This figure, from Pakenham, Suffolk, is unique in Britain. H. 8.4 cm. British Museum.

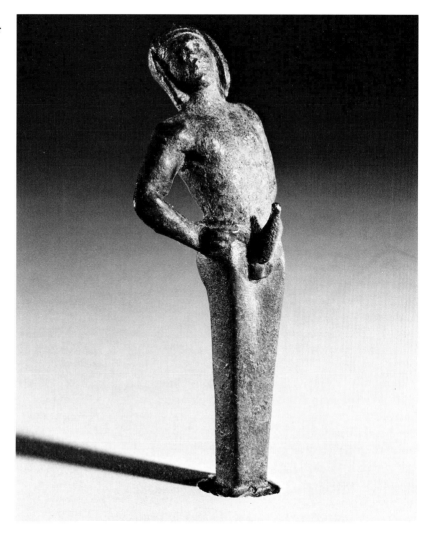

agriculture was Faunus, the first evidence of whose worship in Britain came to light as recently as 1979. The Thetford treasure included spoons inscribed with dedications to Faunus, his name combined with patently Celtic by-names or epithets such as Meddugenus and Blotugus. This treasure dates to the very late fourth century, when Christianity had become the official religion of the empire. The classical literary evidence indicates that Faunus was a Pan-like nature-god with power over fertility, the growth and health of crops and stock, the protection of boundaries and property, and the interpretation of dreams and visions. By the late Roman period he may have been wholly conflated with Pan, and would thus have become part of the retinue of Dionysus. The evidence from Thetford suggests that in Britain he was also assimilated to some native deity with similar characteristics.[13]

Another major focus of religious feeling, closely connected with concern about fertility and health, is expressed in reverence for the sun and sky and for celestial phenomena such as thunderstorms. As in the case of the mother-goddess cult (the 'earth' side of the earth-sky equation), Mediterranean and northern European peoples shared these beliefs.

In classical myth, Jupiter, the Greek Zeus, is a sky and thunder god, as well as the chief of the Olympian deities. Apollo, though a god of music and healing, is closely identified with the sun itself. In Roman iconography the sun was personified as Sol, the counterpart of Luna, the personification of the moon. Deities of eastern religions, such as Mithras and Serapis, were also connected with the sun and the sky, so that in Graeco-Roman religion there was no single, clear-cut system of symbolism in this area, any more than there was in the related field of fertility. We can be quite sure that it was equally complex in the Celtic lands, but as we know far less about the names and the myths involved, we should not be surprised that it is difficult to follow the links between Roman and Celtic sun and sky cults. What is certain, however, is that Celts and Romans would have understood each other's perceptions. There is no sharp dichotomy between classical and Celtic thought in this matter.

The wheel was a universal sun-symbol from early prehistoric times, and was recognised as such by both Romans and Celts. The Gaulish god Taranis, whose name was derived from the word for 'thunder', was mentioned by Lucan as one of the three chief Gaulish deities.[14] He was generally equated with Jupiter, and the wheel is known to have been his attribute. Certainly the Gaulish statuettes which show a mature, bearded god with wheel and thunderbolt can plausibly be identified as Jupiter-Taranis: Jupiter was the Thunderer. But where the sun symbolism of the wheel was paramount, the closest classical deity would seem to be Apollo. Numerous Celtic manifestations of Apollo are known in Britain and other provinces, such as Apollo Maponus in dedications from Corbridge and Apollo Grannus at Inveresk; there was a major temple complex dedicated to Apollo Grannus at Trier in Germany.[15] Ravens, important birds of omen in Celtic super-

70 Gold necklace and necklace-clasp from Dolaucothi, near Llandovery, Dyfed. First to second century AD. Diam. of large wheel, 3.2 cm. British Museum.

stition, were also linked with the classical Apollo, and so an association of wheels and ravens should represent the specifically solar aspect of the sky god. One of the finest illustrations of this is found on a silver vessel from the treasure of Notre-Dame-d'Allençon in Gaul, where we see a traditional classical Apollo with tripod, raven and wheel.[16]

The sun wheel, often paired with a crescent moon, is found on wholly Roman objects such as jewellery of Hellenistic and Roman type from Italy, Egypt and the eastern empire as well as the Celtic north. In Britain, the gold necklaces and bracelet from the Backworth hoard exemplify the type; similar pieces have been found at Dolaucothi in west Wales, and silver wheel- and-crescent pendants occur in the Romano-British jeweller's hoard from Snettisham, Norfolk. Also from Norfolk is the Felmingham hoard, a 71 remarkable collection of bronzes which gives some tantalising glimpses of religious ritual connected with a sun and sky cult. It contains fragments of headdresses, perhaps items of priestly regalia, as well as part of a sceptre and a complete bronze rattle: it is not known whether the latter was simply a noisemaker or had some role in divination. There are also heads of Jupiter and Minerva, a small mask of Sol crowned with sun-rays and the crescent of Luna, a raven, and a fine model wheel.[17]

Another important facet of Romano-Celtic sky cults is exemplified in

71 Hoard of votive bronzes from Felmingham, Norfolk. The object on the left is a rattle, possibly used in some religious ritual. British Museum.

the monuments known as Jupiter-Giant columns. Though most surviving examples are in Gaul and the Rhineland, small fragments are known from three British settlements (Chesterford, Cirencester and Catterick), and there may be others as yet unrecognised.[18] They take the form of tall, tree-like columns on polygonal bases ornamented with figures of deities; the columns are surmounted by a sculptured group depicting a horseman riding down a serpent-legged monster. The allegory evidently concerns gods and giants, the sky and the earth, light and darkness. We cannot put a name to the god, but the column itself indicates a celestial connection. Though images of a rider god are especially common in Celtic areas, and the column itself is also very likely to be a pre-Roman symbol, both have classical aspects as well. The rider trampling a foe is a familiar Roman military motif, and the single column, or a group of four set at a crossroads (a tetrastylon) is an emblem of triumph which would have been understood throughout the Roman world.

At Brigstock (Northamptonshire) and other Romano-British temple sites, a rider god was worshipped who may have more in common with the Roman Mars than with Jupiter. One of the finest small statuettes of this deity, who appears in Roman cavalry armour, comes from Lincolnshire, 73 near the site of Brough (Nottinghamshire); this equestrian Mars may also be referred to in the stylised enamelled bronze brooches of riders which are known from several temple complexes.[19] The delight which Celtic peoples took in war is amply documented in the Greek and Latin sources, while the medieval Welsh and Irish writings describe a warrior élite and a cult of individual heroes or champions reminiscent of Greek legend. It is to be expected that war gods and goddesses should feature prominently in Celtic religion, and such gods would generally have been equated with Mars. We should also bear in mind that the classical Mars was not solely a war god but was very much concerned with agriculture and the protection of territory. In some cases where a local god was identified with Mars it

72 A section from the base of a Jupiter-Giant column, with figures of deities carved in niches. The object was discovered in the early eighteenth century at Chesterford, Essex, in use as a horse-trough. British Museum.

may have been these aspects rather than his warlike characteristics which served as the basis for the comparison.

Inscriptions to Mars and representations of him are very common in Roman Britain. Some of these are clearly connected with the presence of the army. There are conventional statuettes and military inscriptions, often to Mars and Victory, which could be paralleled anywhere in the empire, but there are also some markedly non-classical dedications, such as an altar from Bisley (Gloucestershire) and numerous inscriptions where the name of Mars incorporates a Celtic name or epithet: Alator, Belatucadrus, Cocidius, Condatis, Lenus, Loucetius, Nodens, Olludius, Rigisamus, Thincsus and Toutatis are examples. It is not always clear when we are dealing with a particular aspect of the god (e.g. 'Belatucadrus' means 'fair shining one'; 'Loucetius', also used with the name of Jupiter, means 'brilliant'), and when we have to do with a separate Celtic deity conflated with Mars. The latter would appear to be the case with Toutatis and Cocidius. Cocidius is often

73 Statuette of a Romano-Celtic warrior-god dressed in Roman armour and riding a pacing parade-horse. Found in Lincolnshire, near Brough, Nottinghamshire. H. of horse 9.3 cm. British Museum.

invoked independently, and his name is also sometimes combined with that of another Roman god, Silvanus, a deity of woodland and hunting.

It did not appear contradictory to the Celts, or indeed to the Romans, that a god of war should also be a god of healing; aggression towards an enemy equals the protection of one's own, so the protective role was fundamental to the god's character. The Celtic Mars was also sometimes associated with water ('Condatis' denotes a watersmeet), and hence with healing shrines. At Lydney (Gloucestershire) he is twice equated with the presiding deity Nodens, a healing god who was accompanied by a dog, like the Greek healer Asclepius. Silvanus, a Roman god of woodlands and hunting, also had a dog, in this case the companion of the hunter, but he, too, is conflated with Nodens at Lydney. In Roman mythology, one of Mars' attributes was a wolf.[20]

These are a few threads in the intricate tapestry of beliefs which formed Romano-Celtic religion, and it is clearly futile to expect precise correspondence between any Roman deity and a Celtic one. Mars in some guise seems to have been honoured at many Romano-Celtic shrines. At Barkway (Hertfordshire) silver votive plaques were dedicated to Mars Alator and Mars Toutatis, and at Brigstock (Northamptonshire) and Uley (Gloucestershire) miniature votive weapons indicate worship of a warrior god; yet at the latter site, it is Mercury rather than Mars who represents the local deity.

Caesar remarked that Mercury was the god most often revered among the Gauls.[21] Even in the classical world, the nature of Mercury was complex, and the Greek Hermes and Roman Mercury were by no means precise equivalents. Above all, Mercury was a god of commerce of all kinds, including theft; of travel, of the protection of property and boundaries, of some aspects of fertility, and of a range of crafts and skills. Local Celtic gods who protected a particular region or tribal grouping, and would thus be invoked in trading or other intercourse with a neighbouring group, might be equated by the Romans with Mercury. In Britain, written dedications to Mercury are not particularly numerous, giving the impression that he was not as pre-eminent as Mars and Jupiter, but this is corrected by the frequency with which the god is depicted in art. Where such inscriptions do occur, as at Uley, Celtic epithets are absent. The Celtic elements which can be detected in the worship of Mercury are somewhat different, for instance the tendency for him to become one of the horned gods, and the presence of a female consort, the Celtic Rosmerta or Maia. The latter would appear to have been a tribal goddess with connotations of fertility and plenty, symbolised by the cauldron, bucket or barrel which stands beside her. In a typical relief sculpture of Mercury and Rosmerta from Gloucester, the god has his customary attributes of cockerel, purse and snake-entwined staff, the caduceus, while Rosmerta has a dish, a bucket and an implement which appears to be a long-handled double axe. On occasion, she herself appears with the attributes of Mercury.[22]

74 Head of the cult statue of Mercury from the Romano-Celtic temple at Uley, Gloucestershire. Carved in local limestone, this is a sophisticated piece in a wholly classical tradition. British Museum.

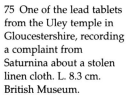

The temple to Mercury at Uley was unknown and undisturbed when it was accidentally discovered in the late 1970s, and subsequent excavations there produced valuable evidence about the nature of a Romanised Celtic shrine. An existing pre-Roman sacred site was developed after the conquest by the addition of a temple building of typically Romano-Celtic form. Worshippers attended the sacrifices of animals appropriate to the god, namely sheep, goats and domestic fowl, masses of whose bones were found: they dedicated votive gifts and exacted vengeance against their enemies by way of curses invoking the aid of Mercury and other gods. In due course, a superb over-lifesize limestone statue of the deity was placed within the temple to serve as the cult-statue. The picture is of a thriving rural community whose reliance upon supernatural aid and approval permeated all aspects of their existence, and who expressed this religious devotion in their traditional way. Newly introduced Graeco-Roman concepts such as large, naturalistic stone statues or written dedications and curses in Latin, were merely embellishments or refinements of age-old customs and beliefs.[23]

Nearly 200 lead curses were found at Uley, and they provide intriguing insights into the problems and concerns which preoccupied the ordinary working men and women of Roman Britain.[24] For example, Cenacus complains to Mercury about his draught animal which was stolen, he says, by Vitalinus and his son Natalinus. Curses such as these normally call down a variety of ills upon the heads of the malefactors, known or unknown, and either promise a payment to the god if the criminals are brought to book or sometimes dedicate to the god the value, or a part of the value, of

75 One of the lead tablets from the Uley temple in Gloucestershire, recording a complaint from Saturnina about a stolen linen cloth. L. 8.3 cm. British Museum.

the stolen goods, so that it is up to the deity to recover his own. Formulae of a legalistic kind are often used, and it is easy to imagine the inscriptions being written to order by professional scribes who were based, with other vendors of goods and services, in the temple precincts.

The making of a direct contract with a deity by asking for help and promising to give something in return is typical of traditional Graeco-Roman paganism, and was apparently also normal practice amongst the Celts. This attitude has sometimes been misunderstood by modern commentators, and taken to imply a cynical and selfish approach to worship. While it is certainly a rational and perhaps unemotional form of religious devotion, it should not be seen as cold or superficial; rather, it is an expression of the sense of the fitness of things, of a deep respect for the natural order, which is one of the many attractive qualities of classical paganism. To those with this view of the world, religious experience does not depend on flashes of insight or mystical emotions (though it does not necessarily preclude such feelings) but on correct observance of the rituals, and a relationship with the supernatural in which both the human and divine parties play their allotted role. During the very centuries when Britain was a province of Rome, this approach was increasingly augmented and ultimately undermined by the growth of a more emotional and personal attitude to religious experience.

Though we have seen that the Celts venerated many goddesses, in Caesar's list of the gods of the Gauls only one female deity is mentioned, Minerva. Roughly equivalent to Athena in Greek mythology, Minerva was a goddess of wisdom and of art, crafts and technology. She was also a war goddess, and is represented wearing a helmet and cuirass and bearing a spear and shield. Clearly, with this range of responsibilities, Minerva was likely to be perceived as the Roman equivalent of a variety of native goddesses, including in all probability tribal deities who combined warlike characteristics with a protective role towards their devotees. The number of written dedications to Minerva in Britain is not very great, but she is quite frequently depicted in statuettes and other small bronzes. However, there was at least one major shrine in her honour, devoted to her not as a war goddess or the mistress of knowledge and wisdom, but in one of her other capacities, as a healing goddess: at Bath, the presiding Celtic goddess of the healing waters was Romanised as Minerva.[25]

We can infer that the natural hot mineral springs at Bath had been venerated from very early times. Such sites have universally been held in awe and respect. After the Roman conquest, the place was rapidly developed into a spa and healing shrine of classical type, complete with magnificent classical buildings, and the altars, sculpture and votive objects from the site identify the goddess who was honoured there as Sulis Minerva, a healing power who, like many of her kind, had links with the healing properties of water and of the sun.

The second great period of Bath as a spa was in the late eighteenth and

76 The broken handle from a silver skillet found with other fragmentary silver items at Capheaton, Northumberland, in 1747. The principal figure on the handle is probably Minerva, holding spear and shield. Below her is a worshipper offering at a large altar which stands before a temple. Close to the temple there appears to be a cave with a stream or spring issuing from it, and two conventional river deities, male and female, flank the foreground. The entire scene is reminiscent of the temple precinct of Sulis Minerva at Bath. Some details are gilded. Second to third century. L. 8 cm. British Museum.

early nineteenth centuries, and the major building programmes of that era revealed, and in part destroyed, much evidence from the time of the town's Roman *floruit*. Contemporary antiquaries made invaluable observations and records of these discoveries, and recent excavations have now augmented them, producing an abundance of new information. The architectural remains are sadly fragmentary, but we can still reconstruct a picture of the elaborate complex of buildings which formed the sacred precinct, including the spendid central temple, its classical façade featuring four tall

77 A silver votive leaf from Barkway, Hertfordshire, dedicated to Vulcan. The god is shown dressed in his characteristic cap and tunic and standing by an anvil. He holds the hammer and tongs of his craft. H. 16.8 cm. British Museum.

Corinthian columns raised on a podium and supporting a pediment richly sculptured in a style which displays a brilliant combination of classical tradition and Celtic vigour. This temple was in existence by the late first century, a mere generation or so after the Roman conquest. The impact of such an imposing and exotic edifice on the native population can well be imagined. Even if resentment may have been felt against the wholesale changes wrought by the Roman administration, the Celtic inhabitants could surely not fail to be gratified by this wholehearted glorification of one of their own sacred places. The contrast with imperialism of modern times is very marked.

The mineral waters were piped and controlled by Roman engineers to create sophisticated bathing facilities, and thousands of votive offerings consigned to the waters by worshippers have been recovered in excavation. These include the expected small valuable objects, mainly coins and jewellery, but larger items, such as pewter and silver table utensils, were also frequent gifts. As at Uley, many curses have been found inscribed on lead or pewter sheet and rolled or folded up before being passed to the goddess for her attention.[26]

Bath epitomises the harmonious blending of Roman and British in a religious precinct which would have looked seemly and familiar to an urbane visitor from Italy or Greece, but which was nevertheless firmly based on the traditional beliefs and practices of the local population. Evidence can be found for the worship of virtually all the Olympian deities in Britain. As we have already seen, at Barkway in Hertfordshire there was a temple to Mars where silver votive plaques of leaf or feather form were found with dedications to a Celtic Mars (Mars Toutatis and Mars Alator); but one of the plaques bears a dedication to Vulcan, the smith god. There must have been Celtic equivalents of this deity, since the mysteries of metalworking are associated with supernatural aid and supervision in virtually all cultures, but we do not know their names. Other representations of Vulcan are not very common, and when he appears it is in fully classical guise, with his anvil, hammer, tongs and smith's clothing. Pottery vessels decorated with representations of these smith's attributes occur, and must also refer to his cult.

Other classical gods and goddesses depicted in art and invoked in inscriptions found in Britain include, for example, Neptune, Diana, Ceres and Venus. Victory was often called upon, together with Mars, by the Roman soldiery, and her image, complete with wings, wreath and palm-branch, is almost a decorative cliché on military inscriptions. Personifications of good fortune, Bonus Eventus and Fortuna, were also very widespread. The most common motifs engraved on the carnelian ring-settings from the Snettisham jeweller's hoard were Ceres and Bonus Eventus, both bringers of fertility and good luck. The motifs used decoratively on personal adornments such as ring bezels, brooches, hairpins and the like were not chosen haphazardly, but were regarded as having a protective power for the wearer. Representations of deities on mosaics form another important class of material, and reveal that general knowledge of classical mythology in Britain was both wide and detailed.

Before we consider the so-called mystery cults which formed a significant element in religious life from the early empire onwards, one or two wholly Roman aspects of religious practice should be noted. The most political manifestation of religion in the Roman state was the imperial cult, which formed an integral part of the structure of administration in the army and in the government of the provinces. The emperor was the chief priest of the state, the *pontifex maximus*, responsible for seeing that the proper religious rites were carried out on all occasions. Like all priests, he claimed a special relationship with the gods, and the custom grew up of elevating him after his death to the status of a god himself. Strictly speaking, a living emperor was not deified, though his *numen*, the spirit of his power and authority, was worshipped. The distinction is a fine one, and it is unlikely that the average citizen would have fully appreciated it. In the provinces, the imperial cult, embracing the major Graeco-Roman gods and the emperor as their priest and representative, was a central element in Roman authority, demanding the declared allegiance of the local inhabitants. In Britain, we know that the centre of the cult was initially at Colchester, where a classical temple to the deified Claudius was built during the early years of the occupation.[27] This temple was attacked at the time of Boudicca's rebellion, being perceived as a symbol of Roman domination. Large statues of the emperor, such as the Claudius found at Saxmundham, Suffolk (thought to be from Colchester) or the Hadrian from the Thames in London, could have been cult-images, though of course colossal or life-size figures of this kind would also have been appropriate in other public and official contexts.

11
41

Certain aspects of state religion were mirrored in microcosm on a domestic level. The head of the family *(paterfamilias)* played the same priestly role within the family as the emperor did in the 'family' of Roman society as a whole. He was responsible for conducting the proper ceremonies on all occasions and ensuring that the household shrine, the *lararium*, was suitably honoured with prayers and offerings. No doubt in practice the mistress of the household saw to this duty. The *lararium* contained a variety of religious images, including statuettes of gods and goddesses to whom members of the family owed special devotion. The universal feature of domestic religion concerned reverence for the spirits of the place, the gods of the household and its everyday affairs, and the spirits of the family's ancestors. These were symbolised by statuettes of the Lares, household gods depicted as dancing figures with libation bowls and drinking horns; by the snakes which had links with the underworld and thus with the spirits of the departed, and indeed also with the spirits of place; and by the *genius*, a local and personal spirit who appears as a figure performing a sacrifice or libation.

We cannot say how widespread traditional Roman religious observance within the family would have been in Britain or other provinces. Many of the small statuettes of gods and goddesses which have been found in great numbers may well have come from household shrines, as well as from temples and other public places. Statuettes of Lares have been found in Britain, and these will certainly be from domestic shrines. The feeling of reverence for the spirits of place and of the departed was inherent in Celtic as well as Roman religion, but it is probable that the formal rituals of Roman family worship would have been usual only among people of Mediterranean origin, for in the family circle men and women tend to adhere to the customs of their own ancestors.

The contractual nature of Roman religion has already been mentioned. The overall plan and order of the universe was perceived and respected, and the human and divine creations took their allotted places within it. If they fulfilled their obligations towards one another, the appropriate results would ensue, which were in everyone's best interests. It was material comfort and safety which was sought, rather than spiritual growth: the latter was not neglected, but was seen as belonging more to the realm of philosophy than that of religion, and was consequently an intellectual discipline suitable only to a small proportion of highly educated men. The *Meditations* of the emperor Marcus Aurelius are concerned with the doctrine of Stoic philosophy in its practical applications, yet to post-classical perceptions they read more as a religious text, one of outstanding power and dignity.[28]

The Romans believed in an after-life and provided for it in the objects which they buried with their dead, but even at its finest, the life of the shades after death was not regarded as very desirable; it was a poor thing compared with the best which could be striven for on earth.

Philosophy and traditional paganism were both in many ways hard taskmasters. Both required the individual to perceive himself or herself as part of a greater whole, that of human society and the natural world. 'That which is not good for the beehive,' says the philosopher emperor with gentle implacability, 'cannot be good for the bee.'[29] The appeal of religious cults which give more recognition to each individual's sense of centrality and uniqueness is not to be wondered at, and such cults were already growing in importance well before Rome started to emerge as a world power, but it was during the period of imperial expansion that the 'mystery religions' gathered strength. These cults, of eastern or Egyptian origin, were based on a more overtly emotional response from the worshipper: in return for a specific personal commitment, the devotee hoped for personal salvation in the after-life, a sense of community, or even unity, with the deity. Such beliefs can reach great heights of nobility, but they can also easily overlook the awareness of society as a whole which characterised classical paganism.

The worship of the wine god Dionysus (Bacchus) was such a cult;

possibly originating in Thrace, it had become thoroughly incorporated into Greek life by early classical times. The characteristic rituals of Bacchic worship were of enormous importance to the history of western civilisation, since they constituted the foundation of Greek drama and thus gave rise to a continuing and developing tradition, as well as to a literature which is considered to be one of the enduring achievements of ancient Greece.

Though especially concerned with the cultivation and use of the vine, Bacchus was essentially a fertility god. His worship involved feasting and

78 A marble statuette of Bacchus, from Spoonley Wood, Gloucestershire. The god holds a wine-cup and is accompanied by a panther. A grape-vine grows around the support on which he leans. H. 39.9 cm. British Museum.

drinking, music and dancing, and the attainment by these means of a state of ecstasy in his devotees, in which they partook of the very nature of the god himself. The *thiasos*, or retinue of Bacchus, was made up of maenads (female worshippers) and a host of gods, demi-gods and animals – Pan, Silenus, satyrs, centaurs, panthers, snakes, deer: they signify a celebration of the powers of nature in a vigorous and untramelled form.

There is ample evidence for Bacchic cults in Britain, especially in the late Roman period when they became a central element in the opposition to Christianity. There are some sculptural representations of fine quality, such as the pieces from the London mithraeum and the marble statuette from Spoonley Wood, Gloucestershire.[30] We have already suggested that the Celticised Faunus invoked on the spoons from the Thetford treasure is a manifestation of Pan/Silvanus, who is in turn one of the participants in the Bacchic *thiasos*; such evidence is important, as it underlines the fact that this major empire-wide religion had a following among Celtic Romans.

Many of the exquisite items of silver tableware in the Mildenhall treasure display the typical Bacchic iconography of the later empire. The outer frieze of decoration on the Great Dish shows the god himself presiding over a 47 riotous dance of maenads and satyrs; Pan is present, as is Hercules, who has just been predictably worsted in a drinking contest with the father of wine. The inner frieze of the dish is a sea-*thiasos* of nymphs, tritons and other marine creatures, which carries overtones of the journey of the soul after death to a happy after-life.[31] Objects like the Mildenhall silver vessels would be exceptional anywhere, and they would not have been made in Britain, but the iconography was familiar and widespread. Scenes of the Bacchic rout frequently appear on late Roman sarcophagi elsewhere in the empire, emphasising that the superficial appearance of undisciplined hedonism is somewhat misleading. The cult was deeply mystical, and was concerned with personal salvation and the profundities of religious experience.

There were other foreign mystery cults in Rome, some so secret in their own time that we have little information about them, and we certainly cannot say how far they might have penetrated into the remoter provinces. One of the widely accepted ones was the cult of the near-eastern (Phrygian) *Magna Mater* Cybele and her consort Attis. Cybele's worship had been officially recognised in Rome since 204 BC. As an archetypal mother-goddess, she shared many characteristics with the Graeco-Roman Demeter/Ceres and with the Egyptian Isis. She was often depicted with a mural crown (castellated like a town wall to symbolise her protective territorial powers), and was accompanied by lions. There is no certain evidence for the worship of Cybele in Roman Britain, but some representations of the shepherd Attis have been found, and it would be surprising if there had not been at least a limited group of devotees here. An object which has been taken as evidence for the cult is a remarkable bronze implement from the Thames. In shape it resembles the iron castration clamps used in Roman veterinary medicine, but it is decorated with busts of Roman deities, including Cybele and Attis themselves: since the priests of the goddess underwent ritual castration, it has been suggested that the implement was used for that purpose. However, the evidence is inconclusive, and no other castration clamp of this kind has been found.[32]

We should remember that in a Celtic province with an ancient tradition of honouring the Matres, the worship of a mother-goddess may have been subsumed within certain local cults, or indeed within the cult of the other great eastern Mother, Isis. Perhaps some of the simple and anonymous images we find of the Matres may have borne not only Celtic names now lost to us, but the titles of Cybele and Isis. We have seen, in the quotation from Apuleius' *Golden Ass* above, that a devotee of Isis had no doubt that she embodied the universal female power, and that other mother-goddesses were simply Isis in a local guise.

Isis was an ancient Egyptian deity. In Roman art she is characterised by her distinctive hairstyle and headdress, by her shawl-like upper garment, knotted between the breasts, and by the *sistrum* (rattle) used in her noisy rites and processions. Many statuettes from the time of the empire depict Isis as a pantheistic deity, combining her attributes with those of Fortuna, Venus and other goddesses and underlining her universality. A beautiful XI small silver statuette from London of her son Harpocrates (Horus) exhibits some of the same pantheistic traits. Such images of Harpocrates, often in precious metal, are found all over the empire.[33]

Though Apuleius' novel is famous primarily for its erotic content, the account it gives of the feelings of a devotee of Isis is of great interest and importance. The passionate devotion and commitment was balanced by the hope of eternal salvation, and founded upon the conviction of the goddess's universal power. The analogy with Christianity is obvious, and it is taken a step closer in another cult, that of the male Persian deity Mithras, which for a time at least was a serious rival to Christianity.

Mithras, depicted like Attis, Orpheus and some others in the typically Phrygian pointed cap, was basically a god of light and the sun. The creation story central to the cult related his slaughter of the Bull which represented primeval chaos, releasing creative and life-giving forces into the world. Mithras was accompanied by two attendants, Cautes and Cautopates, Light and Dark respectively, holding an upright and a downturned torch. Mithraism was a demanding religion. It involved frightening initiation rites leading to seven different grades of initiate, and required of its members a high standard of moral rectitude and probity in their everyday lives. It was popular amongst men of the relatively powerful officer and merchant class, and women were completely excluded.

Mithraism incensed Christians, who could sneer at the simplicities and contradictions of many of the ancient pagan cults but who saw in this mystical faith a deliberate and devilish parody of their own beliefs. The birthdate of Mithras was the midwinter festival of 25 December, the central

79 The bull-slaying scene from the London mithraeum, found in 1889, long before the site of the temple itself was known. The inscription tells us that the marble relief was dedicated by Ulpius Silvanus, a veteran of the IInd Augustan legion, who was initiated into the cult of Mithras at Orange. W. 50.8 cm. Museum of London.

ritual of his worship was a shared meal, and some of the standards demanded of his followers were not unlike those expected of Christians. Christianity and Mithraism each had their exclusive and élitist elements, but these differed. In common with the other mystery cults, Mithraism did not deny the worship of other deities, but it was discriminating about the sex and class of its members: Christianity accepted all followers, male and female, slave and free, but denied the existence of any other god.

Temples to Mithras can be recognised from archaeological remains. They are unlike most pagan classical temples in that the worshippers, instead of being excluded from the inner sanctum, formed a congregation which occupied the interior of the building and shared it with the divine presence. Mithraea were often built wholly or partly underground, and were comparatively small and narrow, with side benches for the worshippers and a place at one end for the altars and cult-images. In Britain, mithraea have been found and excavated in the military zone of the country, at Carrawburgh, Housesteads, Rudchester and Caernarvon, but the most famous British mithraeum is undoubtedly the one excavated at Walbrook in the City of London in 1954. It contained images of other gods such as Bacchus and Serapis, the Romano-Egyptian consort of Isis, as well as the head from a statue of Mithras in the primal bull-slaying scene which was essential in every temple of the cult. Like other mithraic temples in the empire, the Walbrook mithraeum had suffered attack and deliberate damage in the late Roman period. Such actions are usually attributed to Christians, retaliating after generations of persecution and demonstrating that they could match and surpass the intolerance of their erstwhile oppressors.[34]

The evidence for Christianity in Roman Britain is discussed in the following chapter, but here we may summarise religious life in the province as a whole. The overwhelming impression is one of complexity and – Christianity excepted – of harmony. The introduction by Romans and incomers from other provinces of their own religious customs enriched the spiritual life of Romano-British society, opened doors into the developing religious philosophy of the civilised world and played a major part in integrating Britain into the great tradition of classical culture, without in any way belittling, let alone destroying, indigenous Celtic and pre-Celtic beliefs. This happy effect was facilitated by the fundamental similarities between Celtic and classical cults. Religious integration was undoubtedly a major element in the whole process of Romanisation, that indefinable common factor which has left its mark on all the areas which once formed part of the Roman empire.

FURTHER READING

Works on religion in Roman Britain abound, although they tend to be of somewhat uneven quality. The best is M. Henig, *Religion in Roman Britain* (1984), while the Celtic aspect is examined by M. Green, *The Gods of the Celts* (1986), G. Webster, *The British Celts and their Gods under Rome* (1986) and A. Ross, *Pagan Celtic Britain* (1967). See also the important essay by A.C. King, 'The emergence of Romano-Celtic religion', in T.F.C. Blagg and M. Millett (eds), *The Early Roman Empire in the West* (1990), 220–41. There are some very useful papers in M. Henig and A. King (eds), *Pagan Gods and Shrines of the Roman Empire* (1986), and there is much of value in J.R. and E. Harris, *Oriental Cults in Roman Britain* (1965) and V.J. Hutchinson, *Bacchus in Roman Britain* (1986). On temples see W. Rodwell (ed.), *Temples, Churches and Religion in Roman Britain* (1980), and now A. Woodward, *Shrines and Sacrifice* (1992). Outstanding recent site reports include A. Woodward and P. Leach, *The Uley Shrines* (1992) and B. Cunliffe and P. Davenport, *The Temple of Sulis Minerva at Bath, vol. 1: The Site* (1985), and B. Cunliffe (ed.), *The Temple of Sulis Minerva at Bath, vol. 2: The Finds from the Sacred Spring* (1988). L. Allason-Jones and B. Mackay, *Coventina's Well* (1985) is a splendid report on a much older excavation of a shrine by the Hadrian's Wall fort of Carrawburgh.

THE FOURTH
CENTURY AND
BEYOND

For our Lords Diocletian and Maximian, Invincible, both Augusti, and for Constantius and Maximianus, most noble Caesars, under His Perfection Aurelius Arpagius, the Governor, the ... Cohort restored the commandant's house, which had been covered with earth and fallen into ruin, and the headquarters building, and the bath-house, under the charge of Flavius Martinus, centurion in command.

This inscription,[1] one of the very latest closely datable examples known from Roman Britain, comes from the Hadrian's Wall fort at Birdoswald. Erected at some point between AD 296 and 305, the period of the Tetrarchy set up by Diocletian, the fort's record of extensive restoration has been amply verified by a long series of excavations, not least those of recent years. It is now clear that there was work on the gateways and that the floor of one of the two granaries was relaid, and there is a general archaeological impression of a bustle of activity, as a neglected military base was put back into some sort of order.[2]

The context of the inscription is not far to seek. In AD 296, the Caesar Constantius Chlorus had entered London in triumph, after inflicting a

80 Gold medallion of Constantius I, struck in AD 297 to celebrate his defeat of Allectus the previous year. Britannia kneels in front of the gates of London (LON) while Constantius and his navy approach. Electrotype of original in Arras Museum.

momentous defeat upon the insurrectionary forces commanded by Carausius' assassin and successor, Allectus. The scene is shown on a fine medallion found near Arras in France; here Constantius is welcomed by a figure symbolic of London, kneeling before a gate, and is proclaimed as *redditor lucis aeternae*, 'restorer of the eternal light'. The citizens of London had indeed reason to be grateful, for Frankish mercenaries in Allectus' army had escaped the battlefield and were about to sack the city; only the timely arrival of some of Constantius' troops, separated from the main army by fog in the Channel, saved the day: they 'not only rescued your [i.e. Constantius'] provincials, but gave them the pleasure of witnessing the slaughter, as if it were a public show', wrote Constantius' panegyricist, Eumenius.[3]

For most people in Britain, the return to the imperial fold cannot have made much practical difference, and there seems to have been little disaffection. Constantius was able to return to Gaul within the year and, despite a prevalent view of modern scholarship, there is little evidence to suggest that northern tribesmen took advantage of the situation to overwhelm and sack the frontier. Only at the outpost fort at Bewcastle are there signs of enemy attack, namely the looting and burning of the shrine (*aedes*) and underlying strongroom: an imperial statue was torn down, broken up and largely taken away, while two silver plaques bearing the name of the god Cocidius are all that remain of votive offerings to the deity. However, while it would be perverse to deny this as evidence of hostile action, thirteen coins of AD 268–73, although in some instances fairly worn, nevertheless suggest a date earlier than the period of Constantius, and an isolated assault is the most plausible explanation.[4]

This, however, was to change. New federations may have been forming in Scotland – the Picts are first heard of in AD 297 – and in 306 Constantius was back in Britain, leading an army far into the north. Whatever the precise motives behind the campaign (popularly thought, according to a near contemporary source, to have been a quest for a triumphal victory),[5] the militant activities of the Picts later in the century point to the emergence of a serious enemy: Constantius, who was to die at York on 25 July 306, is unlikely to have gone to war without good reason.

The refurbishment of the fort at Birdsowald may therefore have been connected with a deteriorating military situation in the north, and it has been widely argued that the Constantian period saw a major reorganisation of the frontiers – the beginning of the so-called Wall Period III. The idea has both its attractions and its difficulties. Britain, as we saw in chapter 2, seems largely to have escaped the tribulations of the third century that so affected many other parts of the empire, not least Gaul, and the impression from excavations at many forts is that their garrisons were at that time much reduced. Bowness-on-Solway, at the western end of Hadrian's Wall and therefore of considerable strategic importance, is a case in point: investigations to date, although of limited extent, have yielded little third-century material, and there are signs that some barracks may already have been demolished. Two inscriptions, both set up by a tribune called Sulpicius Secundianus in 251–3, show that there was still a military presence, at least in the middle of the century, but it is unlikely to have been substantial and may have been on a 'care and maintenance' basis.[6] Similarly, the Birdoswald inscription suggests that the garrison had been run down, although other inscriptions, dating to 259–68, 270–73 and 276–82, do imply some activity.[7] Whilst it is still not easy to assess the overall situation on the frontier, diminished garrisons in the forts and little or no use of the milecastles and turrets may well have become the norm in the third century, especially as troops were withdrawn to other more pressing theatres of war. Moreover, a not dissimilar picture emerges from other parts of the province: the military presence in Wales was certainly on a very reduced scale, and the legionary fortresses at Chester and Caerleon were also steadily run down in the second half of the third century.[8] Vexillations of all the legions in Britain were despatched abroad, and are likely never to have returned. When the IInd Augustan legion was finally moved from Caerleon to the new Saxon Shore fort at Richborough, probably constructed in the 270s or 280s, it was to occupy a base one-eighth the size of its original fortress, and perhaps numbered as few as 1,000 men.[9]

The Saxon Shore fortifications, and the realignment of military dispositions that they brought about, were briefly described in chapter 2. The building of these massive bases, numbering at least ten in the south-east, must have been a further drain on military resources, and the northern frontier would surely have been affected: indeed, inscriptions show that, at some point, civilians of the Catuvellauni, Dumnonii and Durotriges, as well as the otherwise unknown 'Bricie', were drafted in to work on Hadrian's Wall, although when is not recorded.[10] But it is hard to imagine a particularly huge programme of work on the frontier in the early fourth century, for the manpower can scarcely have been available, however great the need. Thus, whatever the import of the Birdoswald inscription, the temptation to assign many later Roman military works to Constantius must be resisted, or, at the very least, subjected to close scrutiny. At Vindolanda, for example, the supposedly Constantian stone-built fort is now known to have been built in the 220s, and there may be other erroneous equations of this sort.[11] But there would seem to be exceptions. At Wallsend there was drastic replanning of the fort in the late third or early fourth century, entailing the conversion of four barracks in the southern half of the fort into a series of free-standing 'chalets', and the replacement of most of the barracks in the northern *praetentura* by a haphazard arrangement of shack-like structures, some built of wood: these may have been stables, since the garrison was probably the part-mounted cohort of the IVth Lingones, as it had been in the third century. There were also alterations to the head-quarters and hospital (which was made smaller), and the erection of some buildings of modest size in formerly open spaces. We may suppose that

81 Slab from the fort at Binchester, Co. Durham. It is a dedication to the healing gods Asclepius and Salus for the welfare of the unit, set up by, amongst others, a doctor. High priority was placed on good health in the Roman army. Probably third century AD. Durham University.

the unit underwent a considerable reorganisation, and was sharply reduced in numbers, perhaps to as few as 60–80 men.[12]

Similarly, at Housesteads, it has been shown that barracks 13 and 14 were also turned into separate 'chalets', while an adjoining building became a storehouse or granary. The history of the other barracks is much less well known, but there are hints of not dissimilar conversions, and one calculation is that the garrison may have shrunk to fewer than 100 men. Dating these and other changes (which included work on the defences) is not easy, but the weight of the evidence points to the later third century. There is also a very fragmentary inscription which, if correctly interpreted, may read 'To our Lords Diocletian and Maximian' and should therefore belong in the period between 286 and 305; but its import is lost and it may have no relevance to the new buildings.[13]

A third frontier site potentially connected with the activities of Constantius is South Shields. Excavations still in progress are showing that, in the last quarter of the third century, many of the granaries of the supply base built for Severus' campaigns were converted into barracks. The most completely known had quarters for the officers at one end, a workshop and a mere five suites of rooms, again implying a force of reduced size. A large elaborate courtyard house, presumably for the commandant, was built in the south-eastern corner of the fort, and the headquarters (where there had also been a granary in its cross-hall) was restored. What happened to the granaries in the northern sector of the fort has yet to be fully established, but it is clear that it was largely refurbished for a new unit, probably a *numerus* of Tigris boatmen *(barcarii Tigrisiensium)* which is known to have been stationed here in the later fourth century. The abandonment of granaries that could hold provisions for 15,000 men for at least six months must surely imply a greatly diminished frontier force, and presumably new patterns of supply. The correspondence with the evidence of greatly reduced garrisons at Housesteads and Vindolanda is striking and archaeologically satisfactory.[14]

The new building reflects, therefore, a frontier army that was being modified to suit the rather different needs of the later Roman period. The 'chalets' alluded to above are of great interest in this respect. While by no means universal on later Roman military sites, they have been increasingly recognised in recent years, especially on and near Hadrian's Wall, but also at Segontium (modern Caernarvon) in north-west Wales. Excavations at Vindolanda have established that examples there were built when the later stone fort was constructed in the 220s and 230s, and that they are not, therefore, solely a phenomenon of the fourth century as was first thought. Indeed, other third-century examples are suspected at both High Rochester and Ebchester. The Vindolanda barracks had separate officers' quarters and, it would seem, six double-roomed 'chalets', laid out with a relative degree of symmetry. Later alterations, made initially soon after 270 and then about 370, tended to make their appearance much less regular, so that they resembled the examples from other sites.[15]

There has been much discussion about the role of these 'chalets', and it has been maintained that they served as quarters for soldiers and their families.[16] Prior to the reign of Septimius Severus, those below the rank of centurion were not permitted to marry while in military service, but that was revoked by the Edict of AD 197, which also introduced pay increases and the right to wear a gold ring. In reality, informal marriages must long have existed, especially when units were largely static, and this is not infrequently implied on the certificates granting soldiers citizenship after twenty-five years' service. There was a considerable advantage in this, because until the late third century the army relied upon volunteers, and many must have been born and raised in the *vici* around the forts.

Increasingly, however, it was necessary to supplement the cohorts and *alae* (auxiliary cavalry regiments) with *numeri*, a term that normally applied to regiments of very variable strength raised from less civilised tribes, both inside and outside the empire; *cunei* were their cavalry counterpart. First raised in the early second century, *numeri* became common in the third, and not least in Britain. We have already referred to the Tigris boatmen (*barcarii*) in South Shields; but there were also *barcarii* at Lancaster and Moors from North Africa at the Hadrian's Wall fort at Burgh-by-Sands, while at Housesteads the first cohort of Tungrians was reinforced by Frisian cavalry and the *numerus Hnaudifridi*, 'Notfried's irregulars', from Holland and Germany. The frontiers of the empire were becoming increasingly polyglot, and the Frisians at Housesteads seem even to have used hand-made cooking pots of a type otherwise found only in their homeland.[17]

Diocletian, who seized power in AD 284, had introduced a series of radical administrative, military and financial reforms. The empire was now divided up – Italy apart – into some ninety provinces, each governed by a *praeses*; these were grouped into dioceses, administered by a *vicarius*. There were six dioceses in the West, of which the four new provinces of Britain formed one. In addition, there were separate military commands, under a *dux* ('duke') or general. The *dux Britanniarum* was based at York and was in charge of Hadrian's Wall and the northern forts. Given the complexity of this structure (which generated an expensive bureaucracy of thousands upon thousands of civil servants), it is not surprising that Diocletian resorted to a tetrarchy of rulers to preside over this weighty administrative burden.

It is striking that by Diocletian's reign the new posts were generally filled not by senators, but by people of lower, equestrian rank. Italy's pre-eminence, already much eroded, was finally extinguished and a new social order had come into being. Even at the time of Caracalla's grant of citizenship to all freeborn in the empire, in AD 212 (a move aimed essentially at enlarging the population that could be taxed), a legal distinction was emerging between *honestiores* and *humiliores*. The former included senators, decurions, barristers, *milites* (civil servants and soldiers) and those of similar rank, and were roughly equivalent to early Roman citizens; lower-class *humiliores* made up the rest, as *peregrini* (non-Roman citizens) had done in older days. The distinction, although never closely defined, was important. The greatest punishment for *honestiores*, normally speaking, was deportation and loss of property; *humiliores*, by contrast, could be tortured, and it was a customary, if barbarous, habit to inflict such torture upon both accused and witnesses (if lower class) in most criminal trials and in some civil cases. In this way, all doubt about the verdict could be removed.[18]

Legislation initiated by Diocletian (and extended by his successors) also had the effect of binding *humiliores* to the land or to their trade, as well as tying decurions to their curial tasks in the towns. This was aided by a series of censuses across the empire, so that it became illegal, for example, for a rural peasant to leave the place where he was registered, an obligation that was also hereditary. Similarly, it became binding upon soldiers' sons to enter military service, for Diocletian and his co-rulers had roughly doubled the number of legions, even though numerically they were much smaller, and the pressure upon manpower must have been considerable. In practical terms, this may not have made much difference to a family stationed on, say, Hadrian's Wall, for they are likely to have been in any case static: but now they were legally bound to stay, with heavy preventative measures to discourage those of independent temperament.[19]

The main object of the censuses was to facilitate new forms of taxation, not least to pay for the huge body of soldiers and bureaucrats that so dominated the later Roman world. Although the form of the taxes varied from diocese to diocese, the principle remained the same: the collection of the vast quantities of coin, rations, animals, clothing and labour that were needed to supply and maintain the fabric of empire. There was thus a land tax (*iugum*) for the *annona*, the requisition in kind, and a poll tax (*capitatio*) in money. In many regions, however, Diocletian addressed the widespread problem of a largely non-monetary economy (exacerbated by the collapse of the coinage in the third century), so that the poll tax was in effect paid in kind rather than coin. Gaul and Africa may have been exceptions, while for Britain there is no evidence; but, if our earlier picture (chapter 3) of the make-up of the population in Britain carries any conviction, most will have handled little or no money. Foodstuffs, equipment and labour (such as the work of men of some *civitates* on Hadrian's Wall) will surely have paid most of the tax bills.

It is the verdict of the distinguished historian A. H. M. Jones that this brought about 'a budget in the modern sense, an annual assessment of governmental requirements, and an annual adjustment of taxes to meet these requirements'.[20] But these measures presented difficulties. A reform of the coinage, including the introduction of the gold *solidus* (ultimately an economic mainstay of the fourth century), proved initially less than successful, as was an attempt in AD 301 to freeze prices; but a stability of sorts was achieved. Britain must surely have benefited. Its military presence was very much diminished, as we have seen, and therefore would have been much less of a financial burden; moreover, although divided into four provinces, each with administrative costs, these must have been trifling compared with more urbanised parts of the empire. Indeed, there is an undated inscription from Rome, set up jointly by the British provinces (i.e. of third- or fourth-century date), which must imply a considerable measure of co-operation between them and, quite possibly, a single assembly.[21]

In AD 305, Diocletian decided to abdicate and retired to his fortress-palace at Split. Maximian was also persuaded to stand down, and the following year Constantius, who had succeeded him as Augustus in the West, died at York. The army straight away hailed as the new western ruler his son, Flavius Valerius Constantinus, better known to us as Constantine the Great. He was to prove a remarkable man, who will always be associated with the Edict of Milan (AD 313), which gave particular privileges to the Christian Church, and with the building of the 'New Rome' of Constantinople (modern Istanbul). His reign was a long one – he died in 337 – and for the last thirteen years he ruled alone, after defeating the pagan Licinius, Augustus of the East, in 324. It was a victory redolent with symbolism, as Constantine's troops fought under a banner bearing the monogram of Christ, while Licinius' army carried those representing the old deities. Although adherence to paganism was to remain strong, especially in the West (Africa apart), a new order was in the making.

It was the view of the Greek historian Zosimus, writing about AD 500, that, whereas Diocletian had greatly strengthened the frontiers of the empire, 'Constantine ruined this defensive system by withdrawing the majority of the troops from the frontiers, and stationing them in cities which did not require protection'.[22] Zosimus was an adherent to the old pagan beliefs, and his prejudice towards Constantine in particular is far from opaque. In fact, Constantine played a crucial role in reshaping the army of the late empire. A clear distinction was now made between troops stationed on or near the frontier (*limitanei*) and those in the hinterland, known as *ripenses*. In Britain, Hadrian's Wall was still largely garrisoned by the old cohorts, *alae* and *numeri*, perhaps supplemented now by *areani*, whose role was 'to hasten about hither and thither over the long spaces, to give information to our generals of the clashes of rebellion among neighbouring peoples'. Like the *exploratores* (scouts) of the previous century, the *areani* may have been based in outpost forts like Bewcastle and Risingham, where there is evidence for occupation at this time.[23]

The *limitanei* had otherwise become static, small-scale frontier police, perhaps by now living mainly within the forts, for many *vici*, like that at Vindolanda, seem to have been abandoned by this date. Moreover, unlike the Saxon Shore forts and many towns, the forts were not provided with external towers for archers (or, much less probably, artillery). A frontier like Hadrian's Wall may by now have seemed old-fashioned and inde-fensible, and *ripenses* in the diocese were evidently seen as the more import-ant force. Constantine raised many new units in the empire as a whole, termed *auxilia*, and they are well attested in Britain. Amongst them were the *equites Crispiani*, named after Constantine's son Crispus (who was executed in 326) and based at Danum, the fort at Doncaster. Constantine also created field armies of *comitatenses*, with commanders known as *comes* (count). The broad intentions were twofold: one was to promote the growth of a new class of officer, a process already initiated by Diocletian, while the other was to increase the mobility of an army that might have to respond to threats in any part of the empire.

Deciphering the meaning and impact of these developments is a complex matter, although it is considerably aided by a document called the *Notitia Dignitatum*. This is an illustrated list of civil and military officials, together with army units and their location, in both the eastern and western parts of the empire. Probably compiled in the early fifth century, it survives principally in four manuscripts of the fifteenth and sixteenth centuries, themselves copied, it would seem, from a version of tenth-century date. Not surprisingly, it is prone to error and, as far as the British sections are concerned, there are signs that some of the information was seriously out of date – although to what period, or periods, this relates is a subject of considerable contention amongst scholars.[24]

Three commands are listed for Britain: the *dux Britanniarum*, the *comes* of the Saxon Shore, and a *comes Britanniarum*. The title *comes* seems an odd one for the commander of the Saxon Shore forts, with their garrison mainly of *limitanei*; but it may originally also have included bases along the French and Belgian coast. The historian Ammianus Marcellinus seems to confirm this when in discussing the barbarian attacks upon Britain in AD 367–8 he refers to the *comes maritimi tracti*.[25] Still more problematical is the allusion to a *comes Britanniarum*, for there is no real context for his command. The best explanation is that this was an *ad hoc* force, assembled to cope with a particular situation. Gratian, the father of the future emperors Valentinian and Valens, and himself emperor from 367 to 383, held the title, and it has been conjectured that it related to a visit to Britain by the emperor Constans early in AD 343, itself perhaps prompted by some undocumented military crisis. But there is no mention of a *comes Britanniarum* during the seemingly troubled years of the 360s, which culminated in 367–8 with simultaneous attacks by Picts, Scots (from Ireland) and Attacotti (from Ireland or the Western Isles), and the army of the *comes* listed in the *Notitia* is commonly held to have been assembled rather later. Indeed, events of the last two decades of the fourth century may provide a possible context. In 383, the Spaniard Magnus Maximus staged a rebellion and took over large parts of the West, Britain included. Although he survived a mere five years, a campaign against the Picts and Scots is recorded, and later tradition holds him as responsible for founding the ruling dynasty of the Galloway region of south-west Scotland and, less convincingly, as placing the Scottish leader of the Votadini, Cunedda, and his troops in northern Wales. However this folklore is interpreted, it implies that Maximus, despite his preoccupation with fighting the legitimate Roman forces abroad, was forced to take some military measures within northern Britain. Moreover, there are hints that raiding continued after Maximus' death, and, if a poetic allusion can be trusted,[26] sometime in the period 396–8 the Vandal general Stilicho ordered a punitive expedition. Whilst nothing is really known of it, here at least is an occasion when the *comes Britanniarum* of the *Notitia* may have received his appointment.

In synthesising our meagre and often remote 'historical' data for fourth-century Britain (Ammianus' reports may be counted an exception), it would be easy to build up a picture of acclerating decline and disaster, as the hold on the frontiers became even more fragile, especially during and after the 360s. This may of course have been the case, but it is a view that needs to be carefully tested against other sorts of evidence, not least that of archaeology. We have already seen that it is difficult to envisage a standing army of any size in fourth-century Britain. The XXth Valeria Victrix, for instance, is last attested on coins of Carausius, and its fortress at Chester underwent extensive demolition towards the end of the third century; the legion's very existence much after that date is perhaps to be doubted.[27] Equally, recorded imperial visitations to the diocese of Britannia, in an age when emperors were notably mobile, are few and far between. Constantine may have been there in 313–35 and Constans visited in 343; but thereafter – usurpers like Magnus Maximus apart – no emperor is known to have intervened personally (although there were occasions when high-placed officers were despatched to Britain to deal with specific problems, such as the aftermath of the barbarian incursions of 367–8).[28] The implication is that, for a large part of the century, Britain was a backwater, where troubles, although they undoubtedly occurred, were relatively minor in comparison with what was going on in the empire as a whole. Indeed, even in the 360s, grain was being exported to the Continent, and Ammianus implies that the shipments were a routine matter.[29]

We must now try to assess how far this is true of life in the towns and countryside. Attempts to portray the nature and role of the main towns in late Roman Britain have undergone enormous vicissitudes in the scholarship of the last fifty years or so and, despite a vast increase in the amount of excavation, no synthesis of the results has met with total consensus. This is a measure both of the difficulties in deciphering and dating the structural sequences and, even now, of the very partial way in which towns have been investigated. Views have tended to polarise into two main schools of thought. Put succinctly, one envisages late Romano-British towns as thriving centres, where urban life was maintained well after Roman government ended in AD 410,[30] while the other would portray them as mere shells, serving only some administrative functions and as occasional residences for the rich.[31] Artisans, it is argued, had largely migrated to small towns and villages, which became prosperous centres of industry and commerce, and most of the élite members of society preferred generally to reside on their villas, which multiplied and expanded very considerably in the early fourth century.[32] Seen in this light, the *civitas* capitals would be regarded as costly failures, which were never successfully integrated into Romano-British culture.

One of the difficulties here is that the discussion has tended largely to be cast in the form of 'growth and decline', a perspective that is not always helpful. The archaeological indications are that, right across the empire, towns witnessed profound changes in their nature and appearance in the later Roman period. Public places such as fora often underwent considerable modification (for example, the erection of timber stalls) and were even built over; colonnades lining once gracious streets were blocked up and converted into shops; private patronage became more or less a thing of the past, as the rich put money into their own property; and in the fourth century, especially the latter part, churches built on the fringes of the town and beyond the walls (as cemetery chapels) created new urban foci. Even at a great eastern city such as Ephesus the state agora had been largely abandoned by the early fifth century, while the once magnificent Embolos Street was converted into a shop-lined thoroughfare.[33] Grand private houses there were, for the town's administrative role demanded that the affluent occasionally resided there, to fulfil what became increasingly onerous and unattractive duties; but our literary sources suggest that, particularly in the West, many of the upper classes preferred to live mainly on their country estates and indulge in the pleasures of the countryside.[34]

Late antique towns and cities were therefore rather different places from those of two or three centuries before, lacking in many cases the organised rhythm of their carefully planned predecessors. Indeed, Libanius, when composing a funeral oration for the emperor Julian in AD 365, could write of Gallic towns within which 'oxen were yoked, furrows drawn, the seed set, and the corn grew, was reaped and threshed, all inside the city gates'.[35] Although Libanius attributes this state of affairs, very improbably, to barbarian incursions, and couches his remarks in flowery terms, there is every reason to believe that there is some substance behind them. Populations were falling, so that by the late sixth century the inhabitants of Rome itself, once a city of a million or more, probably numbered fewer than 90,000, a trend that began at least as early as the third century. Thus, even Aurelian's great wall around Rome, begun in 271 and 18 kilometres in length, excluded substantial suburbs, while many more or less contemporary circuits in Gaul enclosed very reduced areas. Most later imperial towns, therefore, not only had a somewhat changed appearance, but their cores became physically smaller. Even so, as Libanius indicates, there were open spaces within the walls, and nowhere more spectacularly than in Rome, where a distinction emerged between the *abitato* and the *disabitato* as the city gradually shrank. The point is strikingly made by late nineteenth-century photographs of the city, showing Roman ruins amidst vast areas of pasture, orchards, fields and trees, all within the Aurelianic walls; many late antique cities may well have come to look the same.[36] Thus many scholars talk not in terms of a decline of the city, but of 'mutations' in the urban landscape and a perceptible 'ruralisation' in its appearance.[37]

This wider background is important if we are to try to understand what happened in Romano-British towns in the third, fourth and fifth centuries. Some scholars dismiss as irrelevant the evidence from other parts of the empire, but this is to ignore the broader political, social and economic changes that affected all provinces in various degrees. Urban fortifications are of interest in this respect, and it is worth setting out something of their overall history in Britain.[38] As in Gaul, few towns were provided with defences in the first century, even Camulodunum, for whose inhabitants this had catastrophic consequences when Boudicca's troops sacked the city in AD 60 or 61. The other two *coloniae*, Lincoln and Gloucester, had their legionary ramparts, while Isca Dumnoniorum (Exeter) was likewise allowed to retain its military defences when it became a *civitas* capital. Verulamium, as a *municipium*, was also given a bank and ditch, as were Chichester, Winchester and Silchester. The last three would seem to have lain within the realm of the client king Cogidumnus and, although the circuits at Chichester and Winchester appear to postdate his death (as may the great palace at Fishbourne), it is difficult not to associate this privileged ruler with these conspicuous marks of status.

The erection of town walls was, in fact, tightly controlled, requiring sanction from the emperor who might, on occasion, also provide funds for a place of sufficient importance; for example, the *coloniae* of Gallia Narbonensis, a region already urbanised by the Greeks, were particularly favoured in this respect, unlike the rest of Gaul. Walls had a symbolic and religious importance, marking the sacred boundary (*pomerium*), and in early imperial times at least were normally constructed only around places of high rank. Indeed, in the second century there were attempts to restrain municipalities from projects such as the building of town walls, which came increasingly to be regarded as excessively expensive ways of enhancing their prestige.[39]

It is all the more surprising, therefore, that most of the Romano-British *civitas* capitals and at least twenty-five minor towns were enclosed by earthen banks and ditches in the latter part of the second century. These can hardly have been things of beauty, but they were relatively quick to put up and therefore not too costly: calculations suggest that at Silchester 600 men could have built the 2.5 kilometres of defences (although not the gates and superstructure) in less than two months.[40] This rash of building is, in the absence of inscriptions, hard to date with any precision, and also difficult to parallel in other parts of the empire. However, attempts to link it to the wars of Commodus' reign, in the early 180s, or with Albinus' abortive move to seize imperial power in 196–7, have met with disbelief, as yet another unwarranted correlation between historical and archaeological 'events'. Civic pride, it is argued, is a much more likely explanation, harking back to the elaborate defences of Iron-Age hillforts and *oppida*.[41]

It is perhaps foolish to take a dogmatic view about the issue, since the chance find of an inscription is probably the only way of resolving what must otherwise remain a contentious matter. What, however, is not in doubt is that during the third century, and especially the second half, there was a very considerable investment in massive masonry walls, closely paralleling the great defences of the Saxon Shore forts. One of the earliest was in London, where the landward sides of the city were enclosed within strong defences 3 kilometres in length, built between about AD 190 and 210.

Either Albinus, before his abortive coup of AD 196–7, or Severus, who arrived to campaign in Britain in AD 208, may have been responsible, and London was certainly embellished in other ways at that time. The wharves along the river were extensively reconstructed, and elements are known of a highly decorated arch, bearing figures of Minerva and Hercules and busts of Mercury and Mars. It, too was probably of Severan date, and may have formed the entrance to a temple precinct. The carved blocks, fifty-two in all, were subsequently incorporated into a further stretch of defensive wall built along the north bank of the Thames about AD 270, as dendrochronological dating has shown. Two altars were also found in the riverside wall, both recording the restoration of temples to Isis and Jupiter, probably in the mid-third century. It is remarkable that monuments so recently built or renovated were being pulled down, and the masonry

82 A stone altar found reused in the riverside wall in London, recording the restoration of the temple of Isis by Marcus Martiannus Pulcher. H. 122 cm. Museum of London.

reused: this, too, smacks of haste or an emergency, which is perhaps also reflected in the construction in the 260s of a watch-tower at Shadwell, to the east of the city, well placed to exercise surveillance over the Thames.[42]

Most major and many minor towns of Roman Britain were also enclosed within masonry walls in the course of the later third century. Whilst the dating evidence is not always very adequate, the emerging pattern seems consistent, and can be set alongside more or less contemporary work in Gaul and elsewhere (including, as we have seen, Rome), and on the Saxon Shore forts. However, Verulamium apart, external towers – probably for the use of archers rather than artillery, as was once thought[43] – were not added until later, probably after about AD 350. Ammianus Marcellinus tells us that Count Theodosius restored the *civitates* after the disaster of AD 367–8, and it is tempting, if speculative (and currently unpopular), to attribute this work of modernisation to him. Certainly, well-preserved examples like those that adorn the southern town walls of Caerwent remain impressive down to this day, implying a scale of investment that was far from feeble.[44]

Within the towns, however, the late third and early fourth centuries mark something of a watershed in their internal organisation. As in some, and perhaps many, towns in the empire, the forum and basilica became of decreased significance, and were sometimes even obliterated completely, as at Cyrene and Paestum. In Britain, similar examples are provided by London and Wroxeter (although a few rooms in the enormous basilica in London may have remained in use),[45] while sensitive re-excavation of the basilica in Silchester has demonstrated that it was given over to metal-working well before the end of the third century.[46] Some fora, like those at Leicester and Cirencester, are thought to have been maintained well into the fourth century, and even beyond; but whether they were the vibrant, elegant places of early Roman times is debatable. Certainly, there are implied changes in the framework of administration, perhaps reflecting the rather different society that emerged in the third and fourth centuries.

In some towns, other public monuments were also going out of use, like the baths at Exeter (by the late third century), Wroxeter (by about AD 330) and Canterbury (early to mid-fourth century), and the amphitheatre at London (by the early fourth century). The pattern is not even, and modern evaluations of the chronology are contradictory; but there is an impression here, too, of changes afoot, above all a sharp drop in private patronage (as again was happening elsewhere). Indeed, a general survey of what we know about the later history of amphitheatres in Britain could provide no definite evidence at all either of fourth-century building or repair, or of their usage. It has been argued that the entertainments of the amphitheatre were unappealing to the largely Celtic population of Roman Britain, a view that much modern taste would welcome, given the emphasis upon blood and violence; but it may be more realistic to conclude that pragmatic considerations, especially cost, may have played a greater part.[47]

We may therefore suggest that some of the administrative and public roles of the principal towns were undergoing considerable change in the later third and early fourth centuries, as least as expressed through the history of some major buildings. Indeed, it is sometimes held that there was also a sharp decline in commercial and industrial activity in these places, seen for example in the closing down of the quays of London and the demise of pottery production at centres like Verulamium, Colchester and Canterbury. The so-called 'strip-house', which would seem to typify the work-place and dwelling of the artisan class, certainly became less common (in contrast to the minor towns), whereas larger and more spaciously arranged residences were increasingly in vogue. At Verulamium, where the evidence is comparatively full, the process seems to have begun as early as the later second century, and excavations have revealed a considerable number of substantial buildings, many handsomely embellished with mosaics and wall-paintings. In the early fourth century many were altered or rebuilt, especially in the southern part of the town. Around the forum, however, very little work was carried out at this time – indeed, insula xxvii, a prime adjacent site, was left entirely vacant – and there is more than a hint here that the civic centre no longer held the importance of former times.[48]

Other large fourth-century town houses, assuredly owned by members of the curial class, are also known at several other *civitas* capitals. Examples include buildings with mosaics at Glyde Park Road and Colliton Park, Dorchester (Dorset); Chapel Street, Chichester; Brook Street, Winchester; and a house with a private suite of baths at Lower Thames Street, London. Many of the thirty or so more elaborate residences at Silchester may have been occupied at this time, while at Cirencester houses with fourth-century mosaics are known at Dyer Street, Watermoor and Beeches Road – the latter two again being well away from the civic centre.[49]

Current investigations at Caerwent in south-east Wales are also proving illuminating. In insula i, in the north-west part of the town, a substantial house, 35 x 45 m, was built around two courtyards in the early fourth century. It had mosaics and decorated wall plaster, but also store-rooms and a so-called corn-drier (which, whatever its exact function, was certainly used for agricultural purposes). Elsewhere in the insula were two more houses, one l-shaped and the other with wings, as well as smaller buildings and walled yards. In the centre of the town, a Romano-Celtic temple was constructed about AD 330, and a nearby workshop refurbished at about the same time. The temple remained in use until the late fourth century, but the town's basilica, which lies nearby and was extensively rebuilt towards the end of the third century, had by AD 350 been pulled down and the area given over to industrial activity.[50]

The agricultural aspect of the insula i house is of great interest, and can be matched at other sites. A granary is known at Colchester; barns and other agricultural buildings have been inferred at Silchester; the Beeches Road complex at Cirencester has been interpreted as a fourth-century farm;

and at Verulamium there are signs of an increased agricultural emphasis in the late Roman period. Indeed, the deposits of so-called 'dark earth' which enveloped structures in many Romano-British towns are often regarded as an agricultural accumulation, although scientists are in sufficient disagreement about this as to render prudent a deferred judgement.[51]

The overall picture, therefore, is of a fourth-century urban landscape which, in the *civitas* capitals at least, was increasingly dominated by large, sometimes sumptuous, private residences, some with an agricultural component. Fora and basilicas became effectively irrelevant, and the duties of the élite were probably carried out mainly in, and from, their private houses. It is perhaps significant in this respect that the streets of at least some of the *civitas* capitals were demonstrably maintained in good repair into the late fourth century, if not later, and that the town walls were made militarily more effective by the addition of towers: there is a clear hint here of priorities in the organisation of urban life, and of the concerns of central government.

83 The Romano-Celtic temple complex at Caerwent (Venta Silurum), Gwent. Built about AD 330, it includes the temple itself (top) and a long hall (foreground) fronting the main street.

84 The *curia* (council chamber) at Caerwent. Traces can be seen of the framework for seats; on the left are the stone supports for the magistrate's dais. The *curia* was dismantled in about AD 350.

Nevertheless, it is evident that the ruling classes preferred to reside as much as possible on their country estates, of which some individuals may have owned several. Villas proliferated in the late third and early fourth centuries, especially in the south, where previously underdeveloped areas such as the Cotswolds became very popular; more than forty such estates are now known in this area alone, the great majority being new foundations.[52] Many were very luxurious establishments, handsomely embellished with mosaics, wall-paintings and other architectural features. They irresistibly recall the elegant life described by aristocrats such as Ausonius and Sidonius Apollinaris on their rural estates in fourth- and fifth-century Gaul, and the country houses and hunting scenes shown in so many contemporary mosaics found in North Africa and elsewhere.[53] Indeed, it 86 may be that the late fourth-century treasure of silver spoons and gold 88 jewellery found at Thetford in Norfolk, with its abundance of references to the silvan god Faunus, is a similar evocation of the joys of rural life.[54]

A visit to such well-known sites as Chedworth or Bignor amply conveys the grandeur and graciousness of these splendid residences. Although also working farms, the owners lived in style, according to the best dictates of the day. The villa at Woodchester (Gloucestershire), for example, had at least sixty-five rooms, laid out around three axially arranged courts. More than a dozen mosaics are known (there were certainly more), including the great Orpheus pavement: it measures some 14.4 metres square, but the measurement hardly does justice to its enormous visual impact. It is as breathtaking a symbol of private opulence as one could want.[55]

Villa owners went, therefore, to considerable lengths to display their wealth and sophistication,[56] and subsidiary buildings could also be highly embellished, as the lucky discovery of the fallen façade at Meonstoke (Hampshire) shows. Moreover, due attention was also paid to the grounds. At Frocester Court in Gloucestershire, for example, the villa possessed a formally laid-out garden, a dovecot and an orchard, while at Bancroft (Buckinghamshire) extensive excavations have brought to light a large walled garden, placed in front of the main house and with an ornamental pool in the centre. The house itself was not particularly extensive, but it was provided with an abundance of mosaics – some of very fine quality – most of which were laid as late as about AD 350. Moreover, there was what could well have been a bailiff's cottage, also with a tessellated floor, placed just outside the walled garden, as well as a considerable number of estate buildings. Some of these were circular in plan, in indigenous tradition, and were presumably the quarters of the lowly farm workers.[57]

Stanwick in Northamptonshire presents a not dissimilar picture in that here, too, were a fairly grand fourth-century villa with mosaics, a possible bailiff's house and a sufficiently numerous series of round houses (all with stone footings) to regard them as comprising an associated village.[58] Unfortunately, we know little of the size of the estates that were farmed from these late Roman villas, although field systems extending for at least 25 hectares around that at Winterton (Humberside) and for 40 hectares around Barnsley Park (Gloucestershire) provide some clues. It is likely that, as elsewhere in the empire, the rich accumulated more and more territory at the expense of the poor, with some being farmed directly and some let out to tenant farmers (coloni); the latter are mentioned in Britain, albeit only once, but it is archaeologically impossible to identify them.[59] What the material evidence does suggest is that the sharp increase in the number of rich villas in late Roman times was accompanied by significant improvements in agricultural techniques, equipment and crops. Botanical studies, for example, suggest that crops were being rotated much more efficiently, and that there was now widespread cultivation of flax and bread wheat (triticum aestivum). The profitable produce of orchards and gardens also figures much more prominently in the plant remains, while there seem to have been improvements in ploughs, allowing the farming of heavy clay lands. The so-called corn-drying ovens (which were probably used for a variety of purposes, including the malting of barley to make beer) also become common, and must again signal important innovations in agricultural strategies.[60]

We alluded earlier to Diocletian's reforms in taxation, and it may well be that these were a significant stimulus to increased production. But the material culture, whether measured by mosaics and wall-paintings or by portable objects such as jewellery, silver plate and fine glassware, gives a picture of a deeper underlying prosperity, certainly amongst the upper classes. This must in part have been acquired during the third century, when Britain was somewhat insulated by the sea from the crises that took place elsewhere; but it may also reflect investment from abroad, in a province which will have appeared relatively stable and peaceful when compared with others in much of the western empire. Indeed, there are other unambiguous signs of wealth and investment at this time. Sixteen milestones dating from the period between AD 238 and 276 point to a steady programme of road maintenance, but there are no fewer than twenty-six from the late third and early fourth centuries. Similarly, the small towns that line these roads do in most instances yield abundant evidence of private and economic affluence.[61] The pottery industry is here often taken as an example; both imports and production centres based on the *civitas* capitals entered a sharp decline in the course of the third century, while industries focused upon small towns or rural areas such as the New Forest rapidly captured the market. They were often sited close to inferred boundaries between *civitas* territories, so as to exploit wider markets, and mass-produced huge quantities of table and cooking wares. Durobrivae, near modern Peterborough, particularly flourished, as the numerous, richly decorated suburban villas clearly show; late Roman sites in one of its main marketing areas, the adjoining Fenland, yield vast quantities of this so-called Nene Valley pottery and, however low-cost the product, evidently were a source of considerable wealth.[62]

Many of the smaller towns may also have prospered as a result of the *annona*, the tax in kind that we referred to briefly earlier in this chapter. It is known that *mansiones* (inns), important centres of the *cursus publicus* (postal service), were often extended to facilitate collection of the produce by soldiers, supervised by an *actuarius*. Godmanchester appears to have benefited in this respect, as other small towns such as Catterick, Wanborough (Wiltshire) and Braughing (Hertfordshire) may well have done.[63] So, too, may some of the larger villages, which appear to have become increasingly numerous in late Roman Britain.[64] Like Stanwick, some must have housed villa estate workers and, perhaps, local *coloni*; but others are remote from villas and surely represent a diverse situation. Thus, in the Fens, substantial villages are a conspicuous element of the fourth-century landscape and, although they originated earlier, it is only at this time that they disclose traces of stone buildings and other signs of greater material affluence. Interestingly, it is also these sites that are most productive of coin finds, as though they were local centres of exchange and tax collection.[65]

Another important element in the late Roman rural landscape, especially in southern and eastern parts of Britain, was the Romano-Celtic temple. The available statistics suggest that these reach a peak as late as the mid-fourth century, nearly half a century after Constantine's famous Edict of Milan, legitimising Christianity (AD 313).[66] Hilltop locations were often preferred, sometimes within old Iron-Age centres such as Maiden Castle and Lydney (Gloucestershire), as though to emphasise the antiquity of the religion. Indeed, as we have seen, excavations at Uley, another major Iron-Age hillfort, have shown that the spot was certainly frequented, and probably venerated, far back into prehistory. Some of the temples seem, moreover, to have developed into centres of pilgrimage with accommodation and other facilities. The temple at Uley was surrounded by at least four other buildings,[67] while at Lydney a complex of late third- or early fourth-century date included a temple in classical style, a grand set of baths, a guest-house and a long building with eleven rooms; this may have been for sick people to pass the night in, for the god at Lydney was Nodens, a minor healing deity who, like the better-known Asclepius, may have been thought to have visited the ill in their dreams.[68] An inscription on a mosaic in the temple has recently been reinterpreted to read 'For the god Mars Nodens, Titus Flavius Senilis, superintendent of the cult, from the offerings [of pilgrims] had this laid; Victorinus, the interpreter [of dreams] gave his assistance.'[69]

The distribution of late temples follows that of villas very closely, and there can be little doubt that it was the villa-owners who promoted and patronised them. Like the villas themselves, they were a vehicle for the display of wealth and status, and the holding of religious offices and the endowment of temples was an important way of exercising power. With the increased emphasis upon country life, there was a greater need for rural sanctuaries, apparently matched, as we shall see, by a corresponding decline in the patronage of many urban temples.

It is sometimes claimed that some villas themselves became foci for religious pilgrimage, but the idea is to be resisted. Many owners did display their pagan beliefs through the media of, for example, floor mosaics, but these were not cult centres. Littlecote (Wiltshire), where a spaciously laid-out villa reached its apogee about AD 360, has yielded an imposing mosaic depicting Apollo (or, much less probably, Orpheus), surrounded by four female figures riding on animals, perhaps representing the four seasons. It lies within a room with three apses (a triconch), which stands at the head of a long rectangular room also decorated with mosaics, depicting panthers and sea creatures. This has been interpreted as an Orphic cult room; however, the plan is that of a type of dining-room that became fashionable in North Africa and Italy at the end of the third century, and it is more likely that the owner was displaying the sophistication of his taste.[70]

A recent study of pagan temples in the towns suggests that, by the fourth century, their main *floruit* was coming to an end. There are exceptions like the new shrines built at Chelmsford and Caerwent in about AD 325–30, but temples were certainly going out of use at Colchester in the first half of the fourth century, and neither the London mithraeum nor the great classical sanctuary of Sulis at Bath seem to have been maintained much after about 350.[71] At first sight, it is tempting to attribute this decline to the activities of Christian zealots, for early Christianity was above all an urban phenomenon. But there is reason to doubt this. Paganism and Christianity may have coexisted more harmoniously together at this time than was once believed, at least until the savage prohibitions upon pagan practices that were enacted towards the end of the fourth century.[72] The decay of urban temples should thus be seen as part of a wider process of change, and especially a falling away of private patronage in the towns.

Indeed, the extent to which Christianity was adopted in Britain at this time has been much debated.[73] A Christian writer such as Tertullian (c.AD 160–240), who lived in distant Carthage, could remark that even 'places of the British not approached by the Romans were now made subject to the true Christ'.[74] But the reality is that he was more concerned to demonstrate how the Christian faith had spread to all parts of the Roman empire and, in the absence of corroborative evidence, it is hard to take this allusion to missionary activity at face value. There were British martyrs – although only Alban, Aaron and Julius are known by name – but when they met their dreadful end is not clear. Modern opinion tends to favour the middle of the third century, when the emperors Decius and Valerian instigated terrible persecutions of Christian believers.[75] Certainly, there were British bishops at London, York and Lincoln (or Colchester) by AD 314, as a well-known reference to their participation in the first Church council at Arles shows; there was also what seems to have been a fourth delegation, made up of a priest and a deacon, but from an unnamed place. These could correspond to the four provinces that by now existed in Britain, and at the very least implies that some form of episcopal organisation had come into being in the course of the previous century.[76]

References to the Church in fourth-century Britain are otherwise fairly sparse and incidental, and have little real value as evidence for the popularity of the religion. There are occasional allusions to Britons at other Church councils, and Victricius, Bishop of Rouen, must have visited the diocese in the 390s since 'the bishops, my brothers in the priesthood, called on me to make peace there'.[77] The nature of the dispute is unclear, but it implies an active and numerous clergy. Britain also produced a notable heretic, Pelagius, whose influential views were countered by no less a personage than St Augustine of Hippo. Pelagius preached mainly in the Mediterranean provinces and, between 394 and 410, especially in Rome itself. There is no reason to suppose, therefore, that Pelagianism was a particularly British phenomenon. It did, however, take root in Britain, prompting an appeal by British churchmen for help. As a result, in 429 the bishops of Auxerre and Troyes, Germanus and Lupus, were sent to Britain to counter the heresy, which they did by debate and preaching. They also visited the shrine of Alban, which is generally assumed to have been on the site of the cathedral of St Albans, just outside Verulamium. Here they performed the miraculous cure of the daughter of a man with tribunician authority, suggesting that some decades after the formal demise of Roman control civic administration still existed; it is an important point to which we shall return below.[78]

The material evidence for Christianity in Roman Britain has been subjected to several detailed scrutinies in recent years, and churches have been particularly sought after. That they have proved elusive is not, however, surprising; even in Rome itself, apart from Constantine's three great benefactions (the Lateran, St Peter's and S. Croce in Gerusalemma), the main thrust of church building did not come until the later fourth and early fifth centuries. Moreover, the 'congregational churches' tended to be built on the edges of the city, away from the old pagan centres, while cemetery churches such as St Peter's were constructed, as the law demanded, outside the city walls. Much worship was carried on in 'community centres', essentially ordinary private houses – Pope Damasus I (AD 366–84) turned his mansion into just such a place – and many of these *titulus* churches remained in use for centuries.[79]

It has been doubted whether *titulus* churches were at all common outside major cities such as Rome; but recognisable ecclesiastical buildings are sufficiently sparse in the Romano-British record as to imply that they may be archaeologically very difficult to recognise. Even the well-known so-called church at Silchester is susceptible of other functional interpretations,[80] and was in any case in decay in the later fourth century, while postulated intra-mural churches at Verulamium, Lincoln and Caerwent carry little real conviction on the evidence available. On the other hand, a substantial fourth-century basilican-style building at Culver Street, Colchester,[81] may prove to be a more plausible candidate, and in the same town a fairly certain extra-mural church, with a large cemetery, has been recently excavated at Butt Road.[82] Verulamium, too, has yielded traces of a probable extra-mural church,[83] and late Roman graves beneath the cathedral at St Albans must surely relate in some way to the cult of that martyr.[84] Wells Cathedral may also have originated as a late Roman *martyrium*, and a similar case has been made out for the church of St Martin, a short distance outside the walls of Canterbury.[85] But the most spectacular evidence comes from large-scale excavation on the site of a cemetery at Poundbury, where many of the dead of fourth-century Dorchester (Roman Durnovaria) were buried. Although not yet fully published, the thousand or more graves were mainly of Christian type, containing simple wooden coffins, oriented east-west and mostly with no accompanying objects. One did, however, include a pierced coin of Magnentius, with the chi-rho on the reverse. There were also some more elaborate tombs, with stone or lead coffins, and dotted round the cemetery were a number of mausolea, one

85 High-level view of the restored foundations of the building at Butt Road, Colchester, thought to have been a extra-mural cemetery church of the fourth century.

bearing painted figures on the walls; here, evidently, were the last resting places of some of Durnovaria's richest burghers.[86]

In more rural areas, a convincing instance of a small church with an associated baptistery and font, and a cemetery, has been identified at Icklingham (Suffolk).[87] It is thought to date to the later fourth century, by which time church building may have become more common, as we hinted earlier. The site also yielded two circular lead tanks, bearing chi-rhos. At least fourteen of these lead tanks are now known, half with the Christian monogram, and a role in the baptismal rite seems plausible enough.[88] The nature of the settlement at Icklingham is unclear, although it was of considerable size – at least 15 hectares – and had an important pagan shrine in earlier centuries, to judge from reports and photographs of recently looted finds.[89] It may be that this was an estate church of a sort known in other parts of the empire. Certainly there were villa-owners in fourth-century Britain who manifested their Christian beliefs, as the well-known mosaics from Frampton and Hinton St Mary, both in Dorset, clearly dem- 40 onstrate, as does the extraordinary series of wall-paintings from the house chapel at the villa at Lullingstone.[90] It is particularly intriguing to wonder at the significance of the scenes with trees, plants and houses; dating to the second half of the fourth century, like the famous *orantes* (praying figures), they may portray some biblical narrative now, alas, obscure to us: one day there must be further study of these precious survivals from the early Christian past.

Equally intriguing are the results of a meticulous excavation of the pagan shrine at Uley – as we saw earlier, an important centre of pilgrimage –

which in the late fourth century may have been converted into a church. Such translations were not uncommon in other parts of the empire – the Parthenon in Athens being a spectacular example – and the sequence at Uley (if correctly interpreted) is unlikely to be an isolated example in Britain. Moreover, a decorated Christian casket was found on the site.[91] The dichotomy between Christian and pagan, however rigid in strict theological terms, was in practice likely to have been relatively elastic amongst those who cared little for scholarly debate. There may have been political, financial and social advantage in becoming a Christian; but the old polytheistic beliefs had thousands of years of tradition behind them, which were not easily set aside.

This point is vividly underlined by many of the fourth-century silver hoards. The treasures from Mildenhall, Canterbury, Traprain Law, Corbridge and Hoxne all combine pagan and Christian motifs, while the silver *lanx* found at Risley Park, Derbyshire, though donated by a bishop

86 Three silver spoons from the Thetford treasure, representing the two types of fourth-century spoon in the hoard. Two of the spoons have Bacchic decoration, respectively a Triton blowing his horn and a running panther, and are enhanced with gilding. The third is engraved with a fish. L. of centre spoon 17.7 cm. British Museum.

called Exuperius, is traditionally pagan in its iconography. Even the Water Newton hoard, probably the oldest known Christian church silver, includes numerous votive plaques of pagan type, half of which bear chi- IX rho monograms. The Hoxne treasure, found in 1992, features in its large XII series of silver spoons and ladles both traditional Bacchic decoration and overtly Christian inscriptions, including many chi-rhos and monogram crosses.[92] The notable exception is the Thetford treasure, with its dedications to the rustic god Faunus, best known from ancient literary classics such as Virgil and Horace. Though an attempt has been made to detect Christian symbolism in the Thetford assemblage, the case is not convincing.[93] The dating of Thetford to the 390s or later, when serious persecution of non-Christians began, is confirmed by stylistic parallels with the Hoxne treasure, itself firmly coin-dated to AD 407–8 or later. It remains likely that the Thetford valuables belonged to traditional pagan intellectuals.

The burden of the material evidence, however, is to suggest that the dividing line between Christian and pagan in the fourth century was a tenuous one. A curse tablet to the goddess Sulis from Bath is here of particular interest. It concerns the theft of six silver coins from a purse, perhaps set aside while the owner took the waters: 'whether pagan or Christian ... whether man or woman, whether boy or girl, whether slave or free' it begins, and it is a hitherto unique epigraphic reference to Christianity in Roman Britain. At first sight, it might be taken as a sign of the ubiquity of Christians, but the word itself is misspelt, implying unfamiliarity, and it has been plausibly pointed out that it may be seen as more of 'a tribute to the universal power of Sulis', not as a comment on the prevalence of Christians.[94]

We are moving, therefore, towards a view (not shared by all scholars) that, outside the really intellectual classes, Christianity in Roman Britain took a somewhat diluted form. This may be partly explained by the fact that, as the fourth century wore on, the towns of Roman Britain began to contract and become steadily more depopulated. The matter is hardly without controversy, and is bedevilled by problems of locating and dating the late Roman levels: coins are of crucial importance for establishing a chronology, but their supply was uneven and declined as state-paid officials and soldiers became ever less numerous. Exeter, for example, although demonstrably occupied into the fifth century, appears to have received little or no coin after about AD 380, and it is hard to resist the conclusion that it had become effectively irrelevant as a centre of administration.[95] Some other towns, such as Chichester and Aldborough (Yorkshire), exhibit a similar pattern, although at Cirencester, Caerwent and Verulamium there are comparatively plentiful coin finds from the later fourth century; here the payment of officials and the collection of taxes surely continued. The picture, then, is rather variable, but probably reflects a gradual breakdown in the administration of some parts of the British provinces in the period after about AD 360–70.

There is no shortage of other archaeological evidence to support this. At Exeter, although the forum and basilica appear to have remained in use into the later fourth century, suburbs had been abandoned by about 360 and occupation may have contracted to the central insulae; indeed, one house built there in the mid-fourth century had an adjacent cattle-yard, a far cry from the splendours of earlier times.[96] Similarly, at Cirencester, what is interpreted as a farm was built in the second half of the fourth century, at the Beeches Road site, just inside the walls on the east side of the town. Some insulae, such as XVII and XVIII, may have been completely abandoned by this date and, while the forum and four other insulae appear to have remained in use, the place was certainly much less populous; coin finds remain conspicuously numerous, however, suggesting a continuing role in adminstration, probably as capital of the province of Britannia Prima.[97]

Verulamium also underwent considerable contraction. In the south-eastern part of the town, only three of the twenty-one buildings investigated in the 1930s produced much evidence of late Roman occupation, while three insulae closer to the centre were also partially or wholly abandoned. Around the forum, however, there was new building in three insulae, including a large courtyard house with mosaics, constructed about AD 380; here is unequivocal evidence for a wealthy patrician who continued to patronise urban life. Interestingly, the dumps in the nearby theatre, which signify its abandonment, do not seem on coin evidence to have been made before 388, also suggesting that the town maintained at least some of its functions into late antiquity.[98]

What is clear is that the pattern is not very consistent. While a small town like Mildenhall (ancient Cunetio) in Wiltshire was provided with a new circuit of walls sometime after AD 354–8, at the same time the south gate of Silchester was becoming choked with rubble and the south-east gate was blocked up.[99] At Colchester, the great and imposing Balkerne gate was also closed, and mid-nineteenth-century excavations at the north-east gate found that it had finally been set on fire, with deposits that included many bones of humans and horses, as well as weapons and 'large pieces of burned fatty material . . . of disagreeable import'.[100] Modern archaeological opinion, with its distaste of recognising 'events' in the material record, would probably reject the evidence of this colourful prose; but it is tempting to accept this as a sign of battle (alas, not well dated) and as a hint of the dangers of later fourth-century Britain.

The weight of the remarks, therefore, is to suggest that many of the major and minor towns did survive into the late fourth and early fifth centuries, but with a diminished population and decreased amenities, albeit to a variable degree. Public baths, for example, seem to have been in almost universal desuetude by the middle of the fourth century, those at Canterbury being replaced by wooden buildings erected within the masonry shell.[101] But coins of AD 367–78 and 383–408, stratified in street make-up layers at Winchester and Lincoln, show that some maintenance work was

87 *Above* Two views of the silver-gilt pepper pot in the form of a bust of a late Roman Empress, from the Hoxne treasure. The hollow vessel would have been filled with ground pepper or other spice. The base has a rotating disc that can be closed completely or opened to reveal fine perforations for sprinkling or larger holes for filling. H. 10.3 cm. British Museum.

Right The cast-silver tigress from the Hoxne treasure, her stripes inlaid in black niello. The tigress was originally a handle for a large two-handled decorated silver vase, no other portion of which survived in the treasure. L. 15.9 cm. British Museum.

being carried out in the later fourth century,[102] implying some form of responsible civic administration in these two towns. As so often, the range of evidence is contradictory and difficult to interpret.

London remains a particular enigma. We have already traced its early commercial decline and, as we pointed out earlier, much ink has been spilt over the problem of the so-called 'dark earth' which appears to have enveloped many buildings, public and private, from as early as the second century.[103] Some of this soil undoubtedly relates to agriculture, as has been brilliantly demonstrated at two sites at Colchester;[104] but other deposits may yet yield traces of buildings that remain elusive even to the most sophisticated archaeological techniques. London certainly retained a political and symbolic importance in the fourth century, for it was the seat of the most important officials and was known by the honorific title of Augusta. But it was no longer a city in the Mediterranean sense. Amphitheatre, baths and palaces had been abandoned, and by the late fourth century it had seemingly contracted to the waterfront area, centred on the present Tower of London. Here have been found massive walls 3.2 metres thick, with coins of AD 388–402 in the construction layers, as well as silver ingots of a sort that were sometimes used in the late fourth century to pay officials. At nearby Pudding Lane, a house with heated rooms was rebuilt in or after 367–75, and recently excavated cemeteries to the east of the city walls suggest a relatively large and affluent population, possibly including mercenary soldiers. Given that the western walls of the city lack external towers, unlike the riverside and eastern defences, it may one day prove to be the case that in the late fourth century London was protected by its own, much diminished, circuit.[105]

It is sometimes supposed that this contraction of the towns was accompanied by a rise in the size of the rural population, especially in the villas. Certainly there are country sites which provide evidence of modest expansion in the later fourth century, although they are not numerous. Baths, for example, were built at the villas at Frocester Court and Marshfield (Avon) in about 360–70, and the main villa at Barnsley Park dates from about the same period.[106] Moreover, some mosaic workshops which serviced these sites and were seemingly based upon Durobrivae and Cirencester appear to have functioned until about 370–80.[107] But most villas show signs of decline in the later decades of the fourth century. The main house at Barton Court Farm (Oxfordshire)[108] did not outlast the 370s (although farming continued after that), while at Gadebridge, near Verulamium, most of the buildings were pulled down at about the same time and replaced by stockyards.[109] Only one rectangular building remained, as a cottage-like residence. Similarly, at Latimer (Buckinghamshire), the quite elegant villa of about AD 300 was already decaying by the third quarter of the fourth century and was eventually replaced entirely by timber buildings, four phases of which have been identified.[110] We do not know what prompted the concealment in about 394–5 of a hoard of sixteen gold *solidi* not far from the villa at Rockbourne (Hampshire), but the site itself was already in a state of dilapidation by this time.[111] Occupation was confined to only part of the buildings, mosaics had been torn up, and hearths and areas of burning in various rooms point to a dramatic drop in the quality of life. Rural establishments that were still luxurious in the late fourth and early fifth centuries may yet come to light; but the present indications are that the aristocracy was by this time living in increasingly impoverished and even squalid surroundings.

Fiscal demands, which became increasingly burdensome, must surely have been a factor. Very little coinage seems to have arrived in Britain after about AD 400, and, with a much diminished army and shrinking towns, the supply of high-value money may have been falling well before that. Certainly, finds of coins from the second half of the fourth century are generally much less prolific, and the pointers are towards an economy that was beginning to function much less well.

There were, however, wealthy individuals, who emphasised their status by a display of richly coloured jewellery and other objects: this is well

88 Three gold finger-rings from the Thetford treasure. The ring in the foreground has a Pan-like head, probably representing Faunus, set with garnets. The large ring on the left, set with an amethyst and alternating emeralds and garnets, has dolphin-shaped shoulders, and the third ring depicts two woodpeckers supporting a cup set with green glass. British Museum.

89 Two gold rings of the late fourth century, from Brentwood, Essex (left), and Suffolk. Both rings are engraved with the Christian monogram, but the Suffolk ring has the additional motif of a bird pecking fruit from a branch: this is a common scene in Christian art. British Museum.

illustrated by the late Roman Thetford and Canterbury treasures and by crossbow brooches.[112] They recall the way in which the Celtic élite of the late Iron Age had also sought to emphasise its power and position more by the possession of fine metalwork, such as gold torcs and highly decorated weaponry, than through elaborate architecture. It is as though these late fourth-century aristocrats were deliberately harking back to the traditions of pre-conquest days, while their buildings crumbled around them.

These people will still have emphatically regarded themselves as Romans; but the reality is that, by the end of the fourth century, Rome had scant authority in the diocese. In 406–7, no fewer than three successive usurpers for the purple were set up by the army in Britain. One, Gratian, was a *municeps tyrannus*, some sort of urban aristocrat, who ruled for a mere four months; but the last, Constantine III, was an ordinary soldier who is recorded as removing the last troops from Britain and who suffered ultimate defeat in 411, at Arles in southern France. Northern Gaul had effectively been lost in the aftermath of the great Germanic invasion of AD 406, and Zosimus, writing soon after 498, tells us that in 409 'the people of Britain . . . liberated the cities from threatening barbarians . . . and threw out the Roman officials'. The following year, he relates in a famous passage, the emperor Honorius told the British cities 'to look to their own defence'. Roman Britain had, at least in a legal sense, finally come to an end.[113]

What was to happen subsequently has become one of those minefields of scholarly contention, upon which we shall touch only lightly. The essence of the problem lies in the difficulty, so often encountered in this book, of reconciling the testimony of the written word with the material evidence. What *was* the scale, nature and chronology of the Anglo-Saxon takeover? What *did* happen to the culture of Roman Britain that, a century before, had flourished so conspicuously? And how *did* the people respond to the new world that was emerging around them?[114]

It is sometimes argued that Anglo-Saxons, serving as mercenaries, were already present in fourth-century Britain, bolstering up the by now weak Roman army. This view is based mainly on the occurrence, especially in towns and villas, of distinctive types of belt-fittings. However, it is now recognised that these were insignia worn both by soldiers and by civil servants at this time, and their so-called 'Germanic' characteristics are in fact typical of late Roman art generally. There are graves in the Lankhills cemetery at Winchester which from about AD 350 contain these belts, together with crossbow brooches, sometimes a knife and an offering. Best paralleled in Hungary and Bavaria, these may be burials of *foederati* troops. Anglo-Saxons are, however, elusive, apart from a woman from Dorchester-on-Thames, buried with an early Germanic brooch, and an interment from just outside the east walls of London containing a pair of Saxon-style *tutulus* brooches and a comb; it is likely to date to the beginning of the fifth century.[115]

Bede placed the *adventus Saxonicum* in the year 449, and the archae-

90 Silver brooch of crossbow type with inlaid niello decoration. Such brooches were perhaps worn as symbols of authority. Fourth century AD. British Museum.

ological evidence is in broad agreement with that. There is in effect a gap between the last whispers of Roman Britain and the establishment of the new Germanic kingdoms in the south and east. Thus at Canterbury the first structures associated with Saxon material date to about 450–75, and were dug into deposits of 'dark earth' which close the latest Roman levels; a twenty-year gap is inferred.[116] The break with *romanitas* was in other ways equally decisive. Unlike many other parts of the western empire, Roman language, law and institutions did not survive within the areas conquered by the Angles, Saxons, and Jutes. Two factors are probably of particular importance. One is the early decline of Romano-British centres, urban and rural, and, very probably, of the size of the population. In times of difficulty, families tend to reduce their size, and it would be surprising if this were not the case in the dark days which seem to have attended the last decades of Roman Britain.

The second important factor was the Church. In other regions, such as Italy and southern Gaul, leading ecclesiastics played an important role in reconciling *romanitas* with the new Germanic masters; Latin, educational systems, the law and institutions, not least the Church itself survived, albeit in modified forms. In Britain, the towns were contracting and crumbling at precisely the time when elsewhere churches were being built in considerable numbers in and around cities. It is telling that it was not a British but a Gallic bishop, Germanus, who achieved a famous victory over the Saxons and Picts by gathering together a group of Romano-Britons and baptising its members, all of whom then shouted 'Alleluia'. He then returned to Gaul, leaving, one suspects, a rather feeble ecclesiastical organisation.

A much diminished Romano-British population may help to explain its more or less total assimilation into the Anglo-Saxon kingdoms of southern and eastern Britain. Pockets of Romano-Britons undoubtedly survived. For example, the Queenford Farm cemetery, outside Dorchester-on-Thames, was in use from the late Roman period into the sixth century but shows little sign of Anglo-Saxon influence, especially in terms of grave goods.[117] Similarly, it has been suggested that a small group of inhumations amongst the enormous number of Saxon cremations at Spong Hill, in Norfolk, belong to former Romano-Britons.[118] But most of the population accepted cultural changes which had, in any case, been developing for a generation or more before the final demise of the Roman provinces; conspicuous personal ornament, for instance, was as important in early Anglo-Saxon times as it had been in late Roman Britain.

In the areas which escaped early Anglo-Saxon domination, a culture that has been termed 'sub-Roman' emerged. In a few places, settlement may have continued to focus upon the old towns: the results of recent excavations certainly allow for this possibility at Carlisle,[119] while the well-known work at Wroxeter has disclosed a large wooden building, overlying the basilica and somewhat resembling a winged corridor villa, surrounded by ancillary structures, also in timber.[120] It is more likely to be the residence of some fifth-century potentate, and it is intriguing that a tombstone dating to the end of that century records the resting place of an Irishman called Cunorix; found just outside the town wall, it is written in Latin, which, although somewhat debased, nevertheless shows that some literacy (and thus education) still survived.[121]

Most forts seem to have been abandoned, although the headquarters building at York remained standing and was perhaps inhabited; and the discovery of a large wooden hall, constructed on a granary at Birdoswald, may also attest a sub-Roman community.[122] As in many other parts of the western Roman world, building in wood seems to have become the preferred technique in this period (although reusable stone must have been available in abundance), reflecting the long Romano-British ancestry of such structures. At Poundbury, for example, the late Roman cemetery, somewhat curiously, was overlain by a settlement of post-built houses, together with a threshing area and grain driers. The material culture, even the pottery, was poor (although distinct from contemporary Anglo-Saxon domestic assemblages), as it generally is on other sub-Romano-British sites.[123] This much is clear in particular from the excavation of hillforts, a considerable number of which are turning out to have a major post-Roman phase of occupation. Pride of place must go to the work at South Cadbury in Somerset (a site with intriguing Arthurian associations), where it has been shown that the defences, 1.2 km long, of this old Iron-Age centre were elaborately refurbished in the second half of the fifth century.[124] There was a substantial hall, again built in wood; and a few fragments of wine amphorae from the East Mediterranean and red-slipped tableware made in what is now Tunisia hint at sporadic contact with the outside world. Despite the overall poverty of the finds, this was fairly certainly the base of someone powerful and relatively well-to-do, and it is plausible (if totally unprovable) to see him as a descendant of one of the late Roman aristocrats.

The overall number of hillforts reoccupied in late antiquity, especially in western Britain, is considerable.[125] Although the buildings were generally modest and the range of finds limited, it is surely here that one finds the heirs of the leading classes of Roman Britain. Sites such as Tintagel in Cornwall are comparatively rich in imported pottery, an evident mark of their higher status.[126] Fifth-century churches, on the other hand, have so far proved elusive, although some will surely one day come to light. For Christianity certainly survived in the Celtic west, represented by British monks like Gildas; an ecclesiastic, he wrote in about 540 about the ruin and conquest of Britain (*De Excidio et Conquestu Britanniae*). Gildas' primary concern was to castigate the British rulers and clergy for their sinful attitudes and behaviour; already punished by the victories of the Saxons, they would suffer further if they did not repent of their wicked ways. Alaric's sack of Rome in AD 410 had brought a similar response from churchmen of the time, as Gildas was doubtless well aware.

By Gildas' day, however, most other parts of the former western empire were also beginning to lapse into economic and material decline. The Byzantine reconquest of parts of Italy and North Africa, in the second quarter of the sixth century, brought about not increased prosperity but profound disruption and decay. It was the true beginning of a Dark Age, which affected town and country, prince and pauper alike. That it began so much earlier in Britain is not a matter of simple explanation; but a root cause was probably that, for most of the population, Romanisation was rarely more than skin-deep. Britain gained a remarkable amount from Rome during its time as a province, but this is merely one strand in the complex weave that makes up the nation today.

FURTHER READING

As a field of study, the fourth and fifth centuries are currently as fashionable as they are controversial, a matter highlighted in two excellent recent studies, A.S. Esmonde-Cleary, *The Ending of Roman Britain* (1989) and now N. Higham, *Rome, Britain and the Anglo-Saxons* (1992). For military matters, there is much of importance in D.A. Welsby, *The Roman Military Defence of the British Provinces in its Later Phases* (1982), and in S.T. James, 'Britain and the late Roman army', in T.F.C. Blagg and A.C. King (eds), *Military and Civilian in Roman Britain* (1984), 161–86; see also V.A. Maxfield (ed.), *The Saxon Shore* (1989), and V.A. Maxfield and M.J. Dobson (eds), *Roman Frontier Studies 1989* (1991). On the fate of the towns, the reader should compare R. Reece, 'Town and country: the end of Roman Britain', *World Archaeology* 12 (1980), 77–92, with S.S. Frere, *Britannia* (3rd edn, 1987), chapters 15 and 16. Much is emerging from urban excavations, as indicated in the text and notes: N. Holbrook and P.T. Bidwell, *Roman Finds from Exeter* (1991) provides a particularly sensitive analysis. For religion, and especially Christianity, C. Thomas, *Christianity in Roman Britain to AD 500* (1981) is fundamental, supplemented by R. Morris's delightful *Churches in the Landscape* (1989) and now (somewhat controversially) by D. Watts, *Christians and Pagans in Roman Britain* (1991), and by A. Woodward, *Shrines and Sacrifice* (1992). For the sub-Roman period the reader can now be referred to Higham's book, cited above.

Gazetteer of sites to visit

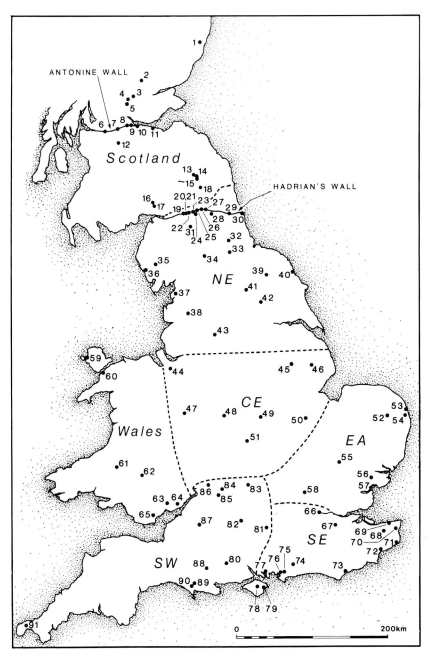

26 Carrawburgh
27 Chesters
28 Corbridge
29 Benwell
30 South Shields
31 Whitley Castle
32 Binchester
33 Piercebridge
34 Rey Cross
35 Hardknot
36 Ravenglass
37 Lancaster
38 Ribchester
39 Wheeldale Moor
40 Scarborough
41 Aldborough
42 York
43 Castleshaw
44 Chester
45 Lincoln
46 Horncastle
47 Wroxeter
48 Wall
49 Leicester
50 Orton Longueville
51 Baginton, The Lunt
52 Caistor St Edmund
53 Caister by Yarmouth
54 Burgh Castle
55 Bartlow Hills
56 Colchester
57 Mersea Island
58 Verulamium, St Albans
59 Caer Gybi
60 Caernarvon
61 Dolaucothi
62 Brecon Gaer
63 Caerleon
64 Caerwent
65 Cardiff
66 London
67 Lullingstone
68 Canterbury
69 Reculver
70 Richborough
71 Dover
72 Lympne
73 Pevensey
74 Bignor
75 Chichester
76 Fishbourne
77 Portchester
78 Newport
79 Brading
80 Rockbourne
81 Silchester
82 Littlecote
83 North Leigh
84 Chedworth
85 Cirencester
86 Great Witcombe
87 Bath
88 Hod Hill
89 Dorchester
90 Maiden Castle
91 Chysauster

KEY

1 Raedykes
2 Inchtuthil
3 Parkneuk
4 Kaims Castle
5 Ardoch
6 Bearsden
7 Bar Hill

8 Rough Castle
9 Watling Lodge
10 Kinneil
11 Cramond
12 Bothwellhaugh
13 Pennymuir
14 Woden Law
15 Chew Green
16 Burnswark

17 Birrens
18 High Rochester
19 Birdoswald
20 Willowford
21 Poltross Burn
22 Cawfields
23 Peel Crag
24 Chesterholm (Vindolanda)
25 Housesteads

The visitor to Roman sites in Britain is extremely well catered for in terms both of maps and guides. The Ordnance Survey map of Roman Britain is now in its fifth edition (1991), and is presented as an overlay upon lightly printed modern roads and places; although nothing like as attractive, informative and clear as its predecessor (1978), it does have some practical advantages for the traveller. Also very useful are the 1:50,000 series of Ordnance Survey maps, which often mark a good deal of archaeological material, and are cartographically excellent.

Amongst the guides, R.J.A. Wilson's *A Guide to the Roman Remains in Britain* (3rd edition, London 1988; new edition in preparation) is first class, and for Scotland is extended by L.J.F. Keppie's similarly excellent *Scotland's Roman Remains* (Edinburgh 1986). P. Ottaway has provided an attractive *Traveller's Guide to Roman Britain* (London 1987) for the armchair reader, and there are very detailed guides to both Hadrian's Wall (J. Collingwood Bruce, *Handbook to the Roman Wall*, 13th edition, revised C.M. Daniels, Newcastle 1978) and the Antonine Wall (Anne S. Robertson, *The Antonine Wall*, 4th edition, revised L.J.F. Keppie, Glasgow Archaeological Society 1990). The second edition of the Ordnance Survey map of Hadrian's Wall (1972) is excellent; the recent third edition less so.

The sites listed below are amongst the more spectacular and accessible; the guides cited above list many more, although generally of lesser or more specialist interest. A list of the major museum collections is also provided; many are in towns first settled in Roman times, but with few conspicuous above-ground traces today.
Note: the number beside each site refers to the map; where known, the ancient name of the place has also been listed, in parenthesis.

SCOTLAND
5 Ardoch (Alauna): fort
17 Birrens (Blatobulgium): fort
12 Bothwellhaugh: fort bath-house
16 Burnswark: hillfort, siege camps, catapult mounds
11 Cramond: fort, 'Eagle Rock' (figures of Mercury)
2 Inchtuthil: earthworks of legionary fortress
4 Kaims Castle: fortlet
3 Parkneuk: watch-tower
13 Pennymuir: camps
1 Raedykes: marching camp
14 Woden Law: hillfort and siege works

ANTONINE WALL
7 Bar Hill: headquarters, baths of fort
6 Bearsden: bath-house
10 Kinneil: fortlet
8 Rough Castle: fort, Wall ditch, pits (*lilia*)
9 Watling Lodge: Wall ditch

NORTHERN ENGLAND (NE)
41 Aldborough (Isurium Brigantum): walls, mosaics
32 Binchester (Vinovia): fort, headquarters
43 Castleshaw (?Rigodunum): fort
15 Chew Green: military camps
35 Hardknot (Mediobogdum): fort, baths, parade ground
18 High Rochester (Bremenium): fort, Dere Street, tombs
37 Lancaster: military bath-house
33 Piercebridge: fort, bridge
36 Ravenglass (Glannoventa): military bath-house
34 Rey Cross: marching camp
38 Ribchester (Bremetenacum Veteranorum): military bath-house
40 Scarborough: signal station
39 Wheeldale Moor: road
31 Whitley Castle (Epiacum)
42 York (Eboracum): walls, tower, Minster excavations

HADRIAN'S WALL, AND ENVIRONS
29 Benwell (Condercum): temple of Antenociticus, Vallum
19 Birdoswald (?Banna): fort walls, gates, granaries
26 Carrawburgh (Brocolitia): temple of Mithras, Coventina's well
22 Cawfields: milecastle
24 Chesterholm (Vindolanda): fort, *vicus*
27 Chesters (Cilurnum): fort, bath-house, bridge abutment
28 Corbridge (?Coriosopitum): fort, town
25 Housesteads (Vercovicium): fort, *vicus*, the Wall
23 Peel Crag: the Wall, milecastle
21 Poltross Burn: milecastle
30 South Shields (Arbeia): fort, reconstructed gate
20 Willowford: bridge

CENTRAL ENGLAND (CE)
51 Baginton, The Lunt: partially reconstructed fort
44 Chester (Deva): legionary amphitheatre
46 Horncastle (?Bannovalium): walls
49 Leicester (Ratae ?Corieltauvorum): baths (Jewry Wall)

45 Lincoln (Lindum): gates, especially Newport Arch, walls
50 Orton Longueville: villa
48 Wall (Letocetum): baths, ?inn (*mansio*)
47 Wroxeter (Viriconium Cornoviorum): baths

EAST ANGLIA (EA)
55 Bartlow Hills: burial mounds
54 Burgh Castle (Gariannum): Saxon Shore fort (walls)
53 Caister by Yarmouth: walls, house
52 Caistor St Edmund (Venta Icenorum): town walls
56 Colchester (Camulodunum): temple of Claudius (museum basement), walls, Balkerne Gate
57 Mersea Island: burial mound
58 Verulamium: walls, houses, theatre

WALES
62 Brecon Gaer (?Cicucium): fort gate
59 Caer Gybi, Holyhead: late fort walls
63 Caerleon (Isca): legionary fortress, baths and amphitheatre
60 Caernarvon (Segontium): fort
64 Caerwent (Venta Silurum): town walls, houses, temple, basilica
65 Cardiff: gate
61 Dolaucothi: gold mines

SOUTH-EAST ENGLAND (SE)
74 Bignor: villa
68 Canterbury (Durovernum Cantiacorum): house, St Martin's Church
75 Chichester (Noviomagnus Regn(i)orum): Cogidumnus inscription
71 Dover (Dubris): house with paintings, lighthouse
76 Fishbourne: palace
66 London (Londinium): walls, temple of Mithras
67 Lullingstone: villa
72 Lympne (Portus Lemanis): Saxon Shore fort (walls, gate)
73 Pevensey (Anderitum): Saxon Shore fort (walls)
77 Portchester (?Portus Ardaoni): Saxon Shore fort (walls)
69 Reculver (Regulbium): Saxon Shore fort (walls, gate)
70 Richborough (Rutupiae): Saxon Shore fort, and earlier base (walls etc.)

SOUTH-WEST ENGLAND (SW)
87 Bath (Aquae Sulis): baths, temple
79 Brading: villa
84 Chedworth: villa
91 Chysauster: native settlement
85 Cirencester (Corinium Dobunnorum): amphitheatre, walls
89 Dorchester (Durnovaria): amphitheatre, house
86 Great Witcombe: villa
88 Hod Hill (?Dunum): hillfort, Roman fort
82 Littlecote: villa
90 Maiden Castle: hillfort, Romano-Celtic temple and house
78 Newport: villa
83 North Leigh: villa
80 Rockbourne: villa
81 Silchester (Calleva Atrebatum): walls, amphitheatre

MAIN MUSEUM COLLECTIONS
Bath, Caerleon, Cambridge (Archaeology and Ethnology), Canterbury, Cardiff, Carlisle, Chester, Chesters, Chichester, Cirencester, Colchester, Dorchester (Dorset), Edinburgh (Royal Museum of Scotland), Glasgow (Hunterian), Gloucester, Hull, Leicester (Jewry Wall), Lincoln, London (British Museum, Museum of London), Newcastle (Museum of Antiquities), Newport (Gwent), Norwich, Oxford (Ashmolean), Reading, Ribchester, St Albans (Verulamium), Taunton, Vindolanda, Winchester, York (Yorkshire Museum).

Notes

The study of Roman Britain has generated so vast a literature that many works have been cited here in shortened form, and have not been included in the general bibliography; these comprise mainly articles of more specialist interest.

The following abbreviations have been used:

Ant. J.	Antiquaries Journal
Arch. Ael.	Archaeologia Aeliana
Arch. J.	Archaeological Journal
CIL	Corpus Inscriptionum Latinarum
CSIR	Corpus Signorum Imperii Romani I (Great Britain)
CW	Transactions of the Cumberland and Westmorland Archaeological and Antiquarian Society
Herts. Arch.	Hertfordshire Archaeology
JBAA	Journal of the British Archaeological Association
JRA	Journal of Roman Archaeology
JRS	Journal of Roman Studies
Northants. Arch.	Northamptonshire Archaeology
OJA	Oxford Journal of Archaeology
PPS	Proceedings of the Prehistoric Society
PSAS	Proceedings of the Society of Antiquaries of Scotland
RB Guide	Guide to the Antiquities of Roman Britain (3rd edn, 1964), by J.W. Brailsford
RCHM	Royal Commission on Historical Monuments
RIB	Roman Inscriptions of Britain. Vol. I (ed. R.G. Collingwood and R.P. Wright, Oxford 1965); vol. II, 1 (ed. S.S. Frere, M. Roxan and R.S.O. Tomlin, Gloucester 1990); vol. II, 2 (ed. S.S. Frere and R.S.O. Tomlin, Stroud 1991).
SHA	Scriptores Historiae Augustae (Loeb edition)
TBGAS	Transactions of the Bristol and Gloucestershire Archaeological Society
TLMAS	Transactions of the London and Middlesex Archaeological Society
VCH	Victoria County History

Introduction

1. T.D. Kendrick and C.F.C. Hawkes, *Archaeology in England and Wales 1914–31* (1932), 209.
2. *JRS* 23 (1933), 101.
3. *Proc. British Academy* 1943, 476.
4. Richmond 1963, 8.

5. Wheeler and Wheeler 1936; cf. generally Potter 1986 and now R. Hingley in *Scottish Archaeological Forum* 8 (1991), 90–101; and P.W.M. Freeman's counter-reply in *ibid.*, 102–4.
6. Pitts and St Joseph 1985.
7. Pottery production centres: Swan 1984.
8. *Antiquity* 58 (1984), 178.
9. *Antiquity* 64 (1990), 954.
10. *Antiquity* 59 (1985), 120.
11. Stead 1991b.

1 Britain before AD 43

1. Solinus, *Collectanea rerum memorabilium* 22, 1–12.
2. Cassius Dio 76, 12, as reported by the eleventh-century writer Xiphilinus, in *Epitome Dionis Nicaeensis*, 321–2.
3. Pliny, *Nat. Hist.* 7, 197.
4. Herodotus, *Histories* 3, 115.
5. Hawkes 1977.
6. Herodotus, *Histories* 4, 152.
7. K. Muckelroy, *PPS* 47 (1981), 275–98.
8. Polybius 34, 10, 6; Strabo 4, 2, 1.
9. For land-transport costs, cf. Duncan-Jones 1982, 366–9; Greene 1986, 39f.
10. Strabo 3, 5, 10–11.
11. Strabo 3, 5, 11; see Rivet and Smith 1979, 43.
12. Diodorus Siculus, *Hist.* 5, 22. For the site of Ictis see B. Cunliffe, *OJA* 2 (1983), 123–6; C.F.C. Hawkes, *OJA* 3 (1984), 211–34; and now B. Cunliffe, *Mount Batten, Plymouth. A Prehistoric and Roman Port* (Oxford 1988).
13. C.F.C. Hawkes, *Antiquity* 33 (1959), 170–82.
14. Caesar, *De Bello Gallico* 5, 12 (henceforth cited as Caesar).
15. A. Birchall, *PPS* 31 (1965), 241–367; Cunliffe 1990.
16. Influential early papers include F.R. Hodson, 'Reflections on the ABC of the British Iron Age,' *Antiquity* 34 (1960), 138–40; *idem*, 'Cultural groupings within the British pre-Roman Iron Age', *PPS* 30 (1964), 99–110; and J.G.D. Clark, 'The invasion hypothesis in British archaeology', *Antiquity* 40 (1966), 172–89.
17. D.G. Coombes and F.H. Thompson, *Derbyshire Arch. J.* 99 (1979), 7–51.
18. Strabo 4, 4, 2.
19. Wheeler 1943; see now Sharples 1991.
20. Alcock 1972; Cunliffe 1984b.
21. R. Palmer, *Danebury, an Aerial Photographic Interpretation of its Environs* (RCHM 1984).
22. Celtic society: Ross 1967, 1986; Rankin 1987. Metalwork: Megaw and Megaw 1986, 1989; Stead 1985.
23. Strabo 4, 4, 4; Caesar 1, 1.
24. P.A. Brunt, *Italian Manpower* (Oxford 1971), 121f.
25. I.M. Stead *et al.*, *Lindow Man: the Body in the Bog* (London 1986).
26. R. Whimster, *Burial Practices in Iron Age Britain* (Oxford 1981); Stead 1979, 1991a.
27. J.S. Dent, *Antiquity* 59 (1985), 85–92.
28. Stead 1991a.
29. Caesar 1, 1; Polybius 2, 28–9; see also J.S. Dent, *Arch. J.* 140 (1983), 120–8.
30. Powell 1980, 18–21.
31. Ptolemy 2, 3, 10; Rivet and Smith 1979, 435–6.
32. E.g. Haselgrove, *Arch. J.* 143 (1986), 364f.; more generally Collis 1984, 15f.
33. R. Palmer, *op. cit.* (n. 21).
34. G. Bersu, *PPS* 6 (1940), 30–111.
35. Wainwright 1979.
36. M. Spratling in Wainwright 1979. J. Foster, *The Iron Age Moulds from Gussage All Saints* (London 1980).
37. Cf. for example the very limited evidence for metalworking

at the Iron-Age settlement at Winnall Down (P. Fasham, *The Prehistoric Settlement at Winnall Down near Winchester* (Winchester 1985), 92).

38. F. Pryor, *Excavations at Fengate, Peterborough: Fourth Report* (1984); P.J. Drury, *Excavations at Little Waltham* (1978).
39. D.L. Clarke, *Models in Archaeology* (London 1972), 801–70.
40. See B. Cunliffe and D. Miles (eds), *Aspects of the Iron Age in Central and Southern Britain* (Oxford 1984).
41. E.g. G. Lambrick and M. Robinson, *Iron Age and Roman Riverside Settlements at Farmoor, Oxfordshire* (London 1979).
42. Lamb 1981; T. Darvill, *The Archaeology of the Uplands* (London 1986).
43. Diodorus Siculus 5, 26, 3. Cf. Cunliffe 1988.
44. A Fitzpatrick, *OJA* 4 (1985), 305–40; D.P.S. Peacock in Macready and Thompson 1984, 37–42; C. Haselgrove in Blagg and King 1984, 27.
45. Cunliffe 1987; D.P.S. Peacock in M. Jesson and D. Hills (eds), *The Iron Age and its Hillforts* (Southampton 1971), 161–88; Cunliffe 1987 (Hengistbury).
46. Exports: Strabo 4, 5, 2; Delos: Strabo 14, 5, 2.
47. L. Langouët in Macready and Thompson 1984, 67–77.
48. R.E.M. Wheeler and K.S. Richardson, *The Hillforts of Northern France* (Oxford 1957).
49. Caesar 3, 8; Strabo 4, 5, 1.
50. Cunliffe 1981, 34–5; *idem., OJA* 1 (1982), 39–68.
51. Stead and Rigby 1986, 51.
52. Stead 1967.
53. Cunliffe in Macready and Thompson 1984, 19; Caesar 5, 12.
54. Frontinus, *Strategemata* 2, 13, 11.
55. Fulford 1987.
56. *Res Gestae* 32.
57. R. Hobbs, *British Iron Age Coins in the British Museum* (London 1996), nos 765–6; C.E.A. Cheesman, 'Tincomarus Commi Filius', *Britannia* 29 (1998), 309–14.
58. *Res Gestae* 3.
59. Strabo 4, 5, 3.
60. Cassius Dio 53, 22.
61. *Res Gestae* 32.
62. Partridge 1981; Potter and Trow 1988.
63. *Britannia* 13 (1982), 325–6.
64. Tacitus, *Annals* 2, 62.
65. G. Alföldy, *Noricum* (1974), 44f.
66. Suetonius, *Caligula* 44, 2; Van Arsdell (*op. cit.*, n.57), 361f.
67. C. Saunders, *Herts. Arch.* 8 (1980–82), 33f.
68. Frere 1983, 3f.
69. Stead and Rigby 1989.
70. Rodwell 1976; Niblett 1985; Dunnett 1975.
71. Foster 1986.
72. Barton Court Farm: Miles 1986.
73. Rodwell 1976; Collins and Rodwell in Cunliffe 1981, 53f.
74. D.F. Allen, *Britannia* 6 (1975), 1–19.
75. Dio 60, 20, 2 (who, however, says 'Bodunni' rather than 'Dobunni').
76. R.S.O. Tomlin (*Ant. J.* 63 (1983), 353–5) argues that the reading for 'Coritani' is Corieltauvi'; Todd (1991, 20) still prefers 'Coritani'.
77. D.F. Allen, *Britannia* 1 (1970), 1–33.
78. The events of AD 47: Tacitus, *Annals* 12, 31. Cenimagni: Caesar 5, 21.
79. R.R. Clarke, *PPS* 20 (1954), 27–86; Stead 1991b.
80. Stead 1985.
81. Ph. Leveau, *Caesarea de Maurétanie* (Rome 1984).

3. Published in Haverfield and Macdonald 1924, 75.
4. Haverfield 1912; Collingwood 1930; Collingwood and Myres 1937; Rivet 1958; Frere 1987.
5. E.g. Hanson 1987.
6. Suetonius, *Div. Claud.* 17; see also Duncan-Jones 1990, 30f.
7. For the possibility that the VIIIth legion was also involved, cf. *Britannia* 2 (1971), 149f.
8. Cunliffe 1968, 232f.
9. Hind 1989.
10. *CIL* vi, 920.
11. Erim 1982.
12. Crummy 1977; 1984, 3f., 94–8.
13. Braund 1984.
14. Frere and St Joseph 1974.
15. Dannell and Wild 1987.
16. Maxfield 1986, 65f.; Coulston 1988; Lepper and Frere 1988, 266–8.
17. Maxfield 1989.
18. Webster 1958.
19. Tacitus, *Ann.* 12, 39.
20. Zonaras 2, 7.
21. Wheeler 1954; Haselgrove and Turnbull 1987; M. MacGregor, *PPS* 28 (1962), 17–57; and now Haselgrove *et al.*, *Arch. J.* 147 (1990), 1f.
22. Tacitus, *Ann.* 12, 39.
23. Tacitus, *Ann.* 12, 32.
24. Crummy 1984, 1988.
25. Niblett 1985.
26. Hawkes and Hull 1947, 38; Niblett 1985.
27. Hull 1958, 259–70; R. Dunnett, *Britannia* 2 (1971), 27–47.
28. Richmond 1968.
29. Frere and St Joseph 1983, 89; Maxfield 1986, 65.
30. M. Todd, *Ant. J.* 64 (1984), 251–68; Todd 1985.
31. Wheeler 1943, 62.
32. See Sharples 1991, 125 for further discussion.
33. *Antiquity* 53 (1979), 31–8.
34. Suetonius, *Div. Vesp.* 4.
35. Elkington 1976; see also G. Clement Whittick, *Britannia* 13 (1982), 113–23, for (unconvincing) arguments for not accepting the date.
36. R. Brill and J. Wampler, *American J. Arch.* 71 (1967), 63–77.
37. Henderson 1988; Holbrook and Bidwell 1991; Cunliffe in Down 1978, 177–83; *Britannia* 13 (1982), 384 (for Lake); R. Bradley, *Archaeologia* 105 (1976), 1–97 (for Dorchester).
38. Bidwell 1979; Henderson 1988.
39. Webster 1988.
40. Hurst 1988 and references.
41. Manning 1981, 1989; *Britannia* 19 (1988), 423–5; D.R. Evans and V.M. Metcalf, *Britannia* 20 (1989), 23–68.
42. *Current Arch.* 113 (1989), 184–6.
43. Frere 1987.
44. Tacitus, *Ann.* 14, 30.
45. Crummy 1988, fig. 2.2 (p. 26); Classicianus: *RIB* 12.
46. M.J. Jones 1988, 146.
47. Tacitus, *Hist.* 1, 60; *Agric.* 16.
48. Cf. generally Hanson and Campbell 1986.
49. I. Caruana, *Minerva* 1, no. 7 (1990).
50. H. Mattingly, *Tacitus on Britain and Germany* (London 1948), 13.
51. Cf. J.K. St Joseph, *Britannia* 9 (1978), 271–87; Hanson 1987, 134–7.
52. C.M. Daniels, *Arch. Ael.* 5, 16 (1988), 260, reviewing Hanson 1987. See also Breeze 1982, 53.
53. W.S. Hanson *et al.*, *Arch. Ael.* 5, 7 (1979), 1–98.
54. Hanson and Yeoman 1988.
55. Tacitus, *Agric.* 24.
56. Frere and Wilkes 1989; Pitts and St Joseph 1985.
57. Maxwell 1984; Maxwell and Wilson 1987.
58. Tacitus, *Hist.* 1, 2. See also Hobley 1989 on the date of the withdrawal, and now Breeze 1991, 40.

2 Conquest and Occupation

1. R. Reece, *Arch. J.* 139 (1982), 456.
2. Frere 1987, Todd 1989, Millett 1990.

59. G.D.B. Jones 1982; Higham and Jones 1985; and now Jones 1991.
60. Bishop and Dore 1989.
61. Bowman and Thomas 1983, 1986, 1987; Bowman, Thomas and Adams 1990; Bowman and Thomas 1991.
62. Bowman and Thomas 1994, no. 291.
63. Bowman, Thomas and Adams 1990.
64. Cf. Wacher 1971, 170 for evidence of military tanning at Catterick.
65. Bowman and Thomas 1983, tab. 22 (p. 105f.).
66. *Britannia* 19 (1988), 496.
67. *SHA Hadrian* 5, 2; see Frere 1987, 109, for signs of warfare in Britain in the Trajanic period.
68. *RIB* 1051.
69. Frere 1987, 122; Birley 1981, 220f.
70. Birley 1981, 237f.
71. *Current Arch.* 108 (1988), 14–17; see also now Crow 1991.
72. G.D.B. Jones 1976, 1982; Bellhouse 1989.
73. Pending a definitive report, usefully summarised in Daniels 1989, 77–83.
74. Dobson 1986. See also G.H. Donaldson, *Arch. Ael.* 5, 16 (1988), 125–37.
75. Robertson 1990. See also L.J.F. Keppie, *Scotland's Roman Remains* (Edinburgh 1986) and G.S. Maxwell, *The Romans in Scotland* (Edinburgh 1989).
76. Aristides, *To Rome*.
77. *RIB* 1147, 1148.
78. *RIB* 1276.
79. J.P. Gillam, *Scottish Archaeological Forum* 7 (1978), 51–6.
80. D.J. Breeze in *Studies in Scottish Antiquity* (ed. D. Breeze, Edinburgh 1984), 32–68; B.A. Knights *et al.*, *J. Arch. Science* 10 (1983), 139–53.
81. Frere and Wilkes 1989.
82. *RIB* 1389.
83. *RIB* 1322. This inscription is highly controversial. Cf. J.J. Wilkes, *Zeitschrift für Papyrologie und Epigraphik* 59 (1985), 291–5; S.S. Frere, *Britannia* 17 (1986), 329; M. Speidel, *Britannia* 18 (1987), 233–7.
84. Dio 76, 12, 1. Cf. F. Millar, *A Study of Cassius Dio* (Oxford 1964), 28–40.
85. The literature is voluminous. Breeze (1982), *inter alii*, supports the conventional 'low' chronology of *c.*163; Mann (1988) argues compellingly for a 'high' chronology; Daniels (1991) now prefers 168–9. See also Breeze and Dobson 1987, 124–7; A. Robertson, *PSAS* 113 (1983), 425–6.
86. *SHA Severus*, 18.
87. R.P. Wright, *Britannia* 5 (1974), 289–92; Frere 1987, 152f.
88. P. Bidwell in Daniels 1989, 83–9.
89. James 1984; Breeze and Dobson 1987, 13f.; Frere 1987, 173 (and generally for Britain in the third century).
90. R. Brulet in Maxfield 1989, 65f.
91. J.C. Mann in Maxfield 1989, 5, for hints of naval engagements in this period.
92. Williams 1991.
93. Maxfield 1989 is an excellent recent, and up-to-date, review, with full references.
94. *SHA Probus* 13, 8; 14, 5–7; Johnson 1983, 249f.
95. Frere 1987, 243.
96. Potter 1979.
97. *RIB* 605.

3 The Romanisation of Town and Country

1. Eumenius, *Panegyric to Constantius* 11, 1.
2. Haverfield and MacDonald 1924, 265; for mosaics Neal 1981, 17; Smith (1969, 72) suggests a much lower total of about 400.
3. Ph. Leveau, *Caesarea de Maurétanie* (Rome 1984), 79.
4. Millett and Graham 1986, 154.
5. Higham and Jones 1985, 78.
6. Phillips 1970, 71.
7. C.C. Taylor in P.J. Fowler (ed.), *Recent Work in Rural Archaeology* (Bradford on Avon 1975), 107–20; cf. also RCHM, *Northamptonshire: an Archaeological Atlas* (1980). Hingley (1989, 164, n. 16) presents further density figures.
8. See now Millett 1990, 181f., for an excellent discussion, concluding with a figure of 3,665,000. For Italy, P.A. Brunt, *Italian Manpower* (Oxford 1971), 121f.
9. F. Millar, *JRS* 58 (1968), 126–34.
10. Tacitus, *Agric.* 21.
11. G. Jobey, *Arch. Ael.* 4, 47 (1970), 51–96; *Arch. Ael.* 5, 1 (1973), 11–54.
12. N. Higham and G.D.B. Jones, *Britannia* 14 (1983), 45–72.
13. G.D.B. Jones, in Blagg and King 1984, 80.
14. P. Fifield in Potter 1979, 305.
15. Usefully summarised in Higham 1986, 201f. See also M.K. Jones 1989.
16. R.G. Collingwood, *CW* 9 (1909), 295f.
17. Macgregor 1976.
18. Carvetii: *RIB* 933 (Old Penrith); *JRS* 55 (1965), 224 (Brougham); cf. also *RIB* 2283 (Middleton milestone).
19. *RIB* 1695.
20. Lloyd-Jones 1984; Davies 1984, 113–19; *idem* 1991; cf. also C.A. Smith, *PPS* 40 (1974), 157–69; Burnham and Davies 1990.
21. G.J. Wainwright, *Britannia* 2 (1971), 48–116.
22. B.D. Shaw, 'Rural markets in North Africa', *Antiquités africaines* 17 (1981), 37–83.
23. Cwmbrwyn: *Arch. Cambrensis* 7 (1907), 175–212; Trelissey: *Bull. Board of Celtic Studies* 18 (1953), 295–303.
24. Ty Mawr: *Arch. Cambrensis* 133 (1984), 64–82. Din Lligwy: *Arch. J.* 132 (1975), 285–6.
25. Bidwell 1979, Henderson 1988, Holbrook and Bidwell 1991.
26. Todd 1987; Tregurthy: *Cornish Arch.* 12 (1973), 25–30.
27. Carvossa: Todd 1987, 202, 222–3.
28. Caerloggas: *Arch. J.* 113 (1956), 33–81.
29. Ph. Leveau, *Rev. Epigraph. A.* 76 (1974), 293–304.
30. Bowman and Thomas 1983, 107–10.
31. *RIB* 583, 587; I.A. Richmond, *JRS* 35 (1945), 15–29.
32. Usefully discussed in a British context by Burnham and Wacher 1990, 33f.
33. Bowman and Thomas 1991.
34. Sommer 1984.
35. Salway 1965, 180f.
36. Birley 1977.
37. Salway 1965, 17f.; see also Birley 1979.
38. Allason-Jones 1989, 50f.
39. Bowman and Thomas 1983, tab. 1 (p. 78).
40. H.G. Pflaum, *Le cursus publicus* (Paris 1940); Pauly Wissowa, *s.v. Annona*; Jones and Walker 1983.
41. M.K. Jones 1989, 133.
42. Cassius Dio 56, 18; cf. G.D.B. Jones 1984.
43. *RIB* 707.
44. Blagg (1990) stresses the evidence for corporate rather than individual patronage.
45. See Burnham and Wacher 1990.
46. R. Hingley, *OJA* 4 (1985), 201–14.
47. Wedlake 1982.
48. B.W. Cunliffe, *Roman Bath Discovered* (1984); Springhead: now usefully discussed by Burnham and Wacher 1990, 192f.
49. D. Mackreth, *Durobrivae* 7 (1979), 19–21; J.P. Wild, *Arch. J.* 131 (1974), 140–70.
50. Burnham and Wacher (1990, 103f.) gather together the numerous references.
51. Trenico: *JRS* 52 (1962), 192; M. Todd, *The Roman Town at Ancaster* (Exeter and Nottingham 1981).
52. Cf. Florus 2, 33, 60 for an analogous situation in Spain.

53. Burnham and Wacher (1990, 122f.) provide a useful summary.
54. *RIB* 2250.
55. Garnsey and Saller 1987, 48f.; M.I. Finley, *Economy and Society in Ancient Greece* (rev. edn 1981); D. Engels, *Roman Corinth. An Alternative Model for the Classical City* (Chicago 1990).
56. Perring and Roskams 1991.
57. Wallace-Hadrill 1991, 260.
58. Tacitus, *Ann.* 14, 32.
59. J. Dillon, *Britannia* 20 (1989), 229–31.
60. Wallace-Hadrill (1991) provides an important assessment on the relationship between the élite and trade.
61. Note that Milne (1985) takes a much more negative view of the importance of trade to the growth of the city.
62. *RIB* 12.
63. Perring 1991 is the latest in a long line of important general surveys of Roman London.
64. *RIB* 21.
65. Frere 1983, 7, 55f.
66. Tacitus, *Agric.* 14; J.E. Bogaers, *Britannia* 10 (1979), 243–54.
67. Fulford 1985, 1989a.
68. Down 1988.
69. *RIB* 92, 91.
70. *Britannia* 19 (1989), 300; *Current Arch.* 120 (1990), 410f.
71. P. Bennett in Maxfield 1989, 118–28, is a most useful summary of recent work in Canterbury
72. R.P. Duncan-Jones in F. Grew and B. Hobley, *Roman Urban Topography in Britain and the Western Empire* (London 1985), 28–33.
73. Webster 1988.
74. Henderson 1988; Bidwell 1979; Holbrook and Bidwell 1991.
75. Tacitus, *Agric.* 21.
76. *RIB* 288.
77. Webster 1988, 120f.
78. McWhirr 1981.
79. *RIB* 110.
80. Trow 1990, esp. 111f.
81. S.D. Trow, *TBGAS* 106 (1988), 19–85; *Britannia* 17 (1986), 411–12; S.D. Trow and S. James in Branigan and Miles 1989, 83–8.
82. Theatre: McWhirr 1981, 37.
83. Columella, *De Agric.* 1, 6.
84. Varro, *Res rustica* 2, 10, 6.
85. King and Potter 1990.
86. Millett 1990.
87. Duncan-Jones 1982, 17f.
88. Cunliffe 1971.
89. King 1990.
90. Todd 1978, 201; see also Blagg in Blagg and Millett 1990, 194–209.
91. Detsicas 1983, 120f.
92. Tidbury Ring: D.R. Wilson, *Britannia* 5 (1974), 252.
93. Neal, Wardle and Hunn 1990.
94. Southwick: S.E. Winbolt, *Sussex Arch. Coll.* 73 (1932), 13–32.
95. Mileoak: C. Green and J. Draper, *Northants. Arch.* 13 (1978), 22–66.
96. Fingringhoe: *VCH Essex* III (1963), 130f.; barrows: Rodwell in Todd 1978, 18–19; Rivenhall: Rodwell and Rodwell 1985.
98. D. Jennings, in press; Lexden: Foster 1986.
99. *VCH Essex* III (1963), 39f.
100. *VCH Essex* III (1963), 43f.
101. M.K. Jones 1989.
102. RCHM 1983.
103. R.M. and D.E. Friendship-Taylor, *Current Arch.* 117 (1989), 316–21; *Britannia* 21 (1990), 332–3.
104. *Britannia* 21 (1990), 370–71; M.W.C. Hassall (pers. comm.) is less certain about this, however.
105. Miles 1986.
106. Neal 1989.
107. *Britannia* 16 (1985), 324; *Britannia* 22 (1991), 252–3.
108. G.D. Keevil, *Current Arch.* 122 (1990), 52–5.
109. For a legal document concerning a property dispute, dated 14 March 118, found in London, cf. Perring 1991, 47; for a bill of sale from Chew Stoke, Somerset, E.G. Turner, *JRS* 46 (1956), 115–18.
110. Crawford 1976.
111. *RIB* 230.
112. J.T. Smith 1978; but see Millett 1990, 197f.; Hingley 1989, 149f.
113. Jarrett and Wrathmell 1981.
114. Brewer 1990 and references.
115. R.J. Zeepvat in Mynard 1987, 60f. See also reports in *Britannia*, espec. 18 (1987), 325–6.
116. D.R. Wilson, *Britannia* 5 (1974), pl. xxiib.
117. Maddle Farm: Gaffney and Tingle 1989; Wharram: C. Hayfield in Price and Wilson 1988, 99–122.
118. A.B. Sumpter in Price and Wilson 1988, 171–96.
119. See *inter alia* Branigan 1976, 46f., and Duncan-Jones 1990, 121f., for different sorts of land tenure.
120. D. Miles in A. Savile, *Archaeology in Gloucestershire* (1984), 197–203; *Current Arch.* 86 (1983), 88–92.
121. E.g. Snettisham (Stead 1991b) and Thetford (Johns and Potter 1983).
122. Hingley 1989, 159.
123. Phillips 1970.
124. Gurney 1986.
125. J.S.P. Bradford, *Ancient Landscapes* (London 1957).
126. Goldcliff: *RIB* 395. J.R.L. Allen and M.G. Fulford, *Britannia* 17 (1986), 91–117; *idem, Ant. J.* 67 (1987), 237–89.
127. Potter 1989.
128. J.E. Bogaers, *Bonner Jahrbücher* 164 (1964), 45–52; *idem, Bonner Jahrbücher* 172 (1972), 310–32.
129. D. Mackreth, *Durobrivae* 9 (1984), 22–5; *Britannia* 14 (1983), 303–5.
130. O.A.W. Dilke, *The Roman Land Surveyors* (Newton Abbot 1971), 188f.
131. Phillips 1970, 288 and pl. xiib; *JRS* 45 (1955), pl. xx.
132. *RIB* 179; *VCH Somerset* I (1906), 309–12.
133. *RIB* 2411.37.
134. *Current Arch.* 85 (1982), 43–8.
135. F. Pryor *et al., The Fenland Project* 1 (1985).

4 Architecture and Art

1. For Roman architecture in general, see Ward-Perkins 1981 and Sear 1982. De la Bédoyère 1991 is a useful survey of Romano-British buildings, with conjectural reconstruction drawings.
2. Vitruvius, *De Architectura*, 5, 1, 4, ed. and trans. F. Grainger (London 1970).
3. Boon 1974, 108.
4. T. Brigham, *Britannia* 21 (1990), 54.
5. DeLaine 1988; de la Bédoyère 1991, 107.
6. K. Kenyon, *Archaeologia* 84 (1935), 213.
7. R. Dunnett, *Britannia* 2 (1971), 27.
8. *RIB* 707.
9. R.E.M. Wheeler, *Archaeologia* 78 (1928), 111; H. Thompson, *Archaeologia* 105 (1975), 127.
10. *Current Arch.* 109 (1988), 49.
11. Hill, Millett and Blagg 1980.
12. Cunliffe and Davenport 1985.
13. Cunliffe and Davenport 1985, 179.
14. D. Fishwick, *Britannia* 3 (1972), 164; P.J. Drury, *Britannia* 15 (1984), 7.
15. Horne 1981; Horne 1986.
16. Downey, King and Soffe 1980; King 1990.

17. D.J. Smith, *Arch. Ael.* (4th series) 40 (1962), 59; J.P. Gillam, I. MacIvor and E.B. Birley, *Arch. Ael.* (4th series), 32 (1954), 176.
18. Thomas 1981; Watts 1991.
19. King and Potter 1990.
20. De la Bédoyère 1991, 121.
21. For Roman gardens, see W.F. Jashemski, *The Gardens of Pompeii* (New Rochelle 1979).
22. Cunliffe 1971, vol. I, 120.
23. S. Applebaum, 'Roman Britain', in H.P.R. Finberg, *The Agrarian History of England and Wales*, vol. I (Cambridge 1972); M.K. Jones 1989.
24. Davey and Ling 1982; R. Ling, *Romano-British Wall-Painting* (Princes Risborough 1985).
25. Rainey 1973.
26. Neal 1981.
27. Smith 1969 (especially p. 117).
28. D. Johnston, 'The Central Southern Group of Romano-British mosaics', in Munby and Henig 1977, 195.
29. Smith 1977.
30. Stupperich 1980.
31. Smith 1969; Neal 1981.
32. M. Henig, in Woodward and Leach 1992.
33. M. Green 1986: while providing many valuable insights, this work presents a view which takes insufficient account of the Roman element in Romano-Celtic society, and effectively denies the existence of varying individual levels of artistic competence: see also Johns, review of M. Green 1986, *JBAA* 140 (1987), 204.

5 Personal Possessions

1. Quoted in N. Lewis, *Life in Egypt under Roman Rule* (Oxford 1983), 52.
2. Henig 1984, fig. 84.
3. W. Drack and R. Fellman, *Die Römer in der Schweiz* (Stuttgart 1988), Taf. 13.
4. T. Potter and C. Johns, *Ant. J.* 66 (1986), 391.
5. *RB Guide*, fig. 12.
6. Hull 1958, 264, pl. XL.
7. *RB Guide*, pl. XIII, 1.
8. Toynbee 1964, 83, pl. XVIII.
9. *RB Guide*, pl. XIV, 11.
10. A. Kaufmann-Heinimann, 'La petite statuaire romaine en argent', *Archéologia* 255 (Dijon, March 1990), 36; Potter 1983, 62, fig. 85; a survey of the type is in preparation by R.A. Lunsingh Scheurleer, for publication in *Ancient Jewelry and Archeology*, ed. W. Rudolph and A. Calinescu (Bloomington, Ind., forthcoming).
11. C. Johns, *Minerva* 1 (9) (November 1990), 47; C. Johns, *Ant. J.*, in press.
12. C. Johns, *Ant. J.*, in press.
13. For general background, Strong 1966 is still indispensable. See also Baratte and Painter 1989; Henig, 'The Luxury Arts', in Henig 1983, 139; and for a survey of recent research and publications, Johns 1990.
14. Stead 1967.
15. C. Johns, *Archaeologia* 108 (1986), 1.
16. Walters 1921, nos 183–7.
17. Painter 1977a.
18. Painter 1977b.
19. A.O. Curle, *The Treasure of Traprain* (Glasgow 1923).
20. Johns and Potter 1983; C. Johns and R. Bland, 'The Hoxne late Roman treasure', *Britannia* 25 (1994), 165–73.
21. J.M.C. Toynbee and K.S. Painter, *Archaeologia* 108 (1986), 15.
22. *Britannia* 22 (1991), 259.
23. *RIB* 2415.2.
24. *RIB* 2415.11, 2415.48.

25. Rivet and Smith 1979, 232.
26. C. Johns, 'An enamelled bronze *pyxis* from a Roman grave at Elsenham, Essex', *Ant. J.* 73 (1993), 161–5.
27. *RB Guide*, pl. XVIII, iv, 14; silver pepper-pot in the form of a black slave from the Chaourse treasure, Walters 1921, no. 81.
28. *RB Guide*, fig. 5, 11.
29. D. Brown, 'Bronze and pewter', in Strong and Brown 1976, 25; N. Beagrie, *Britannia* 20 (1989), 169; C.A. Peale, *Proc. Camb. Arch. Soc.* 40 (1967), 19.
30. Appleshaw: G.H. Engleheart, *Archaeologia* 56 (1898), 1; Icklingham: J.G. Rokewode, *Archaeologia* 29 (1842), 389; J. Liversidge, *Proc. Camb. Arch. Soc.* 52 (1959), 6.
31. J. Price, 'Glass', in Strong and Brown 1976, 111; J. Price, 'Glass', in Henig 1983, 205; Tait 1991.
32. Potter 1983, fig. 72.
33. Harden 1987, no. 27, no. 68.
34. Harden 1987, no. 89.
35. J. Price, *Ant. J.* 54 (1974), 291.
36. Stead 1967.
37. Peacock and Williams 1986.
38. Greene 1992, Peacock 1977 and 1982, Swan 1988. The literature on Roman pottery in general, on the terra sigillata industries, and on Romano-British pottery are all immense, and defy any attempt to devise a representative and succinct bibliography. De la Bédoyère 1989 has a helpful list of references. Much of the material in this chapter is based on discussions with the authors' colleague Valery Rigby.
39. Hull 1963.
40. Hayes 1972.
41. C. Johns, *Ant. J.* 43 (1963), 288: C. Fischer, *Germania* 69 (1991), 163.
42. There is an example of a small lead-glazed bowl in the Elsenham grave-group which contained the fine *millefiori* bronze box.
43. Stead 1991b.
44. C. Jones 1991, 28 ff. and catalogue entries.
45. L. Allason-Jones, *Ear-rings in Roman Britain* (Oxford 1989).
46. C. Johns, *The Snettisham Roman Jeweller's Hoard* (London 1997).
47. M. Henig, *The Content Family Collection of Ancient Cameos* (Oxford and Houlton, Maine, 1990).
48. Tait 1986, 217, no. 539.
49. C. Jones 1991, 31, fig. 4, 6.
50. Tait 1986, 96 (no. 214).
51. C. Jones 1991, 140 ff., 162 ff.
52. The filigree bracelet from Rhayader (*RB Guide*, pl. III) has blue and green enamel in an ancient Mediterranean tradition. There is a small pin in silver with red enamel from a fourth-century coin hoard found at Oldcroft (Glos.), a type which foreshadows the hand-pins of the Celtic west in the early medieval period; C. Johns, *Ant. J.* 54 (1974), 295; S. Youngs, *The Work of Angels* (London 1989), no. 1.
53. R. Tomlin, *Britannia* 10 (1979), 343; Tomlin in Woodward and Leach 1992; Tomlin in Cunliffe 1988.
54. J.P. Wild, *Textile Manufacture in the Northern Roman Provinces* (Cambridge 1970), 9.
55. P. Rashleigh, *Archaeologia* 14 (1803), 221; S. Walker, *Catalogue of Roman Sarcophagi in the British Museum* (London 1990), no. 72.
56. Liversidge 1955; Allason-Jones 1989.
57. *RIB* 769.
58. Allason-Jones 1989, fig. 5.
59. D.M. Bailey, 'Pottery lamps' in Strong and Brown 1976, 93; D.M. Bailey, 'Terracotta revetments, figurines and lamps', in Henig 1983, 191; D.M. Bailey, *Catalogue of the Lamps in the British Museum*, vol. 2 (London 1980) and vol. 3 (London 1988). For a review of recent research and literature, see D.M. Bailey, *JRA* 4 (1991), 51.

60. Toynbee 1964, 359, pl. LXXXII.
61. H. Cleere, 'Ironmaking', in Strong and Brown 1976, 127; W.H. Manning, 'Blacksmithing', in Strong and Brown 1976, 143; W.H. Manning, *Catalogue of the Romano-British Iron Tools, Fittings and Weapons in the British Museum* (London 1985).
62. Jackson 1988; R. Jackson, *JRA* 3 (1990), 5; R. Jackson, *Britannia* 21 (1990), 275; R. Jackson and K. Leahy, *Britannia* 21 (1990), 271.

6 Pagan Gods and Goddesses

1. Henig 1984 is the best general discussion, and M. Green 1986 is also an important survey. For background, see J. Ferguson, *The Religions of the Roman Empire* (London 1970).
2. Caesar 6, 17.
3. K. Jackson, *The Oldest Irish Tradition: a Window on the Iron Age* (Cambridge 1964).
4. M. Green 1986.
5. Lucius Apuleius, *The Golden Ass*, 11, 47.
6. *RIB* 88.
7. Walters 1921, nos 183–7; *RIB* 2414.36.
8. M. Green 1986, 72.
9. C. Johns, *Brit. Mus. Quarterly* 36 (1971/2) 37; *RIB* 2177.
10. Johns 1982.
11. The solitary occurrence of the horned or antlered god with the name *Cernunnos* (albeit incomplete) is on the *Pilier des Nautes*, the fragments of which were discovered in Paris in 1711. They are now in the Musée de Cluny. See J.-P. Caillet, in *Lutèce: Paris de César à Clovis* (Paris 1984), 397 ff.
12. For general discussion of Priapus, see Johns 1982, 50 ff; for the Pakenham statuette, C. Johns and M. Henig, *Ant. J.*, in press.
13. Johns and Potter 1983, 47 ff. and C. Johns, 'Faunus at Thetford: an early Latian deity in late-Roman Britain', in Henig and King 1986, 93.
14. Powell 1980, 181.
15. *RIB* 583, 1120, 1121, 1122, 2132. E. Gose, *Der Gallo-römische Tempelbezirk im Altbachtal zu Trier* (Mainz 1972).
16. F. Baratte, *Le Trésor d'Argenterie Gallo-Romaine de Notre-Dame-d'Allençon* (Paris 1981), no. 5, pl. X.
17. G.C. Boon, *Ant. J.* 63 (1983), 363; H.M. Gilbert, *Bull. B. Celt. Stud.* 28 (1980), 159.
18. The type is discussed in M. Green 1986, 61 ff. The fragment from Chesterford, Essex, not noted by Green, was discovered by the early antiquary John Horsley, who recognised it as Roman but took it to be a sarcophagus of some kind. It was published by Horsley in his *Britannia Romana* (London 1733), 331 (with a wildly inaccurate engraving on p. 192/no. 75), and was acquired by the British Museum in 1803. See also *RB Guide*, 55 and pl. XIX, 4. Catterick: *JRS* 50 (1960), pl. XXII, 2.
19. C. Johns, *Ant.J.*, in press.
20. Henig 1984; R.P. Wright, *Britannia* 16 (1985), 248.
21. Caesar 6, 17.
22. G. Webster, *The British Celts and their Gods under Rome* (London 1986).
23. Woodward and Leach 1992.
24. R. Tomlin, in Woodward and Leach 1992.
25. Cunliffe and Davenport 1985, and Cunliffe 1988.
26. R. Tomlin, in Cunliffe 1988.
27. D. Fishwick, *Britannia* 3 (1972), 164; P.J. Drury, *Britannia* 15 (1984), 7.
28. Marcus Aurelius Antoninus, *Meditations*, trans. by M. Casaubon (London 1634).
29. Ibid., 6, 49.
30. J.M.C. Toynbee, *The Roman Art Treasures from the Temple of Mithras* (London 1986); V. Hutchinson, *Bacchus in Roman*

Britain: the Evidence for his Cult (Oxford 1986); Potter 1983, 63, fig. 86.
31. J.M.C. Toynbee and K.S. Painter, *Archaeologia* 108 (1986), no. 1.
32. *RB Guide*, 60, pl. XXIV, 1; Potter 1983, 63, fig. 87.
33. R.A. Lunsingh Scheurleer, in W. Rudolph and A. Calinescu (eds), *Ancient Jewelry and Archeology* (Bloomington, Ind., forthcoming).
34. Henig 1984; E. Harris and J.R. Harris, *The Oriental Cults in Roman Britain* (Leiden 1965).

7 The Fourth Century and Beyond

1. *RIB* 1912.
2. T. Wilmott in Daniels 1989, 35–6; *Britannia* 21 (1990), 316.
3. Discussed further by Salway (1981, 309f.).
4. I.A. Richmond, K.S. Hodgson and J.K. St Joseph, *CW* 38 (1938), 195–239.
5. Salway 1981, 315.
6. *RIB* 2057, 2058; Potter 1979. Cf. generally Welsby 1982; Breeze and Dobson 1987.
7. *RIB* 1886; *JRS* 51 (1961), 194, no. 12.
8. Cf. most recently Davies 1991, with references.
9. James 1984, 166, 169.
10. *RIB* 1672, 1673, 1843, 1962, 2022.
11. Bidwell 1985, 77f.; see generally Welsby 1982, 68f.
12. Daniels 1989. See also Holder 1982, 98.
13. *RIB* 1613. See Daniels 1989, 57, for a recent summary.
14. Bidwell in Daniels 1989, 83–9.
15. Bidwell 1985, 83f.
16. On chalets generally: Daniels 1980; Bidwell 1991, who does not favour the idea of them housing family units; Allason-Jones 1989, 60–61.
17. I. Jobey, *Arch. Ael.* 5, 7 (1979), 127–43. On *numeri*: Holder 1982, 55; P. Southern, *Britannia* 20 (1989), 81–140.
18. A.H.M. Jones 1973, 519.
19. A.H.M. Jones 1973, 37–76; see also T.D. Barnes, *The New Empire of Diocletian and Constantine* (Cambridge, Mass. 1982); S. Williams, *Diocletian* (London 1985).
20. Jones 1973, 66.
21. M. Beard, *Britannia* 11 (1980), 313–14.
22. Zosimus 2, 34.
23. Ammianus Marcellinus 28, 3, 1; Welsby 1982, 103.
24. Welsby 1982, 133f.; Goodburn and Bartholomew 1976; J.C. Mann, *Britannia* 20 (1989), 75–9.
25. Ammianus Marcellinus 28, 8, 1; on the date of the Barbarian Conspiracy, R.S.O. Tomlin, *Britannia* 5 (1974), 303–9.
26. Claudian 22, 247f.
27. Holder 1982, 106–7.
28. Cf. *inter alii*, Esmonde Cleary 1989, 44–5; Welsby 1982, 104f.
29. Ammianus Marcellinus 18, 2, 3; cf. James 1984, 175.
30. Frere 1966, 1987.
31. Reece 1980. See also Brooks 1986, 1988; Esmonde Cleary 1989.
32. Millett 1990, 143f.
33. C. Foss, *Ephesus after Antiquity* (Cambridge 1979).
34. Sidonius Apollinaris, *Litt.* 2, 2.
35. Libanius, *Orat.* 18, 34–5.
36. R. Krautheimer, *Rome. Profile of a City, 312–1308* (Princeton 1980).
37. E.g. the excellent essay by Y. Thébert, 'L'évolution urbaine dans les provinces orientales', *Opus* 2 (1983), 99–132.
38. Crickmore 1984.
39. See particularly Frere 1984; for a contrary view, stressing the factor of civic pride, see B.R. Hartley in Hartley and Wacher (eds), *Rome and her Northern Provinces* (Gloucester 1983), 84–95.

40. D.W.A. Startin in Fulford 1984, 223–4; Fulford 1984, 236; Fulford and Startin, *Britannia* 15 (1984), 240–4.
41. Millett 1990, 137f.
42. Cf. generally Perring 1991 and references; Hill, Millett and Blagg 1980; D. Sanket and A. Stephenson in Maxfield and Dobson 1991, 117–24; T. Brigham, *Britannia* 21 (1990), 53–98. Shadwell: *TLMAS* 26 (1975), 278–80.
43. Baatz 1983; Millett 1990, 141.
44. Ammianus Marcellinus 28, 3, 2; 28, 3, 7. The provision of towers on just the river front of the *colonia* at York, and only the east side of London, could point to an emphasis upon display rather than defence.
45. T. Brigham, *Britannia* 21 (1990), 53–98.
46. Fulford 1985.
47. Fulford 1989a, 191–3.
48. Frere 1983.
49. McWhirr 1986. See also Wacher 1989; Boon 1974; Esmonde Cleary 1989; and J. Draper and C. Chaplin, *Dorchester Excavations* I (1982).
50. Cf. B. Yule, *Antiquity* 64 (1990), 620–8; R. MacPhail in M. Jones and G. Dimbleby (eds), *The Environment of Man: the Iron Age to the Anglo-Saxon Period* (Oxford 1981), 309–31.
52. Branigan 1976, McWhirr 1981.
53. N.K. Chadwick, *Poetry and Letters in Early Christian Gaul* (London 1955); K.M.D. Dunbabin, *The Mosaics of Roman North Africa* (Oxford 1978).
54. Johns and Pottèr 1983.
55. Neal 1981, pl. 87. For the villa, S. Lysons, *An Account of the Roman Antiquities Discovered at Woodchester* (London 1797); G. Clarke, *Britannia* 13 (1982), 197–228.
56. For knowledge of the literary classics in Britain, A.A. Barrett, *Britannia* 9 (1978), 307–13; for the mosaics Neal 1981, Meates 1979.
57. Frocester: McWhirr 1981, 83; Meonstoke: King and Potter 1990.
58. Neal 1981.
59. *Coloni: Theodosian Code* 11, 7, 2.
60. M.K. Jones 1989.
61. Millett 1990, 143f.; see also Burnham and Wacher 1990.
62. Fulford 1989b on the economy generally.
63. Burnham and Wacher 1990, 12f. and 36f.
64. Millett 1990, 205.
65. Potter 1989.
66. Horne 1981, 1986.
67. Woodward and Leach 1992.
68. Wheeler and Wheeler 1932.
69. R.P. Wright, *Britannia* 16 (1985), 248–9.
70. J.M.C. Toynbee, *Britannia* 12 (1981), 1–5; Wilson 1988, 83. For the most recent plans, *Britannia* 20 (1989), 317–18; *Britannia* 21 (1990), 353–4.
71. Horne 1981; Millett 1990, 195–6; Crummy 1984; Cunliffe and Davenport 1985.
72. Salway 1981, 408; cf. *Theodosian Code* 16, 10, 12.
73. Thomas 1981 is definitive; see also now Watts 1991.
74. *Adversus Iudaeos* 7.
75. Thomas 1981, 45f.
76. Rivet and Smith 1979, 49–50; Esmonde Cleary 1989, 47.
77. *De Laude Sanctorum* 1 (cf. Thomas 1981, 198).
78. On Pelagius, Thomas 1981, 53–60 and references. Germanus: *Vita Germani* 12.
79. R. Krautheimer, *Rome. Profile of a City* (Princeton 1980).
80. *Tituli:* Thomas 1981, 158. Silchester: A.C. King, *OJA* 2 (1983), 225–38.
81. *Current Arch.* 103 (1987), 244.
82. P. Crummy in Rodwell 1980, 243–83.
83. I.E. Anthony, *Herts. Arch.* 1 (1968), 9–50.
84. W. Rodwell, *Antiquity* 56 (1982), 215–18 (Wells); Morris 1989, 15f. (St Martin's, Canterbury).
85. (see 84 above)
86. C.J.S. Green 1982.
87. S.E. West and J. Plouviez, *East Anglian Arch.* 3 (1976), 63f.

88. C.J. Guy, *Britannia* 12 (1981), 271–6; *Britannia* 20 (1989), 234–7; Thomas 1981, 212f.; Watts 1991, 158f.
89. *Minerva* 2, no. 4 (1991), 5.
90. J. Liversidge and F. Weatherhead in Meates 1987, 5–44.
91. Woodward and Leach 1992.
92. C. Johns and R. Bland, 'The Hoxne late Roman treasure', *Britannia* 25 (1994), 165–73; R. Bland and C. Johns, *The Hoxne Treasure: an Illustrated Introduction* (London 1994).
93. Johns and Potter 1983; Watts 1991, 146f.
94. R.S.O. Tomlin, in Cunliffe 1988, 232, no. 98.
95. Holbrook and Bidwell 1991, 11–14.
96. Holbrook and Bidwell 1991.
97. McWhirr 1981, 1986.
98. Frere 1983; R. Niblett, *Herts. Arch.* 9 (1987), 22–78.
99. Mildenhall: *Wilts. Arch. Mag.* 60 (1965), 137. Silchester: Fulford 1984, 237.
100. Hull 1958, 41, citing P.M. Duncan.
101. Brooks 1988.
102. M. Biddle, *Proc. British Academy* 69 (1983), 93–135; M.J. Darling, *A Group of Late-Roman Pottery from Lincoln* (London 1977), 3.
103. B. Yule, *Antiquity* 64 (1990), 620–8.
104. Crummy 1984, espec. 138–40.
105. Perring 1991 is the most recent summary. Cf. also B. Barber, D. Bowsher and K. Whittaker, *Britannia* 21 (1990), 1–12; T. Brigham, *Britannia* 21 (1990), 99–184.
106. Frocester: McWhirr 1981 (with references). Marshfield: K. Blockley, *Marshfield. An Iron Age and Romano-British Settlement in the South Cotswolds* (Oxford 1985). Barnsley Park: G. Webster and L. Smith, *TBGAS* 100 (1982), 65–190.
107. Smith 1984.
108. Miles 1984.
109. Neal 1974.
110. K. Branigan, *Latimer* (Bristol 1971); *Town and Country. The Archaeology of Verulamium and the Roman Chilterns* (Bourne End 1973), 129f.
111. RCHM 1983.
112. Johns and Potter 1983; Canterbury Treasure: *Ant. J.* 65 (1985), 313–52. For crossbow brooches, Clarke 1979, 257f., espec. 129.
113. Zosimus 6, 5, 3; 6, 10, 2.
114. The literature is enormous. Cf., for example, Bartholomew 1982; Casey 1979; Esmonde Cleary 1989; Thompson 1977, 1983, 1984; and Wood 1987.
115. Lankhills: Clarke 1979; Dorchester: Esmonde Cleary 1989, 54–5; London: *Britannia* 21 (1990), 11.
116. Brooks 1988.
117. R.A. Chambers, *Oxoniensa* 52 (1987), 35–70.
118. C.M. Hills, 'Spong Hill III', *East Anglian Arch.* 34 (1984).
119. McCarthy 1990.
120. Barker 1981; *Britannia* 6 (1975), 106–17.
121. *JRS* 58 (1968), 206.
122. York: Carver 1987, 41; Birdoswald: *Britannia* 19 (1988), 436–7; T. Wilmott in Daniels 1989, 35f.; *Current Arch.* 116 (1989), 288–91.
123. C.J.S. Green 1988, 71f.
124. Alcock 1972. See also Alcock 1987.
125. Burrow 1979, 1981.
126. C.D. Morris *et al.*, *Antiquity* 64 (1990), 843–9

Bibliography

For abbreviations used, see p.221

ALCOCK, L. 1972. *By South Cadbury is that Camelot* (London).

ALCOCK, L. 1987. *Economy, Society and Warfare among the Britons and the Saxons* (Cardiff).

ALLASON-JONES, L. 1989. *Women in Roman Britain* (London).

BAATZ, D. 1983. 'Town walls and defensive weapons', in Maloney and Hobley 1983, 136–40.

BAILEY, D.M. 1988. *A Catalogue of the Lamps in the British Museum, vol.3: Roman Provincial Lamps* (London).

BARATTE, F. and PAINTER, K.S. 1989. *Trésors d'Orfèvrerie Gallo-Romains* (Paris).

BARKER, P. 1981. *Wroxeter Roman City: Excavations 1966–1980* (London).

BARTHOLOMEW, P. 1982. 'Fifth-century facts', *Britannia* 13, 261–70.

BÉDOYÈRE, G. DE LA 1989. *The Finds of Roman Britain* (London).

BÉDOYÈRE, G. DE LA 1991. *The Buildings of Roman Britain* (London).

BELLHOUSE, R.L. 1989. *Roman Sites on the Cumberland Coast* (Kendal).

BENNETT, P., FRERE, S.S. and STOW, S. 1982. *Excavations at Canterbury Castle* (Maidstone).

BIDDLE, M. 1983. 'The study of Winchester: archaeology and history in a British town, 1961–1983', *Proc. British Academy* 69, 93–135.

BIDWELL, P. 1979. *Exeter Archaeological Reports, vol.1: The Legionary Bath-House, Basilica and Forum* (Exeter).

BIDWELL, P. 1985. *The Roman Fort at Vindolanda* (London).

BIDWELL, P. 1991. 'Later Roman barracks in Britain', in Maxfield and Dobson 1991, 9–15.

BIRLEY, A.R. 1979. *The People of Roman Britain* (London).

BIRLEY, A.R. 1981. *The Fasti of Roman Britain* (Oxford).

BIRLEY, R. 1977. *Vindolanda. A Roman Frontier Post on Hadrian's Wall* (London).

BISHOP, M.C. and DORE, J.N. 1989. *Corbridge. Excavations of the Roman Fort and Town, 1947–80* (London).

BLAGG, T.F.C. 1979. 'The date of the temple at Bath', *Britannia* 10, 101–8.

BLAGG, T.F.C. 1990. 'Architectural munificence in Britain: the evidence of inscriptions', *Britannia* 21, 13–32.

BLAGG, T.F.C. and KING, A.C. (eds) 1984. *Military and Civilian in Roman Britain* (Oxford).

BLAGG, T.F.C. and MILLETT, M. (eds) 1990. *The Early Roman Empire in the West* (Oxford).

BLOCKLEY, R.C. 1980. 'The date of the "Barbarian Conspiracy"', *Britannia* 11, 223–5.

BOON, G.C. 1974. *Silchester: the Roman town of Calleva* (Newton Abbot).

BOWMAN, A.K. and THOMAS, J.D. 1983. *Vindolanda: the Latin Writing-Tablets* (London).

BOWMAN, A.K. and THOMAS, J.D. 1986. 'Vindolanda 1985: the new writing tablets', *JRS* 76, 120–23.

BOWMAN, A.K. and THOMAS, J.D. 1987. 'New texts from Vindolanda', *Britannia* 18, 125–42.

BOWMAN, A.K. and THOMAS, J.D. 1991. 'A military strength report from Vindolanda', *JRS* 81, 62–73.

BOWMAN, A.K., THOMAS, J.D. and ADAMS, J.N. 1990. 'Two letters from Vindolanda', *Britannia* 21, 33–52.

BRANIGAN, K. 1976. *The Roman Villa in South-West England* (Bradford-on-Avon).

BRANIGAN, K. 1977. *Gatcombe: the Excavation and Study of a Romano-British Villa Estate, 1967–1976* (Oxford).

BRANIGAN, K. 1985. *The Catuvellauni* (Gloucester).

BRANIGAN, K. and MILES, D. (eds) 1989. *Villa Economies* (Sheffield).

BRAUND, D.C. 1984. *Rome and the Friendly King: the Character of Client Kingship* (London).

BREEZE, D.J. 1982. *The Northern Frontiers of Roman Britain* (London).

BREEZE, D.J. 1991. 'The frontier in Britain, 1984–1989', in Maxfield and Dobson 1991, 35–43.

BREEZE, D.J. and DOBSON, B. 1987. *Hadrian's Wall* (3rd edn, Harmondsworth).

BREWER, R.J. 1990. 'Caerwent – *Venta Silurum*: a civitas capital', in Burnham and Davies 1990, 75–85.

BRODRIBB, A.C., HANDS, A.R. and WALKER, D.R. 1978. *Excavations at Shakenoak V* (Oxford).

BROOKS, D.A. 1986. 'A review of the evidence for continuity in British towns in the fifth and sixth centuries', *OJA* 5 (1), 77–102.

BROOKS, D.A. 1988. 'The case for continuity in fifth-century Canterbury re-examined', *OJA* 7 (1), 99–144.

BURNHAM, B.C. and DAVIES, J.L. 1990. *Conquest, Co-existence and Change. Recent Work in Roman Wales*, Trivium 25 (Lampeter).

BURNHAM, B.C. and WACHER, J.S. 1990. *The 'Small Towns' of Roman Britain* (London).

BURROW, I.C.G. 1979. 'Roman material in hillforts', in Casey 1979, 212–29.

BURROW, I.C.G. 1981. *Hillfort and Hill-top Settlement in Somerset in the First to Eighth Centuries AD* (Oxford).

CARVER, M.O.H. 1987. *Underneath English Towns* (London).

CASEY, P.J. (ed.) 1979. *The End of Roman Britain* (Oxford).

CLARKE, G.N. 1979. *Pre-Roman and Roman Winchester, part 2: The Roman cemetery at Lankhills* (Oxford).

CLARKE, G.N. 1982. 'The Roman villa at Woodchester', *Britannia* 13, 197–228.

COLLINGWOOD, R.G. 1930. *The Archaeology of Roman Britain* (London).

COLLINGWOOD, R.G. and MYRES, J.N.L. 1937. *Roman Britain and the English Settlements* (Oxford).

COLLINGWOOD, R.G. and RICHMOND, I.A. 1969. *The Archaeology of Roman Britain* (London).

COLLIS, J.R. 1984. *Oppida: Earliest Towns North of the Alps* (Sheffield).

COULSTON, J.C. (ed.) 1988. *Military Equipment and the Identity of Roman Soldiers* (Oxford).

CRAWFORD, D.J. 1976. 'Imperial estates', in *Studies in Roman Property*, ed. M.I. Finley (Cambridge), 35–70.

CRICKMORE, J. 1984. *Romano-British Urban Defences* (Oxford).

CROW, J.G. 1991. 'Construction and reconstruction in the central sector of Hadrian's Wall', in Maxfield and Dobson 1991, 44–7.

CRUMMY, P. 1977. 'Colchester, the Roman fortress and the development of the colonia', *Britannia* 8, 65–105.

CRUMMY, P. 1984. *Excavation at Lion Walk, Balkerne Lane and Middleborough* (Colchester).

CRUMMY, P. 1988. 'Colchester (*Camulodunum/Colonia Victriciensis*)', in Webster 1988, 24–47.

CUNLIFFE, B.W. 1968. *Fifth Report on the Excavations of the Roman Fort at Richborough, Kent* (London).

CUNLIFFE, B.W. 1971. *Excavations at Fishbourne 1961–1971* (Leeds).

CUNLIFFE, B.W. 1973. *The Regni* (London).

CUNLIFFE, B.W. (ed.) 1981. *Coinage and Society in Britain and Gaul* (London).

CUNLIFFE, B.W. 1983. *Danebury: Anatomy of an Iron Age Hillfort* (London).

CUNLIFFE, B.W. 1984a. 'Relations between Britain and Gaul in the first century BC and the first century AD', in Macready and Thompson 1984, 3–23.

CUNLIFFE, B.W. 1984b. *Danebury: an Iron Age Hillfort in Hampshire* (London).

CUNLIFFE, B.W. 1987. *Hengistbury Head, Dorset, vol.1: The Prehistoric and Roman Settlement 3500 BC – AD 500* (Oxford).

CUNLIFFE, B.W. 1988a. *Greeks, Romans and Barbarians: Spheres of Interaction* (London).

CUNLIFFE, B.W. (ed.) 1988b. *The Temple of Sulis Minerva at Bath, vol.2: The Finds from the Sacred Spring* (Oxford).

CUNLIFFE, B.W. 1990. *Iron Age Communities in Britain* (3rd edn, London).

CUNLIFFE, B.W. and DAVENPORT, P. 1985. *The Temple of Sulis Minerva at Bath, vol.1: The Site* (Oxford).

DANIELS, C.M. 1978. *J. Collingwood Bruce's Handbook to the Roman Wall* (Newcastle upon Tyne).

DANIELS, C.M. 1980. 'Excavations at Wallsend and fourth-century barracks on Hadrian's Wall', in Hanson and Keppie 1980, 173–94.

DANIELS, C.M. (ed.) 1989. *The Eleventh Pilgrimage of Hadrian's Wall* (Newcastle upon Tyne).

DANIELS, C.M. 1991. 'The Antonine abandonment of Scotland', in Maxfield and Dobson 1991, 48–51.

DANNELL, G.B. and WILD, J.P. 1987. *Longthorpe II: the Military Works Depot* (London).

DAVEY, N. and LING, R. 1982. *Wall-Paintings in Roman Britain* (London).

DAVIES, J.L. 1980. 'Roman military deployments in Wales and the Marches from Claudius to the Antonines', in Hanson and Keppie 1980, 255–77.

DAVIES, J.L. 1984. 'Soldiers, peasants and markets in Wales and the Marches', in Blagg and King 1984, 93–127.

DAVIES, J.L. 1991. 'Roman military deployment in Wales and the Marches from Pius I to Theodosius I', in Maxfield and Dobson 1991, 52–7.

DELAINE, J. 1988. 'Recent research on Roman baths', *JRA* 1, 11–32.

DETSICAS, A. 1983. *The Cantiaci* (Gloucester).

DOBSON, B. 1986. 'The function of Hadrian's Wall', *Arch. Ael.* 5(14), 1–30.

DOWN, A. 1978. *Chichester Excavations III* (Chichester).

DOWN, A. 1988. *Roman Chichester* (Chichester).

DOWNEY, R., KING, A. and SOFFE, G. 1980. 'The Hayling Island temple and religious connections across the Channel', in Rodwell 1980, 289–304.

DUNCAN-JONES, R.P. 1982. *The Economy of the Roman Empire* (2nd edn, Cambridge).

DUNCAN-JONES, R.P. 1990. *Structure and Scale in the Roman Economy* (Cambridge).

DUNNETT, R. 1975. *The Trinovantes* (London).

DYSON, T. (ed.) 1986. *The Roman Quay at St Magnus House, London* (London).

ELKINGTON, H.D.H. 1976. 'The Mendip lead industry', in *The Roman West Country*, ed. K. Branigan and P.J. Fowler (Newton Abbot), 183–97.

ERIM, K.T. 1982. 'A new relief showing Claudius and Britannia from Aphrodisias', *Britannia* 13, 277–82.

ESMONDE-CLEARY, A.S. 1987. *Extra-Mural Areas of Romano-British Towns* (Oxford).

ESMONDE-CLEARY, A.S. 1989. *The Ending of Roman Britain* (London).

FITZPATRICK, A.P. 1985. 'The distribution of Dressel I amphorae in North-West Europe', *OJA* 4 (3), 305–40.

FOSTER, J. 1986. *The Lexden Tumulus: a Re-appraisal of an Iron Age Burial from Colchester, Essex* (Oxford).

FRERE, S.S. 1966. 'The end of the towns in Roman Britain', in *The Civitas Capitals of Roman Britain*, ed. J.S. Wacher (Leicester), 87–100.

FRERE, S.S. 1971. *Verulamium Excavations*, vol.I (Oxford).

FRERE, S.S. 1982. 'The Bignor villa', *Britannia* 13, 135–95.

FRERE, S.S. 1983. *Verulamium Excavations*, vol.II (London).

FRERE, S.S. 1984. 'British urban defences in earthwork', *Britannia* 15, 63–74.

FRERE, S.S. 1985. 'Civic pride: a factor in Roman town planning', in *Roman Urban Topography in Britain and the Western Empire*, ed. F. Grew and B. Hobley (London), 34–6.

FRERE, S.S. 1987. *Britannia: a History of Roman Britain* (3rd edn, London).

FRERE, S.S. and ST JOSEPH, J.K. 1974. 'The Roman fortress at Longthorpe', *Britannia* 5, 1–129.

FRERE, S.S. and ST JOSEPH, J.K. 1983. *Roman Britain from the Air* (Cambridge).

FRERE, S.S. and WILKES, J.J. 1989. *Strageath. Excavations within the Roman Fort* (London).

FRERE, S.S., STOW, S. and BENNETT, P. 1982. *Excavations on the Roman Defences of Canterbury* (Maidstone).

FULFORD, M.G. 1975. *New Forest Roman Pottery* (Oxford).

FULFORD, M.G. 1979. 'Pottery production and trade at the end of Roman Britain: the case against continuity', in Casey 1979, 120–32.

FULFORD, M.G. 1982. 'Town and country in Roman Britain – a parasitical relationship?', in Miles 1982, 403–19.

FULFORD, M.G. 1984. *Silchester Defences 1974–80*, Britannia Monograph 5.

FULFORD, M.G. 1985. 'Excavations on the sites of the amphitheatre and forum-basilica at Silchester, Hampshire: an interim report', *Antiq. J.* 65, 39–81.

FULFORD, M.G. 1986. *Silchester Excavations 1986* (Reading).

FULFORD, M.G. 1987. 'Calleva Atrebatum: an interim report on the excavation of the oppidum 1980–1986', *PPS* 53, 271–8.

FULFORD, M.G. 1989a. *Silchester Amphitheatre*, Britannia Monograph 10.

FULFORD, M.G. 1989b. 'The economy of Roman Britain', in Todd 1989, 175–202.

GAFFNEY, V. and TINGLE, M. 1989. *The Maddle Farm Project. An Integrated Survey of Prehistoric and Roman Landscapes in the Berkshire Downs* (Oxford).

GARNSEY, P.D.A. and SALLER, R. 1987. *The Roman Empire: Economy, Society and Culture* (London).

GOODBURN, R. and BARTHOLOMEW, P. (eds) 1976. *Aspects of the Notitia Dignitatum* (Oxford).

GREEN, C.J.S. 1982. 'The cemetery of a Romano-British Christian community at Poundbury, Dorchester, Dorset', in *The Early Church in Western Britain and Ireland*, ed. S.M. Pearce (Oxford), 61–76.

GREEN, C.J.S. 1988. *Excavations at Poundbury I: The settlements* (Dorchester).

GREEN, M. 1986. *The Gods of the Celts* (Gloucester).

GREENE, K. 1986. *The Archaeology of the Roman Economy* (London).

GREENE, K. 1992. *Interpreting the Past: Roman Pottery* (London).

GURNEY, D. 1986. *Settlement, Religion and Industry on the Fen-edge: Three Romano-British Sites in Norfolk* (Hunstanton).

HANSON W.S. 1987. *Agricola and the Conquest of the North* (London).

HANSON, W.S. and CAMPBELL, D.B. 1986. 'The Brigantes: from clientage to conquest', *Britannia* 17, 73–90.

HANSON, W.S. and KEPPIE, L.J.F. (eds) 1980. *Roman Frontier Studies 1970* (Oxford).

HANSON, W.S. and YEOMAN, P.A. 1988. *Elginhaugh. A Roman Fort and its Environs* (Glasgow).

HARDEN, D.B. *et al.* 1987. *Glass of the Caesars* (Milan).

HARTLEY, B.R. 1972. 'The Roman occupation of Scotland: the evidence of Samian ware', *Britannia* 3, 1–55.

HARTLEY, B.R. and FITTS, L. 1988. *The Brigantes* (Gloucester).

HASELGROVE, C.C. and TURNBULL, P. 1987. *Stanwick: Excavations and Research, Interim Report* (Durham).

HAVERFIELD, F. 1912. *The Romanization of Roman Britain* (2nd edn, Oxford).

HAVERFIELD, F. and MACDONALD, G. 1924. *The Roman Occupation of Britain* (Oxford).

HAWKES, C.F.C. 1977. *Pytheas: Europe and the Greek Explorers* (Oxford).

HAWKES, C.F.C. and HULL, M.R. 1947. *Camulodunum* (London).

HAYES, J.W. 1972. *Late Roman Pottery* (London).

HENDERSON, C. 1988. 'Exeter (*Isca Dumnoniorum*)', in Webster 1988, 91–119.

HENIG, M. 1978. *A Corpus of Engraved Gemstones from British Sites* (Oxford).

HENIG, M. (ed.) 1983. *A Handbook of Roman Art* (London).

HENIG, M. 1984. *Religion in Roman Britain* (London).

HENIG, M. and KING, A. (eds) 1986. *Pagan Gods and Shrines of the Roman Empire* (Oxford).

HESLOP, D. 1987. *The Excavation of an Iron Age Settlement at Thorpe Thewles, Cleveland, 1980–1982* (London).

HIGHAM, N. 1986. *The Northern Counties to AD 1000* (Harlow).

HIGHAM, N. and JONES, G.D.B. 1985. *The Carvetii* (Gloucester).

HILL, C., MILLETT, M. and BLAGG, T.F.C. 1980. *The Roman Riverside Wall and Monumental Arch in London* (London).

HIND, J.G.F. 1989. 'The invasion of Britain in AD 43 – an alternative strategy for Aulus Plautius', *Britannia* 20, 1–22.

HINGLEY, R. 1989. *Rural Settlement in Roman Britain* (London).

HOBLEY, A.S. 1989. 'The numismatic evidence for the post-Agricolan abandonment of the Roman frontier in northern Scotland', *Britannia* 20, 69–74.

HOLBROOK, N. and BIDWELL, P.T. 1991. *Roman Finds from Exeter* (Exeter).

HOLDER, P.A. 1982. *The Roman Army in Britain* (London).

HORNE, P. 1981. 'Romano-Celtic temples in the third century', in King and Henig 1981, 21–6.

HORNE, P. 1986. 'Roman or Celtic temple?', in Henig and King 1986, 15–24.

HULL, M.R. 1958. *Roman Colchester* (London).

HULL, M.R. 1963. *The Roman Potters' Kilns of Colchester* (London).

HURST, H.R. 1988. 'Gloucester (*Glevum*)', in Webster 1988, 48–73.

JACKSON, R. 1988. *Doctors and Diseases in the Roman Empire* (London).

JAMES, S.T. 1984. 'Britain and the late Roman army', in Blagg and King 1984, 161–86.

JAMES, S.T. 1988. 'The Fabricae: state arms factories of the later Roman empire', in Coulston 1988, 257–331.

JARRETT, M.G. and WRATHMELL, S. 1981. *Whitton: an Iron Age and Roman Farmstead in South Glamorgan* (Cardiff).

JOHNS, C.M. 1982. *Sex or Symbol: Erotic Images of Greece and Rome* (London).

JOHNS, C.M. 1990. 'Research on Roman silver plate', *JRA* 3, 28.

JOHNS, C.M. and POTTER, T.W. 1983. *The Thetford Treasure. Roman Jewellery and Silver* (London).

JOHNSON, S. 1976. *The Roman Forts of the Saxon Shore* (London).

JOHNSON, S. 1983. *Late Roman Fortifications* (London).

JOHNSTON, D.E. (ed.) 1977. *The Saxon Shore* (London).

JONES, A.H.M. 1973. *The Later Roman Empire AD 284–602: a Social, Economic and Administrative Survey* (2nd edn, Oxford).

JONES, C. 1991. 'Romano-British jewellery', in *Treasures and Trinkets: Jewellery in London from Pre-Roman Times to the 1930s*, compiled by T. Murdoch (London).

JONES, G.D.B. 1976. 'The western extension of Hadrian's Wall: Bowness to Cardurnock', *Britannia* 7, 236–43.

JONES, G.D.B. 1982. 'The Solway frontier; interim report 1976–81', *Britannia* 13, 282–97.

JONES, G.D.B. 1984. '"Becoming different without knowing it": the role and development of vici', in Blagg and King 1984, 75–91.

JONES, G.D.B. 1991. 'The emergence of the Tyne-Solway frontier', in Maxfield and Dobson 1991, 98–107.

JONES, G.D.B. and MATTINGLY, D. 1990. *An Atlas of Roman Britain* (Oxford).

JONES, G.D.B. and WALKER, J. 1983. 'Either side of the Solway: towards a minimalist view of Romano-British agriculture in the north-west', in *Settlement in Northern Britain 100BC-AD1000*, ed. J. C. Chapman and H.C. Mytum (Oxford), 185–204.

JONES, M.J. 1988. 'Lincoln (*Lindum*)', in Webster 1988, 145–66.

JONES, M.K. 1989. 'Agriculture in Roman Britain: the dynamics of change', in Todd 1989, 127–34.

KING, A.C. 1981. 'The decline of Samian manufacture in the North West Provinces: problems of chronology and interpretation', in King and Henig 1981, 55–78.

KING, A.C. 1990. 'The emergence of Romano-Celtic religion', in Blagg and Millett 1990, 220–41.

KING, A.C. and HENIG, M. (eds) 1981. *The Roman West in the Third Century* (Oxford).

KING, A.C. and POTTER, T.W. 1990. 'A new domestic building façade from Roman Britain', *JRA* 3, 195–204.

LAMB, H.H. 1981. 'Climate from 1000 BC-AD 100', in *The Environment of Man: the Iron Age to the Anglo-Saxon Period*, ed. M.K. Jones and G.W. Dimbleby (Oxford), 53–65.

LEPPER, F. and FRERE, S.S. 1988. *Trajan's Column* (Gloucester).

LEWIS, M.J.T. 1965. *Temples in Roman Britain* (Cambridge).

LIVERSIDGE, J. 1955. *Furniture in Roman Britain* (London).

LLOYD-JONES, M. 1984. *Settlement and Society in Wales and the Marches: 5000 BC to AD 1100* (Oxford).

LUTTWAK, E.N. 1976. *The Grand Strategy of the Roman Empire* (Baltimore).

MCCARTHY, M.E. 1990. *A Roman, Anglian and Medieval Site at Blackfriars Street, Carlisle* (Stroud).

MACGREGOR, M. 1976. *Early Celtic Art in North Britain* (Leicester).

MACREADY, S. and THOMPSON, F.H. (eds) 1984. *Cross-Channel Trade between Gaul and Britain in the Pre-Roman Iron Age* (London).

MCWHIRR, A.D. 1981. *Roman Gloucestershire* (Gloucester).

MCWHIRR, A.D. 1986. *Houses in Roman Cirencester* (Cirencester).

MCWHIRR, A.D., VINER, L. and WELLS, C. 1982. *Romano-British Cemeteries at Cirencester* (Cirencester).

MALONEY, J. and HOBLEY, B. 1983. *Roman Urban Defences in the West* (London).

MANN, J. and PENMAN, R.G. (eds) 1978. *Literary Sources for Roman Britain* (London).

MANN, J.C. 1971. 'Spoken Latin in Britain as evidenced in inscriptions', *Britannia* 2, 218–24.

MANN, J.C. 1974. 'The frontiers of the Principate', in *Aufstieg und Niedergang der römischen Welt*, II/I, ed. H. Temporini (Berlin), 508–33.

MANN, J.C. 1976. 'What was the Notitia Dignitatum for?' in Goodburn and Bartholomew 1976, 1–10.

MANN, J.C. 1988. 'A history of the Antonine Wall: a reappraisal', *PSAS* 118, 131–7.

MANNING, W.H. 1981. *Report on the Excavations at Usk 1965–1976: the Fortress Excavations 1968–1971* (Cardiff).

MANNING, W.H. 1989. *Usk. The Fortress Excavations 1972–1974* (Cardiff).

MARSDEN, P. 1980. *Roman London* (London).

MARSDEN, P. 1987. *The Roman Forum Site in London: Discoveries before 1985* (London).

MAXFIELD, V.A. 1986. 'Pre-Flavian forts and their garrisons', *Britannia* 17, 59–72.

MAXFIELD, V.A. 1989a. 'Conquest and aftermath', in Todd 1989, 19–30.

MAXFIELD, V.A. (ed.) 1989b. *The Saxon Shore* (Exeter).

MAXFIELD, V.A. and DOBSON, M.J. (eds) 1991. *Roman Frontier Studies 1989* (Exeter).

MAXWELL, G.S. 1984. 'New frontiers: the Roman fort at Doune and its possible significance', *Britannia* 15, 217–23.

MAXWELL, G.S. and WILSON, D.R. 1987. 'Air reconnaissance in Roman Britain, 1977–84', *Britannia* 18, 1–48.

MEATES, G.W. 1979. *The Roman Villa at Lullingstone, I: The Site* (Chichester).

MEATES, G.W. 1987. *The Roman Villa at Lullingstone, II: The Wall Paintings and Finds* (Maidstone).

MEGAW, R. and MEGAW, V. 1986. *Early Celtic Art in Britain and Ireland* (London).

MEGAW, R. and MEGAW, V. 1989. *Celtic Art from its Beginnings to the Book of Kells* (London).

MERRIFIELD, R. 1983. *London: City of the Romans* (London).

MILES, D. (ed.) 1982. *The Romano-British Countryside* (Oxford).

MILES, D. (ed.) 1986. *Archaeology at Barton Court Farm, Abingdon, Oxon.* (London)

MILES, D. and PALMER, S. 1982. *Archaeological Investigations at Claydon Pike, Fairford/Lechlade: an Interim Report 1979–1982* (Oxford).

MILLETT, M. 1990. *The Romanization of Britain* (Cambridge).

MILLETT, M. and GRAHAM, D. 1986. *Excavations on the Romano-British Small Town at Neatham, Hampshire, 1969–1979* (Winchester).

MILNE, G. 1985. *The Port of Roman London* (London).

MORRIS, P. 1979. *Agricultural Buildings in Roman Britain* (Oxford).

MORRIS, R. 1989. *Churches in the Landscape* (London).

MUNBY, J. and HENIG, M. 1977. *Roman Life and Art in Britain* (Oxford).

MYNARD, D.C. 1987. *Roman Milton Keynes: Excavation and Fieldwork 1971–82* (Aylesbury).

NEAL, D.S. 1974. *The Excavation of the Roman Villa in Gadebridge Park, Hemel Hempstead 1963–8* (London).

NEAL, D.S. 1981. *Roman Mosaics in Britain* (London).

NEAL, D.S. 1989. 'The Stanwick villa, Northants: an interim report on the excavations of 1984–88', *Britannia* 20, 149–68.

NEAL, D.S., WARDLE, A. and HUNN, J. 1990. *Excavation on the Iron Age, Roman and Medieval Settlement at Gorhambury, St Albans* (London).

NIBLETT, R. 1985. *Sheepen: an Early Roman Industrial Site at Camulodunum* (London).

OGDEN, J. 1982. *Jewellery of the Ancient World* (London).

OGDEN, J. 1992. *Interpreting the Past: Ancient Jewellery* (London).

PAINTER, K.S. 1977a. *The Mildenhall Treasure: Roman Silver from East Anglia* (London).

PAINTER, K.S. 1977b. *The Water Newton Early Christian Silver* (London).

PARTRIDGE, C.R. 1981. *Skeleton Green: a Late Iron Age and Romano-British Site* (London).

PEACOCK, D. 1977. *Pottery and Early Commerce* (London).

PEACOCK, D. 1982. *Pottery in the Roman World* (London).

PEACOCK, D. and WILLIAMS, D. 1986. *Amphorae and the Roman Economy* (Harlow).

PERRING, D. 1991. *Roman London* (London).

PERRING, D. and ROSKAMS, S.P. 1991. *The Archaeology of Roman London, 2: Early Development of Roman London West of the Walbrook* (London).

PHILLIPS, C.W. (ed.) 1970. *The Fenland in Roman Times*, Royal Geographical Society Research Memoir 5.

PITTS, L.F. and ST JOSEPH, J.K. 1985. *Inchtuthil. The Roman Legionary Fortress* (London).

POTTER, T.W. 1979. *Romans in North-West England* (Kendal).

POTTER, T.W. 1983. *Roman Britain* (London).

POTTER, T.W. 1986. 'A Roman province: Britain AD 43–420', *in Archaeology in Britain since 1945*, ed. I.H. Longworth and J. Cherry (London), 73–118.

POTTER, T.W. 1989. 'The Roman Fenland: a review of recent work', in Todd 1989, 147–76.

POTTER, T.W. and TROW, S. 1988. *Puckeridge–Braughing, Hertfordshire. The Ermine Street Excavations 1971–72* (Herts. Arch. 10).

POWELL, T.G.E. 1980. *The Celts* (London).

PRICE, J. and WILSON, P.R. (eds) 1988. *Recent Research in Roman Yorkshire* (Oxford).

RAINEY, A. 1973. *Mosaics in Roman Britain* (Newton Abbot).

RAMM, H. 1978. *The Parisi* (London).

RANKIN, H.D. 1987. *Celts and the Classical World* (London).

RCHM 1983. 'West Park Roman villa, Rockbourne, Hants', *Arch. J.* 140, 129–50.

REECE, R.M. 1972. 'A short survey of the Roman coins found on fourteen sites in Britain', *Britannia* 3, 269–76.

REECE, R.M. 1980. 'Town and country: the end of Roman Britain', *World Archaeol.* 12 (1), 77–92.

REECE, R.M. 1981. 'The third century: crisis or change', in King and Henig 1981, 27–38.

REECE, R.M. 1987. *Roman Coinage in Britain* (London).

RICHMOND, I.A. 1963. *Roman Britain* (2nd edn, Harmondsworth).

RICHMOND, I.A. 1968. *Hod Hill, vol. 2: Excavations carried out between 1951 and 1958* (London).

RIVET, A.L.F. 1958. *Town and Country in Roman Britain* (London).

RIVET, A.L.F. (ed.) 1969. *The Roman Villa in Britain* (London).

RIVET, A.L.F. and SMITH, C. 1979. *The Place-names of Roman Britain* (London).

ROBERTSON, A.S. 1990. *The Antonine Wall* (4th edn, rev. L.J.F. Keppie, Glasgow).

RODWELL, W. 1976. 'Coinage, oppida and the rise of Belgic power in south-eastern Britain', in *Oppida: the Beginnings of Urbanisation in Barbarian Europe*, ed. B. Cunliffe and T. Rowley (Oxford), 181–366.

RODWELL, W. 1978. 'Rivenhall and the emergence of first-century villas in northern Essex', in Todd 1978, 11–32.

RODWELL, W. (ed.) 1980. *Temples, Churches and Religion: Recent Research in Roman Britain* (Oxford).

RODWELL, W. and RODWELL, K. 1985. *Rivenhall: Investigations of a Villa, Church and Village 1950–1977* (London).

ROSS, A. 1967. *Pagan Celtic Britain* (London).

ROSS, A. 1986. *The Pagan Celts* (London).

SALWAY, P. 1965. *The Frontier People of Roman Britain* (Cambridge).

SALWAY, P. 1981. *Roman Britain* (Oxford).

SEALEY, P.R. 1985. *Amphoras from the 1970 excavations at Colchester Sheepen* (Oxford).

SEAR, F.B. 1982. *Roman Architecture* (London).

SHARPLES, N.M. 1991. *Maiden Castle* (London).

SMITH, D.J. 1969. 'The mosaic pavements', in Rivet 1969, 71–125.

SMITH, D.J. 1977. 'Mythological figures and scenes in Romano-British Mosaics', in Munby and Henig 1977, 105–24.

SMITH, D.J. 1984. 'Roman mosaics in Britain: a synthesis', in *Atti del III Colloquio Internazionale sul Mosaico Antico, Ravenna, 1980*, ed. F. Campananto (Ravenna), 357–80.

SMITH, J.T. 1978. 'Villas as a key to social structure', in Todd 1978, 149–86.

SOMMER, C.S. 1984. *The Military Vici in Roman Britain* (Oxford).

STEAD, I.M. 1967. 'A La Tène III burial at Welwyn Garden City', *Archaeologia* 101, 1–62.

STEAD, I.M. 1976. *Excavations at Winterton Roman Villa* (London).

STEAD, I.M. 1979. *The Arras Culture* (York).

STEAD, I.M. 1985. *Celtic Art* (London).

STEAD, I.M. 1991a. *Iron Age Cemeteries in East Yorkshire* (Southampton).

STEAD, I.M. 1991b. 'The Snettisham Treasure: excavation in 1990', *Antiquity* 65, 447–65.

STEAD, I.M. and RIGBY, V. 1986. *Baldock: the Excavation of a Roman and Pre-Roman Settlement 1968–1972* (London).

STEAD, I.M. and RIGBY, V. 1989. *Verulamium: the King Harry Lane Site* (London).

STRONG, D. 1966. *Greek and Roman Gold and Silver Plate* (London).

STRONG, D. and Brown, D. 1976. *Roman Crafts* (London).

STUPPERICH, R. 1980. 'A reconsideration of some fourth-century British mosaics', *Britannia* 11, 289.

SWAN, V.G. 1984. *The Pottery Kilns of Roman Britain* (London).

SWAN, V. 1988. *Pottery in Roman Britain* (4th edn, Aylesbury).

TAIT, H. (ed.) 1986. *Seven Thousand Years of Jewellery* (London).

TAIT, H. (ed.) 1991. *Five Thousand Years of Glass* (London).

THOMAS, A.C. 1981. *Christianity in Roman Britain to AD 500* (London).

THOMPSON, E.A. 1977. 'Britain AD 406–410', *Britannia* 8, 303–18.

THOMPSON, E.A. 1983. 'Fifth century facts?', *Britannia* 14, 272–4.

THOMPSON, E.A. 1984. *St Germanus of Auxerre and the End of Roman Britain* (Woodbridge).

TODD, M. (ed.) 1978. *Studies in the Romano-British Villa* (Leicester).

TODD, M. 1981. *Roman Britain* (Brighton).

TODD, M. 1985. 'Oppida and the Roman army. A review of recent evidence', *OJA* 4(2), 187–99.

TODD, M. 1987. *The South-West to AD 1000* (London).

TODD, M. (ed.) 1989. *Research on Roman Britain 1960–89* (London).

TODD, M. 1991. *The Coritani* (2nd edn, Gloucester).

TOYNBEE, J.M.C. 1964. *Art in Britain under the Romans* (Oxford).

TROW, S.D. 1990. 'On the northern shores of Ocean: some observations on acculturation processes at the edge of the Roman world', in Blagg and Millett 1990, 103–18.

TROW, S.D. and JAMES, S. 1989. 'Ditches villa, North Cerney: an example of locational conservatism in the early Roman Cotswolds', in Branigan and Miles 1989, 83–8.

WACHER, J.S. 1971. 'Yorkshire towns in the fourth century', in *Soldier and Civilian in Roman Yorkshire*, ed. R.M. Butler (Leicester), 165–78.

WACHER, J.S. 1975. *The Towns of Roman Britain* (London).

WACHER, J.S. 1989. 'Cities from the second to fourth centuries', in Todd 1989, 75–90.

WAINWRIGHT, G.J. 1979. *Gussage All Saints: an Iron Age Settlement in Dorset* (London).

WALLACE-HADRILL, A. 1991. 'Elites and trade in the Roman town', in *City and Countryside in the Ancient world*, ed. J. Rich and A. Wallace-Hadrill (London), 241–72.

WALTERS, H.B. 1921. *Catalogue of the Silver Plate (Greek, Etruscan and Roman) in the British Museum* (London).

WARD-PERKINS, J.B. 1981. *Roman Imperial Architecture* (Harmondsworth).

WATTS, D. 1991. *Christians and Pagans in Roman Britain* (London).

WEBSTER, G. 1958. 'The military advance under Ostorius Scapula', *Arch. J.* 115, 49–98.

WEBSTER, G. 1975. *The Cornovii* (London).

WEBSTER, G. (ed.) 1988. *Fortress into City. The Consolidation of Roman Britain, First Century AD* (London).

WEDLAKE, W.J. 1982. *The Excavation of the Shrine of Apollo at Nettleton, Wiltshire, 1956–1971* (London).

WELSBY, D. 1982. *The Roman Military Defence of the British Provinces in its Later Phases* (Oxford).

WHEELER, R.E.M. 1943. *Maiden Castle, Dorset* (Oxford).

WHEELER, R.E.M. 1954. *The Stanwick Fortifications* (London).

WHEELER, R.E.M. and WHEELER, T.V. 1932. *Report on the Excavation of the Prehistoric, Roman and Post-Roman Site in Lydney Park, Gloucestershire* (Oxford).

WHEELER, R.E.M. and WHEELER, T.V. 1936. *Verulamium. A Belgic and Two Roman Cities* (Oxford).

WILLIAMS, T. 1991. 'Allectus' building campaign in London: implications for the development of the Saxon Shore', in Maxfield and Dobson 1991, 132–41.

WILSON, R.J.A. 1988. *A Guide to the Roman Remains in Britain* (London).

WOOD, I. 1987. 'The fall of the Western Empire and the end of Roman Britain', *Britannia* 18, 251–62.

WOODWARD, A. and LEACH, P. 1993. *The Uley Shrines. Excavation of a Ritual Complex on West Hill, Uley, Gloucestershire, 1977–9* (London).

ZIENKIEWICZ, J.D. 1986. *The Legionary Fortress Baths at Caerleon* (Cardiff).

Supplementary bibliography

This brief additional bibliography lists some of the most significant and relevant books published since the original edition of Potter and Johns *Roman Britain* in 1992. Many important articles have also appeared and the reader should refer to journals such as *Britannia* and the *Journal of Roman Archaeology*.

ARNOLD, C.J. and DAVIES, J.L. 2000. *Roman and Early Medieval Wales* (Stroud).

BÉDOYÈRE, G. DE LA 1998. *The Golden Age of Roman Britain* (Stroud).

BÉDOYÈRE, G. DE LA 1999. *Companion to Roman Britain* (Stroud).

BÉDOYÈRE, G. DE LA 2000. *Voices of Imperial Rome* (Stroud).

BIDWELL, P. 1997. *Roman Forts in Britain* (London).

BISHOP, M.C. and COULSTON, J.C.N. 1993. *Roman Military Equipment* (London).

BLACK, E.W. 1995. *Cursus Publicus: the Infrastructure of Government in Roman Britain* (Oxford).

BLAND, R. and JOHNS, C. 1994. *The Hoxne Treasure: an Illustrated Introduction* (London).

Bowman, A.K. 1994. *Life and Letters on the Roman Frontier: Vindolanda and its People* (London).

Bowman, A.K. and Thomas, J.D. 1994. *The Vindolanda Writing Tablets (Tabulae Vindolandenses II)*, (London).

Braund, D. 1996. *Ruling Roman Britain* (London and New York).

Breeze, D.J. 1996. *Roman Scotland* (London).

Breeze, D.J. and Dobson, B. 2000. *Hadrian's Wall* (4th edn, London).

Brewer, R. (ed.) 2000. *Roman Fortresses and their Legions* (London and Cardiff).

Crummy, P. 1997. *City of Victory* (Colchester).

Cunliffe, B. 1998. *Fishbourne Roman Palace* (Stroud).

Dark, K. 2000. *Britain and the End of the Roman Empire* (Stroud).

Dark, K. and Dark, P. 1997. *The Landscape of Roman Britain* (Stroud).

Faulkner, N. 2000. *The Decline and Fall of Roman Britain* (Stroud).

Fulford, M. and Timby, J. 2000. *Late Iron Age and Roman Silchester: Excavations on the Site of the Forum-Basilica 1977, 1980–86* (London).

Henig, M. 1995. *The Art of Roman Britain* (London).

Hingley, R. 2000. *Roman Officers and English Gentlemen* (London).

Hobbs, R. 1996. *British Iron Age Coins in the British Museum* (London).

Jackson, R.P.J. and Potter, T.W. 1996. *Excavations at Stonea, Cambridgeshire, 1980–85* (London).

James, S. 1993. *Exploring the World of the Celts* (London).

James, S. 1999. *The Atlantic Celts* (London).

James, S. and Millett, M. (eds) 2001. *Britons and Romans: Advancing an Archaeological Agenda* (York).

James, S. and Rigby, V. 1997. *Britain and the Celtic Iron Age* (London).

Johns, C.M. 1996. *The Jewellery of Roman Britain* (London).

Johns, C.M. 1997. *The Snettisham Roman Jeweller's Hoard* (London).

Johnson, P. and Haynes, I. 1996. *Architecture in Roman Britain* (York).

Knight, J.K. 1999. *The End of Antiquity* (Stroud).

Ling, R. 1998. *Ancient Mosaics* (London).

Mawer, C.F. 1995. *Evidence for Christianity in Roman Britain* (Oxford).

Milne, G. 1995. *Roman London* (London).

Neal, D.S. and Cosh, S.R. 2002. *Roman Mosaics of Britain, vol.I: Northern Britain* (London).

Price, J. and Cottam, S. 1998. *Romano-British Glass Vessels, a Handbook* (York).

Rook, T. 1992. *Roman Baths in Britain* (Princes Risborough).

Salway, P. 1993. *The Oxford Illustrated History of Roman Britain* (Oxford).

Swift, E. 2000. *The End of the Western Roman Empire* (Stroud).

Tyers, P. 1996. *Roman Pottery in Britain* (London).

Webster, P. 1996. *Roman Samian Pottery in Britain* (York).

Woodside, R. and Crow, J. 1999. *Hadrian's Wall: an Historic Landscape* (London).

Photographic acknowledgements

Cambridge University Collection of Air Photographs: Figs 10, 23, 31, 32, 35. Philip Crummy, Colchester Archaeological Unit: Fig. 85 and Plate III. M. Ali Döğenci (courtesy of Professor K. Erim): Fig. 12. Durham University, Department of Archaeology: Fig. 81. W.S. Hanson (Crown Copyright): Fig. 14. Hull City Museums and Art Galleries: title page. Simon James: Figs 26–7, 33. Graham Keevil, Oxford Archaeological Unit: Fig. 30. Museum of London: Figs 58, 79, 82. National Museum of Wales: Figs 17, 34, 83–4 (Photos R.J. Brewer). A.L. Pacitto: Fig. 6. T.W. Potter: Figs 1, 4, 15, 18–19, 25, 29. St Albans Museums: Figs 22, 48. All other photographs are by the British Museum Photographic Service.

The maps, Figs 36 and 44 and Plate V were drawn by Stephen Crummy.

Index

Numbers in **bold type** refer to illustrations